# BURNING THE CURTAIN

# BURNING THE CURTAIN

## Four Revolutionary Spanish Plays

Translated and Introduced by

## Gwynne Edwards

Francisco Ors: *Contradance*
Alfonso Sastre: *Tragic Prelude*
Antonio Buero Vallejo: *Two Sides to Dr Valmy's Story*
Jaime Salóm: *Almost A Goddess*

**Marion Boyars · London · New York**

Published in Great Britain and the United States
in 1995 by Marion Boyars Publishers
24 Lacy Road, London SW15 1NL
237 East 39th Street, New York, NY 10016

Distributed in Australia and New Zealand by
Peribo Pty Ltd, 58 Beaumont Road, Mount Kuring-Gai, NSW

CIP data for British Library and Library of Congress available.

ISBN 0–7145–3009–3

Typeset in 11pt Times and Switzerland by Ann Buchan (Typesetters), Shepperton
Printed by Redwood Books Ltd, Trowbridge

# Contents

**To Eleri**

# Introduction

It has been said of the great Spanish painter, Francisco Goya, that in his work he defined the true reality of Spain itself: 'a great bullring violently split into two colours: black and white'. The element of sharp contrast is certainly one which can be found throughout Spanish history, not least in the twentieth century, for the horrors of the Civil War (1936-39) and the repression of the Franco dictatorship which followed it have become since 1975, the year of Franco's death, a period of liberation in which all kinds of tensions have been released. In this respect the arts can be seen to be a true mirror of national consciousness, and, in reflecting the enormous changes which have taken place, Spanish theatre and cinema have followed a remarkably parallel course. The trajectory of Spanish cinema, for example, is one which has progressed from the films of Carlos Saura and Victor Erice — wonderful films but many of them made within the constraints of an ever-watchful censorship during the Franco years — to the gloriously uninhibited cinema of Pedro Almodóvar. Both Saura, in films such as *The Hunt* (1965) and *Raise Ravens* (1975), and Erice, in *The Spirit of the Beehive* (1973), discovered and exploited ways of commenting on and criticizing the Franco regime while working within it. Their methods, however cunning, were therefore distinguished by an inevitable reticence, particularly in relation to issues of sex and religion. For Almodóvar, in contrast, there are no inhibitions: rather a total delight in the freedom to portray on screen all manner of sexual licence, heterosexual, homosexual or lesbian. In this he has been followed by others, such as Bigas Luna, the director of *¡Jamón, Jamón!* (1992) and *Golden Balls* (1993). As far as Spanish theatre is concerned, the pattern has been exactly the same. Alfonso Sastre and Antonio Buero Vallejo, like Saura and Erice, worked within the limitations of the Franco period and are generally regarded as the two great dramatists of the dictatorship. Francisco Ors and Jaime Salóm, although writing during the latter part of the Franco years and, in Salóm's case, often successfully, have discovered since 1975 a new freedom which has allowed them to explore subjects and themes which would previously have been denied them. In 1980, for example, Salóm's audacious *The Cock's Short Flight* had Franco's father as its protagonist; Francisco, an unconventional, free-thinking man who abandoned his wife for his mistress; and Ors's *Contradance*, on which he commenced work in 1977, is strongly reminiscent of Almodóvar in its frank treatment of homosexuality.

Despite the essential differences between the periods of dictatorship and democracy, the important work which they have both produced has one thing in common:

the spirit of rebellion and revolt. During the Franco years this, of course, took the form of opposition to the regime itself, and in cinema and theatre alike, artists such as Saura, Erice, Sastre and Buero Vallejo expressed, often obliquely, their disapproval of all it stood for. During the democracy that spirit of revolt has become an open and unfettered rejection of all those conservative, repressive and right-wing values which Franco imposed upon his countrymen for almost forty years and which, of course, continue to be a feature of Spanish life. As far as theatre is concerned, the revolt has embraced both content and form, for it is clear that a theatre which advocates the status quo in terms of its themes will also do so in a conventional and unchallenging form. The important Spanish theatre of the twentieth century has always sought to express challenging ideas in new ways: a true theatre of revolution.

Federico García Lorca, without doubt the most inspirational Spanish dramatist of the twentieth century was, for many years after his death in August 1936, regarded universally as the victim of Fascism: Spain's most famous dramatist picked out and ruthlessly executed by Franco's assassins as an example to those who dared advance liberal values in the face of the growing strength and opposition of the Right. During the last few years of the Second Spanish Republic (1931-1936), and in the last years of his life in particular, Lorca had supported various left-wing organizations: The Association of Friends of the Soviet Union, and the Workers' Party for Marxist Unification. From 1931 he had been a director for several years of the touring student theatre company 'La Barraca' which was part of the Republican government's policy of educating the Spanish people at large. When the General Election took place in February 1936, he strongly supported the Popular Front and not long afterwards made his left-wing stance very clear by reading some of his poems at a mass meeting in the Casa del Pueblo de Madrid. On May Day of that year he published in the Communist magazine, ¡Ayuda!, a message of encouragement to the workers of Spain. He also seems to have watched the May Day parade waving a red tie from a window in the Ministry of Communications.

In addition, Lorca's homosexuality marked him out as someone who, in the eyes of the Right, offended not only their own conservative moral standards but the teachings of the Catholic Church itself. At the première of *Yerma* in 1934, right-wing sympathizers had stopped the performance, calling Lorca a 'queer' and his leading actress, Margarita Xirgu, a 'lesbian'. On the following day the right-wing newspaper, *Gracia y Justicia*, cuttingly alluded to Lorca's 'hangers-on', implying that they were homosexual. Given these circumstances, it is hardly surprising that, one month after Franco's uprising against the left-wing government, Lorca should have been murdered, or that one of the Fascist assassins, Juan Luis Trecastro, should have boasted of putting 'two bullets into his arse for being a queer'.

Lorca's theatre is also one of opposition to the convervatism which plagued the Spanish theatre during his own lifetime and which continued to do so, very predictably, during the Franco years. In some respects Lorca was the 'angry young man' of his generation, venting his spleen on bourgeois theatre and the bourgeois values embodied in the superficial, escapist and commercial plays which dominated the stages of Madrid during the twenties and thirties. In his own work Lorca attempted from the very outset to deal with themes which he considered to be important and which, being based on his own experience, were often to do with individual passions and aspirations which run counter to the expectations of society. In *Blood Wedding*, for example, the Bride, faced with an arranged marriage, runs off with Leonardo, the married man she really loves, and in *The House of Bernarda Alba* Adela, refusing to submit to her mother's domination, has a secret affair with her sister's fiancé. For Lorca, the theatre should be provocative, controversial, prepared to confront difficult and often uncomfortable issues, laying bare in the process the sometimes shameful reality of human nature. In his own words: 'The theatre requires that the characters who walk the stage should be dressed in poetry and that simultaneously we should see their bones, their blood. . . .'

In Lorca's unusual and ambitious play *The Public*, completed in 1930, a debate about theatre contrasts two evocative and peculiarly Lorcan phrases: 'the theatre of the open air' and 'the theatre beneath the sand'. The former refers to the theatre of superficial entertainment to which he was so opposed, the latter to the serious, probing theatre of which he felt himself to be a part. This distinction was, for him, one which defined not only the concerns of theatre but also its relationship to its audience. Although he wrote for traditional proscenium stages designed to foster the 'suspension of disbelief' and to create on stage a self-contained world physically distanced from the audience, Lorca boldly asserted, 'my characters . . . burn the curtain. . . . One must destroy the theatre or live in it!' This intention to involve his audience in the issues and the emotions of the play was powerfully expressed in *Play Without a Title*, written during the last year of his life. In the opening scene, a character called the Author addresses the audience directly: '. . . the author does not want you to feel you are in a theatre but in the middle of the street'. Later in the same play the link between the stage and life is further emphasized: 'We aren't in a theatre. Because they will come to break down the doors.' Lorca's view of what the theatre should be was expressed, of course, before the outbreak of the Civil War in 1936, but his revolutionary cry was one which, during the subsequent dictatorship, was shared by all the important dramatists who wrote in opposition to it. In this respect Lorca is a key-figure in the Spanish theatre of the twentieth century, a voice which in the last resort the forces of extreme conservatism failed to silence.

After the Civil War it was not unnatural that for many the theatre should become a diversion from emotional trauma and economic stagnation, the so-called 'theatre of evasion'. There were, however, those who passionately believed, in circumstances of considerable poverty, political repression and strict censorship, that the theatre should portray the reality of Spain, and do so in a way which involved and engaged its audience. In terms of theme, the plays of Alfonso Sastre and Antonio Buero Vallejo — the two major dramatists of the dictatorship — constitute a 'theatre beneath the sand'; an attempt to penetrate beneath the surface in order to reveal 'the truth of the tombs.' As far as dramatic method is concerned, Lorca's desire to 'burn the curtain' has its counterpart in Buero's 'immersion technique' and Sastre's 'detached penetration', both phrases which — despite the objective implications of the latter — point towards audience involvement and a theatre whose character is closely linked to the social and political circumstances of the time.

Beginning his career in 1945 with the experimental theatre group, Arte Nuevo

(New Art), Alfonso Sastre's intention was to create a theatre which both opposed the commercially orientated, superficial, escapist and bourgeois drama of the post-War years, and offered an alternative which dealt with serious issues and revitalized theatre technique. Initially, the concerns of Sastre's plays were of a more general kind, focusing, for example, on man as victim, lost in a meaningless world. By 1950, however, he had become a member of a new theatre group, Teatro de Agitación Social (Theatre of Social Agitation), whose name reflects its political and social aims and whose purpose was precisely to involve theatre audiences in political and social issues. Although the group failed in practical terms, as was inevitable in a dictatorship, its manifesto signified an important moment in the history of twenti-eth-century Spanish theatre and embodied an ideological position which, with certain modifications, would characterize most of Sastre's future work: a position of protest against the dictatorship and all it represented, and an invitation to the theatre-going audiences of the time to ponder on the political situation in which they found themselves. Sastre's fate, however, was to see his plays either banned after a few performances or, especially during the sixties, not to have them per-formed or published at all. With other dramatists of the sixties who opposed the dictatorship, Sastre became marginalized, his work as divorced from the theatre-going public as the latter was divorced from it.

*Tragic Prelude*, which still remains to be produced in Spain, was the first play to be written by Sastre for the Teatro de Agitación Social. It expresses two ideas which are fundamental to Sastre's thinking: first, the belief that any unjust social order represents a tragic situation whose existence is usually accepted by the ma-jority; and second, the notion of revolution as a tragic event, a sacrifice which involves suffering and bloodshed but which may be the only way to overthrow social injustice. The action of the play itself takes place in an unspecified country ruled over by a cruel dictatorship, which a group of terrorists is attempting to overthrow. Within the terrorist group two contrasting attitudes are seen: Antón's increasing disillusionment with revolutionary action which inevitably involves the death of innocent people; and Pablo's belief that the shedding of blood is a neces-sary sacrifice in the interests of the ultimate good. Early on in the play, Antón voices his doubts about the course of action being undertaken:

> Someone dies because he has to, because he's guilty. But others die with him too. Others who had no cause to die. Do you understand? Innocent people sacrificed. Completely pointless bloodshed.

Pablo's reply is uncompromising:

> We have to regard the thing as a whole — innocent victims as well. It's the only way to move this structure we call the State, and we have to destroy it, whatever the cost.

This moral dilemma is experienced by a third member of the group, Oscar, whose attempt to assassinate a government minister results in the bombing of a bus in which many people die, including, he is led to believe, his own brother. Arrested, tortured, and finally freed by the police, Oscar comes to share Antón's view of the revolution, blames Pablo for his brother's death and murders him. Discovering finally that his brother is not dead after all, that the police have tricked and freed him merely to have him lead them to other members of the group, Oscar gives himself up, assuming the role of victim in the name of the revolution and taking upon himself the suffering of all those who have died in its cause, innocent or otherwise.

Although *Tragic Prelude* advocates revolutionary action, it does not present it as in any way easy. Indeed, both here and in his theatre as a whole, Sastre depicts revolution as an enormously difficult undertaking in every sense, involving the suffering not only of those at which it is directed but also of those who participate in it. Sastre's desire to involve his audience in these issues is expressed through a stage technique based upon naturalism, the action of the play being firmly grounded in a recognizable reality. The characters are given a history and a background with which the audience can identify — for example, the University world depicted at the beginning, and the close-knit family to which Oscar returns every evening. In addition, the hopes, ambitions and fears of the young men are feelings to which we can easily relate. But, having established in this way a close link with his audience, Sastre simultaneously broadens the range of reference. For example, Oscar in his prison cell, bleeding, sick and despairing, becomes before our eyes the universal victim of injustice and brutality, a metaphor of suffering mankind.

Antonio Buero Vallejo, akin to Sastre in his opposition to the Franco regime, chose to work more cunningly within the dictatorship, producing work which attacked the regime in a much more oblique manner. A concern with themes highly relevant to the dictatorship — such as passive acceptance, blindness, truth, guilt — lies at the heart of the fifteen or so plays which he wrote between 1949 and 1975. Very often, however, their contemporary relevance is framed in metaphor, as in the case of the blind-school setting of *In the Burning Darkness* (1950), or distanced in history, as in *Las Meninas* (1960) and *The Sleep of Reason* (1970) in which the liberal ideas of Velázquez and Goya respectively clash with authoritarian regimes. Given the relevance of these issues, Buero regarded it as essential that his audience should become involved in the on-stage action both intellectually and emotionally. He experimented to that end with a variety of dramatic techniques ranging from the symbolic realism of the plays of the 1950s to the more Brechtian approach of the 1960s. In particular, Buero developed what has come to be known as the 'immersion' technique in which the audience is made to share the experience of the characters by a variety of stage effects.

*Two Sides to Dr Valmy's Story* is somewhat unusual in Buero's theatre in that he refused to change or remove certain scenes, and the Franco censorship withheld permission for its performance during the dictator's lifetime. Despite the fact that most of Buero's plays were not only performed but had great success during the dictatorship, *Two Sides to Dr Valmy's Story* was not premièred until 1976. Coming when it did, with the possibility of democracy in the offing, it was the first play to be performed in a commercial theatre which deals with the theme of political torture, and thus exposed the atrocities which the majority of Spaniards knew had taken place in their country but against which they had been unable to speak out for many years. Written in 1964, *Two Sides to Dr Valmy's Story* belongs to a large group of plays, including Sastre's, whose attempts to voice the truth were silenced for that very reason.

The theme of truth, and the different attitudes which people adopt towards it, lies at the very heart of this play. The married couple who appear at the beginning address the audience directly, seeking to convince us that the events we are about to witness are not true, or are greatly exaggerated, and could only happen in other countries. The events in question, which constitute the body of the play, concern Daniel Barnes, a member of the secret police, who tortures a political prisoner, leaving him impotent as a consequence, and then becomes impotent himself. Unable to understand the reason for his condition and alarmed by the effect it has on his marriage, Daniel Barnes consults Dr Valmy, who gradually exposes the cause of his patient's problem. Barnes, however, is unwilling to acknowledge the truth about himself and, in particular, about the cruelty and inhumanity of his profession. As far as Daniel's wife is concerned, the discovery of the truth about her husband and the eventual death of the political prisoner in question drive her to insanity and murder. At the end of the play, the married couple who appeared at its beginning attempt once more to persuade us that what we have just seen is quite untrue, but are immediately seized by the men in white coats and removed to an institution. Barnes' story of political persecution and torture is finally shown to be true, and the efforts to pretend that it does not exist are revealed as the lie. *Two Sides to Dr Valmy's Story* is therefore a play which greatly involves the audience in issues which, in the Spain of the dictatorship, affected it greatly. Such issues, in a broader sense, affect all people at all times, making us ponder on our own relationship to the truth and on the degree to which we are accomplices in the perpetuation of injustice.

During the sixties Buero became attracted to Brecht's dramatic theory and technique and to the Brechtian desire to make the audience think about the significance of what it is seeing. This desire to distance the audience from the on-stage events and thus to make it draw its own conclusions about them, is clearly evident in *Two Sides to Dr Valmy's Story*. But the play's concern with the nature of truth and untruth, with what is real and what is illusion, also indicates a debt to the influence of Pirandello, whose plays *Six Characters in Search of an Author, Henry IV* and *Right You Are, If You Think You Are*, sought to make audiences think about the nature of reality by deliberately breaking down the traditional barriers between stage and auditorium. From the very beginning of *Two Sides to Dr Valmy's Story*, when the husband and wife address the audience directly, Buero's desire to involve us is perfectly clear. Towards the conclusion, when the couple appear again to voice their opinion of what is true, the lights suddenly come up in the auditorium. By obliterating the gap between characters and public, this stage device plunges the audience into those issues of truth and untruth which the characters themselves are debating. This is a very good example of Buero's 'immersion' effect.

Furthermore, the highly theatrical nature of Daniel Barnes' story is staged in a way which underlines precisely its sensational and far-fetched nature and thus make its audience doubt its authenticity. In the first place, the story is presented in a fragmented manner which involves not merely constant movement from Daniel's home to Dr Valmy's office and the police-station where Daniel works, but also leaps in time between the past and the present. Incidents, such as the dream in which Mary sees herself being electrocuted, are extremely dramatic. In addition, Daniel Barnes' story frequently involves powerful, emotionally charged scenes, such as the one in which the prisoner is tortured. Such episodes inevitably draw the audience into the on-stage action. It is with a sense of relief, therefore, that we learn from the married couple that what we are witnessing is not true. But when the couple are revealed to be mentally unbalanced, and we realize that the Daniel Barnes story is authentic, that sense of relief is at once dispelled, and the feeling of anguish intensified.

The sudden transformation from dictatorship to democracy after 1975 appears to have surprised those Spanish dramatists who had opposed the Franco regime as much as it did the rest of the world. Indeed, the question often posed by Sastre in his plays — how do we use our freedom when it is acquired? — became unexpectedly relevant. Ceasing to be outsiders, writers quickly discovered that the new Spanish order for which they had long fought had, by its very creation, deprived them of their accustomed themes. To explore new directions and seek new causes required an ingenuity and energy which in most cases had been exhausted on old targets. In the last fifteen years or so, dramatists like Buero and Sastre have written good, individual plays which seem often unconnected with their earlier work and which certainly lack its vitality. It is surprising, therefore, to note that the experience of the important film-makers of the dictatorship has been essentially different. Since 1975 both Saura and Erice have made outstanding films.

The dramatists who have produced the most interesting work since the arrival of democracy have been either those who were not writing during it or those whose work was not intended to be, openly or otherwise, an assault upon it. Francisco Ors and Jaime Salóm belong to this second category. Neither can be regarded as writers whose principal aims, like those of Buero and Sastre, were mainly 'political' during the Franco years, although this is not to say that they did not oppose the values which the dictatorship embodied. Ors's early work, for example, ran into trouble with the censorship precisely because its concern with homosexual love ran counter to what was approved of; while Salóm's plays of the sixties and early seventies slipped through the net because their preoccupations were considered to be more 'universal' than particular. For both writers, however, the absence of a totally committed anti-Franco stance meant that, when democracy arrived, they were not, like Buero and Sastre, suddenly deprived of the motivation for their work. On the contrary, Ors was now able to write much more freely, and Salóm to explore human nature in more daring and ambitious ways. Nevertheless, both dramatists, given the freedom which they enjoy, continue to exemplify the spirit of revolt, for the society in which they live did not, after Franco's death, easily cast off those attitudes and values which were part of its fabric. The new democracy simply meant that the revolutionary spirit could burn more brightly.

Francisco Ors's *Contradance* was written quickly, between December 20, 1977 and February 1, 1978, and was given its first performance on March 21, 1980, at the Teatro Lara in Madrid. Because much of his work concerned itself with homosexual themes, earlier attempts to publish novels and plays — mainly in the sixties — had been frustrated by the censors, ever eager to pounce on writers whom they regarded as infringing acceptable moral values. As a result, Ors had been obliged

to turn to writing for Spanish television, for which he often produced adaptations
of other people's work. Ors can therefore be regarded as yet another writer who
was effectively silenced during the sixties. The end of the dictatorship meant that
he could at last speak in his own voice on those issues which he regarded as truly
important, particularly that of homosexual love and the need for a society in which
it could be tolerated. Even so, when *Contradance* was staged, just five years after
Franco's death, it undoubtedly shocked audiences who for years had been pro-
tected from such frankness. It is certainly a play which meets Lorca's requirements
for a 'theatre beneath the sand'.

The principal theme of *Contradance* — homosexual love — is embodied in
three groups of characters, although one of these — Elizabeth I of England and her
lover, Lord Henry — appears initially to be a heterosexual couple. In reality, Elizabeth is a man who, from birth, has been brought up as a female, the child's mother
fearing that a boy would quickly be killed by enemies at Court. To all appearances,
therefore, Elizabeth is a woman whose upbringing and education have helped to
develop female attitudes in the growing child, as well as a sexual attraction to men.
Physical contact of a 'normal' sexual nature with male admirers, as well as detec-
tion of Elizabeth's true gender, has carefully been avoided: a leather garment
covering the entire front of her body has prevented both and allowed only for anal
sex. Although this satisfies Elizabeth to the extent that she is a homosexual man,
growing involvement with Lord Henry obliges her finally to reveal her 'secret' in
an attempt to put their relationship on a truly homosexual basis.

The striking device of a male Elizabeth who is thought by her lovers to be a
woman allows Ors to explore both homosexual and heterosexual relationships.
Drawing from Lord Henry the admission that he truly loves her, Elizabeth, prior to
revealing herself to be a man, has Henry promise he will love her in any circumstances: 'I love you for yourself, not for your body.' Faced with the naked truth,
Henry feels only revulsion and finds great difficulty in acknowledging the truth of
his earlier words in this new situation. Predictable as his reaction is, it embodies the
innate intolerance of homosexual love which is expressed by many of the other
characters of the play. Henry's decision to marry Elizabeth is revealed to be moti-
vated by ambition, not love.

The theme of homosexual love is otherwise centred on the relationship of David
Moore, a young courtier, with a young man he has recently brought back from
Spain. Ors himself embodies in the character of Moore the alternative world for
which the play itself is a plea. Elizabeth observes of him: 'you have a way of
looking at things that I've never seen before . . . as if you carried inside you a
different kind of world . . . as if you'd seen a different kind of reality'. There is,
between Elizabeth and David Moore, an understandable if unrealized attraction
and a concern on her part for his safety amongst courtiers who are, almost without
exception, violently homophobic. When Moore is arrested for what is described as
his 'crime', Elizabeth not only defends him but attempts to arrange his escape, as
she has done once before in the case of another young man. When Moore is killed,
Elizabeth laments his passing and with it the snuffing-out of all that he represented:
'You discovered a door and opened it on a different world. . . . And because you
thought and felt like that, they ended up by killing you. They are responsible who

feel that the thrust of a sword is more noble, more beautiful, more manly than a kiss.'

In contrast, heterosexual relationships are presented by Ors as a kind of game indulged in by most of the Court in which love itself is entirely absent. Lord Henry, for example, conducts his relationship with Elizabeth in tandem with an affair with Lady Caroline, and at the same time is rumoured to have a wife hidden away on his country estate. Lady Caroline shares her sexual favours between Lord Henry and Lord Norfolk and also, it would seem, desires her step-son, David Moore. Their relationships are ones in which lust, calculation, duplicity, treachery and cruelty all play their part and in which ambition and self-advancement are often powerful factors: the game of love intertwined with the game of politics. In contrast to the alternative world represented by David Moore, the existing one is portrayed by Ors as a world without hope or compassion.

In this respect the Court of Elizabeth is distinguished by its intolerance towards, and hatred of, homosexuality, embodied by Lord Norfolk, Lady Caroline and Lord Henry himself. Norfolk speaks of homosexual love as an offence which 'goes against Nature itself', and Lady Caroline describes it as 'so hideous and repulsive that those who practice [it] merit execution'. At the end of the play Lord Henry murders David Moore, observing that, 'men like him deserve that kind of treatment'. The intolerance of the Court of Elizabeth is used by Ors as a parallel for the hostility which he had himself encountered in the Spain of the Franco years, offering the clear suggestion that little has changed in the ensuing years.

The direct impact of *Contradance* upon its audience is evident in the very opening scene. Nothing is more guaranteed to seize the attention of an audience than the presentation on stage of a sexual act. From the moment in which the moaning of a woman becomes the inarticulate cries of a couple in the darkness, audience expectations are aroused, the distance between stage and auditorium immediately bridged by the re-creation on the darkened stage of a deeply familiar experience to which few members of the audience can remain indifferent. When the lights come up slowly, and the woman is seen to be Queen Elizabeth being sodomized by her lover, our initial expectations quickly become a sense of shock, both on account of the identity of the woman and of the nature of the act in question. The audience has allowed itself to be drawn cunningly into the scene only to have its feelings disconcerted. What is more, the relationship of the two characters, Elizabeth and Lord Henry, is full of anguish, pleading and recrimination; emotions with which, in sexual relationships, an audience can easily engage. Since the theme of the play is love in its various manifestations, it is important that Ors should involve his audience at the deepest level, and this he does to great effect.

Scenes Three and Five of Act One are brilliant examples of this process. In the first of these Elizabeth obliges Lady Caroline to expose her breasts and attempts to excite her sexually. From the point of view of the audience, as well as of Lady Caroline, the relationship is apparently lesbian. Elizabeth, however, also refers to her own masculine characteristics and asks Lady Caroline to imagine, as she intimately strokes her, that she is indeed a man. The ambiguity of the scene's eroticism is both fascinating and engaging; an effect which is greatly reinforced in hindsight when, in Scene Five, Elizabeth reveals herself to be a man. The 'revelation' to Lord

Henry is as much a shock to him as it is to the audience. Where we might once have been attracted to her, or in some way have identified with Lord Henry's desire and longing to possess her physically, we are now suddenly faced — as is Lord Henry — with the inescapable fact that our attraction and desire has been for a man. It is a moment in the play when the distance between stage and auditorium completely disappears, when the emotions of one of the play's characters are one with those of the audience.

While *Contradance* involves its audience at key moments, it also distances it at others. The historical setting, the often formal nature of life at Court, and the stylization of both language and behaviour oblige us to observe the on-stage action in a more detached way. The technique is particularly evident in Act One, Scene Two, in which, during the ball at Court, Elizabeth passes from one partner to another in a series of movements that are distinguished by their high formality, engaging each of them in conversation which is both polished and stylized. The effect of such distancing is, of course, to highlight the facade of Court life which, at other moments in the play, is stripped away as effectively as the characters' costumes in order to reveal the naked reality of emotion and undisguised prejudice beneath its surface. The on-stage action, when it confronts its audience with scenes of a disconcerting sexual frankness, similarly exposes feelings which for most of the time are contained, and even repressed, by conformity to social niceties. In short, *Contradance* is a play which burns the curtain in the most personal and powerful way of all, obliging each and every member of the audience to confront his or her sexuality.

Jaime Salóm is perhaps the one dramatist whose success has continued unabated both during and after the dictatorship; a success which he attributes to the fact that his plays are less concerned with ideology than with the psychological exploration of human conflict. At first sight his immensely successful *The House of the 'Chivas'* appears to occupy the same kind of territory as the work of Buero and Sastre. Its action is set during the Civil War in a house where a family and a group of Republican soldiers await the consequences of the imminent Nationalist victory. Similarly *The Heirs Apparent,* which examines the problems faced by a son whose father, the autocratic head of the family firm, dies, would appear to be a commentary on the Franco dictatorship. The same could be said for many of Salóm's other plays of the sixties and seventies, but the fact remains that, however much one feels tempted to see them in relation to the political and social background in which they are set, Salóm insists that his main concern is the depiction of humanity in all its variety. His aim is to create an identification between stage and auditorium in terms of human experiences which are common to us all. As far as staging is concerned, Salóm is also a constant experimenter, sometimes employing naturalism, sometimes symbolism, often a mixture of both, in order to broaden the play's relevance.

*Almost a Goddess*, which dramatizes the lives of the surrealist painter, Salvador Dalí, his wife Gala (or Elena), and her first husband, the French poet, Paul Eluard, is a fine example of Salóm's technique. The play focuses on love, money and religion, examined from the different points of view of the three main characters. In the early part of the play, Gala is only seventeen years old, highly impressionable and still a virgin, despite the outrageous story she tells of having been seduced by her stepfather. Fascinated by the young Paul Eluard, whom she meets in a sanatorium where she is a patient, she soon falls in love with him. It is a love which remains with her even after their divorce and his death. For Eluard, however, love means something different: the experience of many different partners and the sharing of Gala with other men, of whom the painter, Max Ernst, is only one example. Despite the fact that Gala's love for Paul will 'dominate any other act of love', she is corrupted by him. Years later in New York she is seen selecting from photographs the string of young men she thinks might satisfy her. In Dalí's vivid phrase she is a woman 'full of uterine frenzy'; a lusting, dissatisfied creature who can never encounter again the pure experience of love which was once hers. Dalí, incapable of a sexual relationship, is mocked by Eluard for that reason, and in later life is obliged to satisfy his sexual desires by hiring young couples whose 'performances' he eagerly observes.

The theme of money is embodied in the name 'Avida Dollars', coined by André Breton to describe Dalí. In the United States both Gala and Dalí pursue material wealth, as she predicts prior to their departure '. . . gold, gold, money, fortune, money!' This proves to be as corrupting as the experience of love, ultimately leading Dalí to sign blank sheets of paper on which forged prints will subsequently be made. The trajectory is one in which both Gala and Dalí become grotesque monsters.

Much of the play's fascination lies in the juxtaposition of opposites; of purity and degradation, of idealism and cynicism, and the point is also well illustrated in relation to the theme of religion. Gala is presented from an early age as intensely religious: 'I also pray a lot. To the icons and the crucifixes I brought with me and that cover the walls of my room.' Later on, after Eluard's death and the fading of her feelings for Dalí, her love affair with the young actor who has the lead in *Jesus Christ Superstar* is imbued with religious feeling. But if she seems convinced that the young man really is Christ, he is also for her a reincarnation of the young Eluard. Their relationship consequently becomes a heady mixture of religion and eroticism.

This thematic complexity is matched by Salóm's dramatic technique, which can only be described as kaleidoscopic. The single highly-stylized setting acts as a frame in which events covering more than half a century ebb and flow with all the shifting qualities of memories and dreams. The action moves forward, presenting events chronologically, yet simultaneously moves backward as memories constantly intrude in the form of flashbacks. The thoughts and feelings of the protagonists frequently take the form of monologues, often highly lyrical which, combined with the confrontations between characters, create the impression of being able to see them both from the inside and from the outside. It requires only the physical movement of one of the characters — turning away, getting up, sitting down — to take the action in an entirely different direction or to create a leap in time either forward or backward, almost in the manner of cinema. At the opposite extreme from naturalism, the dramatic technique of *Almost a Goddess* has the effect of holding and transfixing its audience, and therefore of drawing it into the grotesque emotional lives of its characters. It is as if the stage has become a great distorting mirror in which, despite the disturbing nature of the reflected image, we are able to see ourselves: a telling metaphor for the way in which the four dramatists presented here have extended the boundaries and possibilities of twentieth-century theatre to an astonishing degree.

# CONTRADANCE

# Francisco Ors

Francisco Ors was born in Casinos, Valencia, on January 16, 1933, and was therefore only three years old at the outbreak of the Civil War. His primary and secondary education took place in the city of Valencia itself, but he subsequently pursued his university studies and obtained his degree at the University of Granada. In 1967 Ors settled in Madrid, where he remained for twenty years. Nowadays he lives in Costa Rica, visiting Spain only occasionally in order to see his relatives. He has effectively turned his back on Spain, feeling himself to be marginalized in Spanish society and at odds with the theatre establishment.

Ors's early interests were as much in science as in literature. In the introductory note to the Spanish text of *Contradance*, for example, he observes: 'Personally I consider myself to be less a writer than a man of science, and it is therefore scientific investigation at its deepest level — where physics, biology and sociology combine in order to produce a genuine humanism — which is my true vocation.' Pulled in both directions, he nevertheless pursued his literary interests from an early age in the form of both poems and essays. At the age of twenty-seven he wrote a novel *Prison For the Rain* followed a year later by *Between the Net and the Wind*. Neither succeeded in circumventing the censorship laws which were often applied so rigidly during the Franco years and neither was therefore published, which is not surprising in view of the fact that *Prison For the Rain*, in particular, drew on the author's homosexual experience, so hated in the Franco regime.

As a result of these difficulties, Ors turned from the novel to the theatre in which he had always been keenly interested. In 1966 he wrote *A Thousand and One Nights* and in the following year, when he moved to Madrid, *We Women Are Wonderful*. Plans to produce these plays were thwarted by the censorship. In consequence, Ors turned his attention to television drama and worked as a script-writer for RTVE over a period of eight years, writing about seventy scripts, some of them original, others adaptations of novels. His own work contained such titles as *Romantic Autumn* and *Adolescence*, and his adaptations included Manuel Puig's well-known novel, *Heart-Break Tango*. In the end, however, the constraints of censorship which he had suffered earlier were now repeated in a different form in the attempts by RTVE to control his scripts and introduce whatever changes they deemed necessary. Despite his belief in his ability as a script-writer, Ors resigned and has vowed never to return to the company. The picture of Ors which emerges very clearly from these clashes with censorship is that of a man who, rather than compromise his values and his independence, is willing to suffer the consequences.

Typically, Ors's experience of the Spanish theatre world has been brief, explosive and controversial. *Contradance*, his one true success, was surrounded by major problems. Initially, the play had been read and approved for production by the Centro Dramático Nacional — the Spanish equivalent of a National Theatre — which had been set up in 1978 under the auspices of the Ministry of Culture and whose brief it was to perform both classical and new work. Intended for production in November and December 1979 under the direction of Fabiá Puigserver, an illustrious name in Spanish theatre, *Contradance* ran into problems when the Centro Dramático Nacional itself acquired a new artistic director. Although he continued to express an interest in the play, the new director, José Luis Gómez, suggested changes and set down conditions which Ors found impossible to accept. True to his beliefs and refusing to compromise, Ors simply withdrew the play.

Ors has subsequently denied the suggestion that he withdrew the play in order to secure a commercial production and has gone on to describe his dismay and disappointment in relation to the events of that time. Nevertheless, just two hours after a final telephone conversation with José Luis Gómez, the offer of a commercial production arrived, followed by five more in the following week. The world première, directed by José Tamayo, took place at the Teatro Lara in Madrid in March 1980.

In the new liberal climate of 1980 which saw soft-porn films in the cinemas of Madrid, *Contradance* proved to be a sell-out, as the theatre critic of the Spanish journal, *Cambio 16*, noted at the time: ". . . this first play by the Valencian dramatist, Francisco Ors, had made its audience either extremely nervous or excited, arousing at times passionate debate. For each performance, since its première a week ago, the theatre has been packed. . . .' Undoubtedly, audiences were attracted by what seemed to be the play's sensationalist elements at a time when Almodóvar, for example, was shooting his first professional film, the outrageous *Pepi, Luci, Bom and All the Other Girls on the Heap*.

Despite the publicity which surrounded the production, many of the reviewers appreciated both the seriousness of the play's theme and its formal perfection. In this respect, Angel Fernández-Santos observed in *Diario 16*: 'Contradance . . . is a play . . . which surprises in many respects, not least in its formal perfection. . .; but it is more than a brilliant and formally perfect work: it is one in which its formal qualities contain a subject matter distinguished by its power and intensity.' In other words, *Contradance* was the culmination of all the work which Ors had attempted to produce previously and which had been banned.

Ors has noted that the Madrid production was preceded by production offers from New York, Rio de Janeiro, Buenos Aires, Rome, Paris, and many other places. The well-known Spanish actress and director, Nuria Espert, also showed an early interest, and it is no coincidence, therefore, that in 1994 she directed the play's Japanese première in Tokyo, to be revived there in July, 1995. For this revival Ors has written additional material relating to the character of David Moore, which is incorporated in this English translation.

In many ways Francisco Ors is an isolated phenomenon in the Spanish theatre, an individualist who does not consider himself to be part of it or, indeed, to be integrated into Spanish society in general. His is a combative, uncompromising spirit which has finally expressed itself fully in the new freedom which followed Franco's death. He is thus a lone voice who is also a part of that vital, liberating moment.

# CONTRADANCE

A Play by

## Francisco Ors

## Characters

Elizabeth I of England

The Ghost of Ann Boleyn

Lady Caroline

Lord Henry

Norfolk

Lord Moore

David Moore, his son

The Ambassador of Spain

The deaf-mute guard

An Attendant

A Scribe

Ladies, soldiers

# Act One

## Scene One

*Darkness. Sound of the wind outside, dying away. The sound of Elizabeth pant-*
*ing, almost inaudibly at first but gradually louder. The rhythm becomes quicker*
*and stronger, interspersed with inarticulate cries from both Elizabeth and Lord*
*Henry. The lights slowly come up on the couple. Elizabeth is standing, fully*
*dressed. Lord Henry, also dressed, is sodomising her. As the lights come up and*
*their panting increases, Elizabeth's face reveals very clearly that she feels more*
*anguish and pain than pleasure. She is sweating, transported, almost on the*
*point of collapse, seeking the moment of ecstacy that will not come and which*
*drives her to the very limit of desperation. Finally a great convulsion, followed*
*by a relief and relaxation of all her muscles. Only Lord Henry's arms prevent*
*her falling.*

ELIZABETH:    (*moaning*) No, no. . . .

HENRY:    Elizabeth! You can't do this to me again. Let me enter you . . . properly! Let me come inside you! You said you would. You promised me. You
gave me your word.

ELIZABETH:    Not now. Next time. I promise.

HENRY:    No. Now! I worship you. You are my life, my whole existence. Don't
go! Let me taste your mouth!

ELIZABETH:    Please!

HENRY:    I want to enjoy you as a woman. You deny me that part of your body.
You offer me the most ignoble part. Let me enjoy that at least!

ELIZABETH:    You are hurting me.

HENRY:    You have to suffer to give me pleasure, as any other woman would.
You have to submit. You have to forget that you are the Queen.

*A bell tolls. The ghost of Ann Boleyn appears, silently observing the scene.*

ELIZABETH:   Let me go! (*She pulls away*)

HENRY:   Elizabeth!

ELIZABETH:   Don't touch me! Not now. Perhaps later tonight, when everything's finished. Button my dress.

HENRY:   (*having arranged his own clothing, he buttons Elizabeth's dress at the back*) Always the same excuse. I rode all morning to get here. I could have come to grief more than once. I knew you'd do this. I knew you'd break your word. Whatever I do doesn't seem to matter. I took such risks to get here . . . all for this!

ELIZABETH:   It's getting late.

HENRY:   You always say that when we are together.

ELIZABETH:   I did what I could. Next time I'll try again.

HENRY:   I'm just your servant. Even less than that: you use me for your own convenience, as you do the pick to clean your teeth or that piece of leather that covers the front of your body.

ELIZABETH:   My life is difficult.

HENRY:   You make it difficult.

ELIZABETH:   What do you mean?

HENRY:   You deny me yourself as a woman. Oh, you don't need to tell me why. You are keeping yourself for your future husband. No doubt you've agreed to marry France. I saw his ambassador yesterday. He looked very cheerful. Or is it the King of Spain?

ELIZABETH:   You are jealous.

HENRY:   Don't be absurd. Why should I be jealous of them? I don't seek your hand, only your love.

ELIZABETH:   It's getting late.

HENRY:   Why can't you love and let yourself be loved? Why refuse yourself the most beautiful thing on earth? Elizabeth, listen to me. One day you'll get married, I know. But the man you marry . . . I very much doubt he'll offer you love. He'll simply be your husband. That's not what I want. I want to love you, and make love to you. And you always say no.

ELIZABETH:   I go as far as I can. I'm taking a risk. . . .

HENRY:   You give me no more than you've given all the others. I'm no different from Norfolk. One more on the list of those you've used to satisfy your appetites.

ELIZABETH:    You know that isn't true.

HENRY:    You deny yourself the best thing of all, by which I mean trust . . . to be honest with someone who loves you. You can't relax. When we make love, when you get more and more excited, I know how tense you always are. Continue like that, and you'll lose all human feeling.

ELIZABETH:    Be silent! I know how easily a ruler can become a monster.

HENRY:    Then why behave like this? If you can't be a woman for me, at least show me some feeling.

ELIZABETH:    I love you.

HENRY:    I ask for less than that.

ELIZABETH:    I've told you I love you.

HENRY:    Then show me I exist only for you, that you understand my feelings and my body's needs. That you really want, if only once, to satisfy my desires.

ELIZABETH:    Come back tonight, after the ball. I'll prove to you how much I love you.

*The figure of Ann Boleyn appears again. Lights fade and music leads into Scene Two.*


## Scene Two


*A ball at Court. The Queen, the Spanish Ambassador, Lord Moore, Norfolk, and Lady Caroline participate. Lord Henry is seated.*

ELIZABETH:    What is it you wish to tell me, Norfolk?

NORFOLK:    Your Majesty, the offence such men commit is the worst of all. It goes against Nature itself.

ELIZABETH:    If that's the case, Nature should exact its punishment. I am Queen of England, not of Nature. Crimes against her are not my domain.

NORFOLK:    Such crimes as theirs are covered by our laws. They have always been punished with death. Any court which tries them has no other option.

ELIZABETH:    Then they should not be put on trial. Continue.

*The Queen partners Lord Moore.*

ELIZABETH:   Moore, my friend. You've been observing me since I arrived. That always means that something's occurred of which you are aware and I am not. What is it?

MOORE:   I can't honestly say, your Majesty. I had things on my mind before I came, and all these lights have somewhat dazzled me. The new lights are certainly magnificent. Perhaps their brightness exposes my inner thoughts. Though there may, of course, be another explanation.

ELIZABETH:   You know I regard you as my greatest confidant, someone I truly trust. Your presence here guarantees my peace of mind.

HENRY:   Thank you, your Majesty. Such compliments are always welcome, more so tonight.

ELIZABETH:   Tonight I am happy too. Continue to observe.

*The Queen partners the Spanish Ambassador.*

Ambassador, as you noted this morning, the crown of England is barely settled on my head. Before I even consider marriage, I think it wise to let it settle much more firmly. Don't you agree?

AMBASSADOR:   Your Majesty's good sense is always evident. I should, however, clarify my observation. I think my words, as they have reached your Majesty, have been distorted, either by malice or by accident.

ELIZABETH:   No matter. It expresses the views of many of my courtiers. They seem to think the early bird catches the worm.

AMBASSADOR:   Your Majesty.

ELIZABETH:   Continue. . . .

*The Queen partners Lord Norfolk.*

I see you wish to ask a question.

NORFOLK:   Why is it, your Majesty, these men cannot be brought to trial?

ELIZABETH:   The answer is quite simple: because they cannot be found guilty. Lord Wesley is one of our very best men. We cannot put his only son to death. In any case, the boy is good and most intelligent. I would not sign the warrant.

NORFOLK:   Lord Wesley is a man of honour. He'd surely understand. I doubt he'd wish to intervene for any son who's disgraced himself so.

ELIZABETH:   He is his father. Whether he intervenes or not, he'd want me to be merciful. Continue.

*The Queen partners Lord Moore.*

Lord Moore, have you considered the matter further?

MOORE:    Your Majesty, you told me you are happy. But I think there is more to it than that. Something much deeper.

ELIZABETH:    You are quite right. Something much, much deeper: pure joy.

MOORE:    Ah, yes. Joy. I caught its scent when I arrived. The terrible, disturbing, unsettling scent which always accompanies joy.

ELIZABETH:    Moore, please!

*The Queen partners the Spanish Ambassador.*

Ambassador, you were saying?

AMBASSADOR:    It seems to me, your Majesty, that even if the crown is barely settled on your head, it could be an advantage.

ELIZABETH:    I don't understand.

AMBASSADOR:    I mean as far as marriage is concerned. In affairs of the heart a little haste is surely better than excessive calculation. Take a Spaniard's word for it. In matters such as these, we act on the spur of the moment, without regretting it.

ELIZABETH:    You mean you take the bull by the horns?

AMBASSADOR:    Yes, quite, your Majesty. Our women too. We do not lack passion.

ELIZABETH:    I am aware of it. King Philip seems quite the opposite. Such gloomy features. But beneath it lies an extremely ardent person, anxious, of course, to embrace marriage.

AMBASSADOR:    Your Majesty.

ELIZABETH:    If my dear sister, Mary, did not produce a child, it is because she was too old to do so. She would have seemed their grandmother. But I am well aware of what King Philip has in mind.

*The Queen partners Norfolk.*

What is it, Norfolk?

NORFOLK:    Your Majesty, I encountered Wesley this morning. I inquired about his son, only to be told he had no son. I saw in his eyes the resolution of a nobleman.

ELIZABETH:    I saw him this morning too. I saw in his eyes the bitterness and sadness of the world. When he kissed my hand, he bathed it with his tears.

NORFOLK:    The tears of anger, your Majesty. Of course, a woman is more easily moved.

ELIZABETH:   I am not a woman. I am the Queen. I know how to read the eyes of my subjects. My heart bleeds for Wesley's son.

NORFOLK:   As well as for his accomplice?

ELIZABETH:   Of course. He's younger still, a visitor to our shores. I think him even less to blame.

NORFOLK:   The act is vile and sinful. How can it not be punished?

ELIZABETH:   I know many others equally guilty. They hold themselves in high esteem, and I respect them.

NORFOLK:   You fail to understand, your Majesty. These are two young men. It offends Nature.

ELIZABETH:   Nature is often strange, but wise. It is quite absurd to think it is offended. But let us not discuss philosophy. I have said that I will pardon them. Continue.

*The Queen partners Lord Moore.*

Moore, I speak of joy, and you are full of gloom. You should feel happy on my account. Is this how you reward me?

MOORE:   Experience has taught me much, your Majesty. For any queen, joy may foretell disaster, even death.

ELIZABETH:   Of course, my friend. But bear in mind that where there is no death, there is no life.

*The Queen partners the Spanish Ambassador.*

Yes, Excellency?

AMBASSADOR:   I think I can guarantee that, after two attempts at marriage, King Philip will prove a successful husband. And in one particular area I know you'll have no complaints. He may appear cold and silent, but in reality. . . .

ELIZABETH:   That doesn't concern me. I am English and therefore equally cold. A neat paradox!

AMBASSADOR:   Paradox? Where's the paradox?

ELIZABETH: Continue.

*The Queen partners Lord Norfolk.*

Tonight, when the guards have done their rounds, ensure the doors to the cells are open and the way to the exit clear and well-lit. The horses will be outside. Tomorrow the two young men will sail from Dover.

NORFOLK:    As you command, your Majesty.

ELIZABETH:    Their lives are as precious to me as your own, Lord Norfolk.

NORFOLK:    I shall give the order myself.

ELIZABETH:    I rely on you above all others. Continue.

*The Queen partners Lord Moore.*

Norfolk has his instructions. The escape will be tonight. Is everything arranged?

MOORE:    I'll see that the horses are prepared. I know young Wesley. There'll be no mistake.

ELIZABETH:    I'm grateful. Such loyalty ensures I sleep well.

MOORE:    I am honoured by your confidence. This is, however, a task I undertake with pleasure.

ELIZABETH:    You have a son, I know. I trust he is well. Continue.

*The Queen partners Norfolk.*

Norfolk, you seem somewhat troubled of late.

NORFOLK:    I am not myself tonight.

ELIZABETH:    I am not referring just to tonight. For some time now you've seemed withdrawn and rather dejected. You know I'm very fond of you. What is it that bothers you?

NORFOLK:    Judge for yourself, your Majesty: an ageing wife, incapable of giving me an heir, practically paralysed and yet refusing to die. Some men are much more fortunate. They become widowers when it best suits them.

ELIZABETH:    Norfolk, . . . .

NORFOLK:    There was also a time, my Lady, when you showed me special affection. Now you choose to ignore me, which makes me think you favour someone else. You toy with my happiness.

ELIZABETH:    You are mistaken, Norfolk. In any case, as you well know, it was a game. But now you have Lady Caroline. Her breasts are like two gentle doves.

NORFOLK:    Lady Caroline will not see me. She claims my nature is too harsh.

ELIZABETH:    I don't believe it. Lady Caroline worships you. I've heard her say so. But, as a woman, she needs to know that you love her. Pay her more attention. Continue.

*The Queen partners Lord Moore.*

How is your son?

MOORE:   A source of concern, Majesty.

ELIZABETH:   Not bad news, I hope.

MOORE:   No, quite the contrary. His letters speak of happiness.

ELIZABETH:   And that concerns you?

MOORE:   Indeed it does. I barely sleep. He's in the very heart of Spain yet speaks of happiness. It disconcerts me. I'll order his return, if that does not displease your Majesty.

ELIZABETH:   Of course not, Moore. I want very much to see your son. When you asked my permission to send him to Spain, I gave it with regret. Your marriage prompted it, I know, but now sufficient time has passed.

MOORE:   Caroline has other distractions. The boy will be quite safe from her.

ELIZABETH:   Then tell him to return. As soon as he does, I wish to see him.

MOORE:   My thanks, your Majesty.

ELIZABETH:   But now I wish to speak to your wife, alone. The ball can end whenever you and Norfolk think appropriate.

MOORE:   Of course, your Majesty.

*Moore commands the music to stop. Everyone applauds the Queen.*

ELIZABETH:   The day has been extremely tiring but still I must attend to certain things. (*She looks at Lady Caroline with seeming indifference* ) Lady Caroline shall accompany me. The rest of you continue your enjoyment. Life is sweet. England shall be even greater than she is, but not everyone will survive to taste its pleasures. Enjoy tonight.

*Applause. The Queen goes out with Lady Caroline.*
*They proceed to the Queen's room.*


## Scene Three


*Elizabeth and Lady Caroline.*

ELIZABETH:   Be seated. There's something I wish to ask of you.

CAROLINE:   Your wish is my command, your Majesty.

ELIZABETH:    In the course of what I wish to say, you must be calm. And sec- ondly, sincere. Is that understood?

CAROLINE:    Perfectly.

ELIZABETH:    I want you to help me understand certain mysteries of Nature.

CAROLINE:    What do you mean?

ELIZABETH:    Of the nature of women. Of course, you say that I am a woman. But that's not quite the issue. I am the Queen, which changes everything. My feelings and desires cannot be indulged like those of other women. I hope you understand.

CAROLINE:    Yes, of course.

ELIZABETH:    There are certain things outside my own experience. But because I am the Queen, I ought to try to experience them. That's why I've asked you here tonight. Caroline, you are a very different kind of woman: femi- nine, delicate, beautiful, your skin as white as milk, your lips like roses. What is more, you have experience of many men.

CAROLINE:    My name is much abused. I've always been the object of slander.

ELIZABETH:    No need for modesty. This is between the two of us.

CAROLINE:    Then I shall try not to be childish.

ELIZABETH:    Are you willing to help me?

CAROLINE:    Your Majesty can count on it. Though I can't think what you can learn from me. What can I show you?

ELIZABETH:    Firstly, your breasts.

CAROLINE:    My breasts?

ELIZABETH:    I wish to see them. I have never seen a woman's breasts. Why look so surprised? I am the Queen. I need to know my kingdom, my cities, my subjects. And I need to know more about human nature.

CAROLINE:    Of course. I understand.

ELIZABETH:    Tonight I need to know about a woman's breasts.

CAROLINE:    But, your Majesty, *you* have breasts too.

ELIZABETH:    Indeed, but mine are those of a queen, as is my body. Can't you understand?

CAROLINE:    Why, yes. Whatever you wish.

ELIZABETH:    Then show me your breasts. Let me see them.

*Lady Caroline has first to remove a short cape which is fastened at the nape of her neck. She does so with difficulty.*

CAROLINE:   They are nothing special, your Majesty. Nothing out of the ordinary.

ELIZABETH:   Not according to my reports. Norfolk says they are like two trembling doves.

CAROLINE:   Norfolk drinks too much. Your Majesty, . . . .

ELIZABETH:   Undo your dress. I wish to see them.

*Caroline undoes her dress, exposing her breasts. Elizabeth contemplates them, unmoved.*

ELIZABETH:   Let me touch them.

CAROLINE:   Your Majesty.

ELIZABETH:   I wish to touch the skin that people praise so much. This white flesh whose texture is unforgettable.

*Elizabeth places her hand inside Lady Caroline's dress, caressing her and exploring her body as she speaks.*

This stomach they endlessly speak of. This belly where they find such joy.

CAROLINE:   Your Majesty. . . .

ELIZABETH:   This secret place that offers them pleasure. Norfolk claims he'd willingly sacrifice one hand to be able to introduce the other here.

CAROLINE:   Norfolk's tongue is far too loose.

ELIZABETH:   Don't draw back. Nothing will happen. No need to tremble. This is simply an exploration of the battlefield.

CAROLINE:   I'm sorry, your Majesty. I can't help it.

ELIZABETH:   Your skin is extremely fine. Even so, I fail to understand why it should cause such pleasure and excitement.

CAROLINE:   If you were a man, your Majesty, I think you might.

ELIZABETH:   You think so?

CAROLINE:   I'm perfectly sure.

ELIZABETH:   I rather doubt it.

CAROLINE:   If you were a man, you'd soon be aroused, and you in turn would arouse me.

ELIZABETH:    You think this stroking, done by a man, would give you pleasure?

CAROLINE:    Of course, your Majesty.

ELIZABETH:    Then tell yourself that I am a man.

CAROLINE:    But I know you are not.

ELIZABETH:    Try to use your imagination.

CAROLINE:    But you are a woman. One can't deceive Nature.

ELIZABETH:    Look at my hands. They are more like a man's. Look at my skin. And my duties are more like those of a man than any woman. It shouldn't be difficult for you to believe that I am a man.

CAROLINE:    Try as I might, I could never invest you with that which you would require to be a man.

ELIZABETH:    But I'm not undressed, so how would you know? Just close your eyes. Embrace me. Imagine you're in the arms of a man, that I feel as a man does. Caress me. Let me kiss you.

*Elizabeth kisses her on the mouth. Caroline almost vomits.*

CAROLINE:    I can't, your Majesty. I'm sorry. I cannot do it. It goes against Nature.

ELIZABETH:    I forbid you to mention Nature again.

CAROLINE:    Very well, I shan't, your Majesty.

ELIZABETH:    And try to overcome this feeling of revulsion. Do you think that I don't feel it too?

CAROLINE:    Then why do this at all?

ELIZABETH:    I have to. The reason doesn't matter. Come here. I want you to seduce me. You have to give me pleasure. Close your eyes. Forget everything. Imagine that I am your King, your master. And that, if you succeed in seducing me, anything you want is yours.

CAROLINE:    I'll try. I think I can. I'll do my very best.

*Lady Caroline kisses and caresses Elizabeth. After a few moments, Elizabeth draws away, disappointed and indifferent.*

ELIZABETH:    Enough!

CAROLINE:    Your Majesty. Was I so disappointing? Didn't you enjoy it?

ELIZABETH:    I'm afraid I did not.

CAROLINE:    But I did what I could. I did my very best.

ELIZABETH:   You aren't to blame. You are very sweet. You've helped me a great deal.

CAROLINE:   Have I helped you discover what you wished to know?

ELIZABETH:   I'm really not sure what I wished to know. Perhaps to convince myself of something I knew already. I haven't discovered anything new.

CAROLINE:   There is nothing new to learn, your Majesty. I promise. A man and woman are all that's needed. They long for each other, they undress, and everything follows. There's nothing else to find out.

ELIZABETH:   Life is simple for simpletons.

CAROLINE:   Nature. . . . Forgive me!

ELIZABETH:   It doesn't matter. It was just my curiosity. I had heard Norfolk praise your body so much!

CAROLINE:   Norfolk! Always Norfolk!

ELIZABETH:   Lord Henry too.

CAROLINE:   Lord Henry?

ELIZABETH:   Indeed. My information is that you no longer favour Norfolk. Why is that? Do you find him repugnant?

CAROLINE:   No. He's a very attractive man.

ELIZABETH:   Then why do you not receive him?

CAROLINE:   Because . . . quite frankly, his tongue is far too loose.

ELIZABETH:   You have to remember that men always like to talk, and since they lack imagination, they talk about the things they do. My experience tells me that in the end they conceal nothing.

CAROLINE:   It isn't like that with Norfolk. He talks about it the very same day. I sometimes think he wants to see me just to be able to talk about it afterwards. It angers me.

ELIZABETH:   I do admit it is a serious fault.

CAROLINE:   And I am a married woman. I love my husband. I respect him. He's good and generous.

ELIZABETH:   I love and respect him too. If only he knew how much.

CAROLINE:   That is why I no longer see Norfolk. Don't you think I'm right, your Majesty?

ELIZABETH:   I think it's your affair. Norfolk behaves very badly, of course, but there is good reason. He has a difficult time of it. His wife is sick and extremely unpleasant. She neither gives him pleasure nor children and refuses to let him have them by someone else. It helps to explain his bitterness and lack of warmth. But he is a brave and loyal man, always concerned with our safety. Without such people, you could not amuse yourself. Our enemies would easily destroy us.

CAROLINE:    Of course, your Majesty. I understand.

ELIZABETH:    And how is he rewarded? He drinks alone. I think it unfair he should be so deprived of pleasure.

CAROLINE:    Am I to understand that, were I to take him into my bed, I could rely upon your Majesty's good favour?

ELIZABETH:    Just bear in mind that pleasing him means pleasing me.

CAROLINE:    Thank you, your Majesty. In that case I shall receive him. The fact is he is quite witty, and extremely generous.

ELIZABETH:    Return to the others. The entertainment will not have finished yet. Perhaps you can engage him in pleasant conversation.

CAROLINE:    I shall do my best. It shouldn't be too difficult.

ELIZABETH:    Goodnight, Caroline.


## Scene Four


*Elizabeth, her deaf-mute guard and the ghost of Ann Boleyn. Elizabeth is deep in thought. She looks at herself in a mirror, touches her body. She removes her wig and dress, revealing the piece of leather whch covers most of the front of her body but not her back. She goes to the head of the bed and from behind a tapestry takes hold of a length of rope. A beam of light reveals that the rope extends to a small room above. The deaf-mute guard is seated there in front of a bench on which he is carving a piece of marble. The end of the rope is tied to his arm. On the bench to one side is a gleaming dagger. Elizabeth changes her mind and conceals the rope again. She picks up her nightdress, puts it down once more and begins to untie the ribbons which hold the piece of leather in place. The figure of Ann Boleyn is suddenly illuminated.*

ANN BOLEYN:    Elizabeth, you have to take great care.

ELIZABETH:    (*stops untying the ribbons*) Mother, I can't go on like this. I shall go mad. I cannot keep this secret any more. It poisons my entire being. You tell me to take care, and so I do. I have spent my entire life being careful. And ever since I became Queen, I've been more careful and prudent than ever. Are not my guards outside? Is not Constancio up above, loyal to me because I saved him when Mary had left him deaf and dumb? Every night, while I am asleep, he watches over me, never sleeping himself. At any sign of danger I merely pull the rope and there he is, a tiger ready to kill on my account. . . . Oh, yes, I know. The real danger is within . . . within myself, and the strongest door is never safe if someone else is given the key. . . . You are right. You are always right. But I'm tired of listening. I refuse to listen any more. My life is my own. Remember that you risked your life, so why can't I risk mine? I am weary of it all. I need to trust someone. Lord Henry loves me. I can see it in his eyes. He brings me to life. The warmth of his hand makes beauty even more beautiful, truth much more certain. . . . Oh, yes, I shall be prudent, but things are different now. I'm not afraid. I love Lord Henry.

## Scene Five

*Elizabeth and Lord Henry.*

HENRY:   Twice in a single day you've said you love me. But what do those words mean on the lips of a Queen? That you want my body? That you want to use me?

ELIZABETH:   Of course not. It's rather strange. I suddenly know that when I say those words, I don't know what I've said. Perhaps because I've never said them before.

HENRY:   Elizabeth, . . . .

ELIZABETH:   You've been married once. You must have loved your wife. And then there were other women. I'm sure you must have said those words quite often. So you are the one to tell me what they mean.

HENRY:   Their meaning changes, according to the circumstances. With other women it meant different things: pleasure, possession, domination. With you it's different again.

ELIZABETH:   Why?

HENRY:   Well, I cannot dominate *you*. You deny me complete enjoyment of your body. You are the Queen and therefore inaccessible. But I know you are also a person of flesh and blood. Your smile communicates your pleasure. When I touch you, you tremble. When you kiss me, your lips transmit to mine your fierce longing and desperation. I feel your bitterness and isolation. When I kissed my wife, or any other women, I never felt such things. No woman in the world has ever kissed me as you do. Nowhere else could I find the exquisite pleasure contained in your mouth. It is like experiencing death yet being fully aware of life. Let me kiss you. . . . Do you know now what 'I love you' means? Do you understand?

ELIZABETH:   What you say must be true. No one could lie so convincingly.

HENRY:   Why should I lie? How could anyone feign something quite as intimate? Words, expressions, caresses can, of course, be feigned, but no one can invent the touch of his tongue or the taste of his mouth. When I am with you, my lips become much softer.

ELIZABETH:   I know you want me. When you hold me close, your body grows tense, you can barely speak. But it isn't sufficient. I need something more than that. Something beyond desire.

*They look at each other.*

If my body were not what you imagine. . . .

HENRY:   It would make no difference. You are more than your body, and it's you that I want.

ELIZABETH:   Is that the truth?

HENRY:   I swear it. I've never experienced it before.

ELIZABETH:   Not ever?

HENRY:   Believe me. To love a woman was to love her body. To look at her, to gaze at a woman's body. Nothing more. But to look at you, to gaze deep into your eyes, is to see a person filled with longing and uncertainty. Someone who longs for love but fears finding it. In those moments of greatest tenderness, your eyes reveal the fear of a hunted animal. I don't know why you are so afraid. You are the Queen. What point is there in reaching out if you won't be helped? You are like the person crossing the desert, dying of thirst, who will not accept the drink he's offered. Isn't that right?

ELIZABETH:   More than anything I want to give myself to you.

HENRY:   Then what is stopping you?

ELIZABETH:   My body.

HENRY:   I don't understand.

ELIZABETH:   There's something you don't know, . . . that no one knows. Something you can't imagine. It might put an end to your love.

HENRY:   It would make no difference. If you were deformed, or scarred, or diseased, it wouldn't matter. I love you. I love you for yourself, not for your body.

*They look at each other. A moment of expectant calm.*

ELIZABETH:   Then I shall give you proof, not just of my love, but of my absolute trust.

*Elizabeth begins to undress. After removing her dress which she allows to drop to the floor with a certain fatalism, she begins to undo the ribbons which hold in place the piece of leather.*

HENRY:   Shall I possess you at last?

ELIZABETH:   You've already done so, in the only way you can. Now you can see my body and learn the truth, be part of my life, my secret. The person who loves you is a man.

HENRY:   I don't believe it! Is this some kind of trick, some wicked deception? Do you think I would want to make love to a man, caress a man? It must be a trick!

ELIZABETH:   It isn't a trick. I *am* a man. A man who loves you. Above all questions of sex and the law. Above all matters of custom and education. Above what people call Nature. And you love me.

HENRY:   I do not. I do not.

ELIZABETH:   It's difficult to accept, I know. You feel you've been betrayed. But the truth will out if one is brave enough to face it. And the thousands of words with which they've tried to demean it count for nothing. I love you. I stand naked before you and tell you that I love you. It doesn't matter who is involved, love is always beautiful.

HENRY:   It doesn't matter who is involved!

ELIZABETH:   Words are not precise enough. My hands can explain it better.

HENRY:   Stay away from me! Don't touch me! I'm trying to control myself. Touch me, and I'm likely to react as any man would.

ELIZABETH:   As a man you know my skin, as a man you know my body's warmth, have responded to its softness.

HENRY:   Only because I thought you were a woman. Now I know you aren't.

ELIZABETH:   But my skin is still my skin; the skin you've longed to touch. My lips, the lips you longed to kiss. My scent, the scent which aroused your senses.

HENRY:   And now it's changed.

ELIZABETH:   Our bodies are the same bodies.

HENRY:   Why did you undress?

ELIZABETH:   Because you wanted me.

HENRY:   That piece of leather solved the problem.

ELIZABETH:   Would you have me put it on again? Would you have me conceal the truth and pretend that things are not as they are? Is that what you want?

HENRY:   I'd rather the truth weren't what it is. I wish I hadn't seen what I've seen.

*Lord Henry gives her something with which to cover herself.*

ELIZABETH:   Why do you fear the truth? It cannot be changed.

HENRY:   It all makes sense now. And every word takes on a different meaning.

ELIZABETH:   As do your own. Must I remind you? 'It wouldn't make any difference. If you were deformed, or scarred or diseased, it wouldn't matter.' But now, it seems, my being diseased is better than my being a man.

HENRY:   It makes it . . . impossible.

ELIZABETH:   You often speak badly of women. You even despise them. For you a man is worth much more. If that is so, why doesn't a man merit your love? You said that, when you looked in my eyes, you saw a person, not a woman. . . . Why did you say that?

HENRY:   Because it was true.

ELIZABETH:   You mean it *was* and isn't now? Do you think the taste of my mouth is any different?

HENRY:   You've taken me completely by surprise. Elizabeth, the Queen so praised by poets, is a man. The woman whose hand the Kings of Europe seek is a man. Let me look at you. Let my eyes confirm the truth of this. It is indeed the body of a man. But why? Why did you conceal the fact? Why such an elaborate deceit?

ELIZABETH:   My mother thought it prudent.

HENRY:   But why?

ELIZABETH:   To save me from certain death. She knew that Catherine's supporters would kill a boy. She confided in the midwife, who was also my tutor and governess.

HENRY: Lady Margaret.

ELIZABETH: They agreed that, if the child were born a boy, they would say it was a girl.

HENRY: And no one knew the truth?

ELIZABETH: The boldest schemes are often the most successful.

HENRY: Your mother longed for a son. If it were known that you were a boy, she might not have been put to death.

ELIZABETH: And if I'd been killed, it would hardly have helped her. In any case, this was what she chose to do.

HENRY: You could have revealed the truth later on. Your subjects would have welcomed a King.

ELIZABETH: Undoubtedly. But by that time they considered me a woman. I doubt that they'd have accepted me if I'd suddenly become a man. It would all have been too strange. And there was another reason.

HENRY: What?

ELIZABETH: I wasn't an ordinary man. I knew by then that I desired other men.

HENRY: Perhaps you were conditioned to it, by wearing women's clothes. By acting as a woman, you came to believe you were one.

ELIZABETH: Not true. I was always aware that I was a man. In spite of that, I always dreamed of men.

HENRY: How could you be sure?

ELIZABETH: One always knows. In the end I knew for certain.

HENRY: How?

ELIZABETH: One day when I was still quite young . . . or rather, one night . . . in the garden . . . a boy of my own age kissed me.

HENRY: Who was he?

ELIZABETH: It doesn't matter. My very first kiss, but I knew at once. The longing I felt, the impossible desire. I accepted what I was and learned to contain it. Of course, there were men I used to satisfy my needs . . . how else could I go on? That's what I thought my life would be, until you appeared.

HENRY: Another one to satisfy your needs.

ELIZABETH: I can't think how it could have occurred. I was so afraid. But it did. I watched you smile and began to believe that it meant something. Something I may have imagined but wanted to believe in; needed to believe in. And you gave voice to it. You were very clever. You knew how to match your words to what I wanted to hear.

HENRY:   My words were sincere. I never deceived you.

ELIZABETH:   Perhaps they were. It's all very difficult. Before you arrived tonight, I wondered what to do.

HENRY:   And you decided to be honest.

ELIZABETH:   I decided to say nothing, that everything should continue as before. But then, when you came, I thought it might be possible that, in spite of everything, we could join our lives, our destinies.

HENRY:   How precisely?

ELIZABETH:   By making you my husband. We could be together, love each other.

HENRY:   Be together! It sounds so strange, so odd.

ELIZABETH:   Does it frighten you . . . or repel you so much?

HENRY:   I don't know. It's all so strange. The idea of being your husband.

ELIZABETH:   Do you think it might be possible?

HENRY:   I know I love you. I'm sure of that. I meant it when I said it was you I loved, not your body. How could I love your body when I'd never even seen it? But when I looked into your eyes, I knew I only wanted to protect you.

ELIZABETH:   Nothing has changed.

HENRY:   Oh, but it has. I know now that you are a man. I don't know if it's possible.

ELIZABETH:   I know it is. Listen to me. We are all prisoners. Prisoners of reason, custom, prejudice. The mind is a great jailer. It imprisons our deepest and most natural instincts. Cut the jailer's head off! Break the chains of habit and superstition! Free your body! Let it live! Close your eyes! Forget everything else!

*Elizabeth's enthusiasm grows as she tries to encourage him.*

HENRY:   Come close. Let me touch you.

*Elizabeth goes to him. He closes his eyes and begins to stroke her skin and hair.*

ELIZABETH:   It's the same skin. The same voice. The same warm flesh.

HENRY:   You really want to make me your husband?

ELIZABETH:   I've thought of it so often. I've wanted it so often.

HENRY:   Your skin is so smooth. So warm. It seems smoother than ever.

ELIZABETH:   Your hands express much more. Your touch is much more passionate. You are trembling!

HENRY:   (*opening his eyes, moving away, looking straight at her*) I love you.

ELIZABETH:   Can you say those words and not feel ashamed?

HENRY:   I can. I feel free. A free man who loves you.

ELIZABETH:   (*removing a ring. She gives it to him. He puts it on his finger*) Wear this. It will remind you of those words, this night, this moment.

*They kiss. The sound of galloping horses is heard.*

HENRY:   Do you hear that noise?

ELIZABETH:   Of course.

HENRY:   The sound of horses in full flight. Someone's trying to escape. There seems to be two of them. Who could it be? It's almost dawn.

ELIZABETH:   It must be love and freedom. They ride together tonight.

*They embrace. Lights down. Sound of horses fading.*

# ACT TWO

## Scene One

*Lord Henry and Lady Caroline in bed. Lord Henry laughing.*

CAROLINE:  My dear Henry, what woman makes you laugh as I do?

HENRY:  No one. I admit it. Today you've even surpassed yourself.

CAROLINE:  Then do you not think I deserve a reward?

HENRY:  Your father must have been a friar!

CAROLINE:  If you accuse me of begging, you accuse yourself of being miserly. When a man lacks generosity, a woman is obliged to beg. It's not very pleasant.

HENRY:  Caroline, please! We are enjoying ourselves.

CAROLINE:  Oh, so we are! At least, *you* are!

HENRY:  You mean, you are not?

CAROLINE:  Not quite as much.

HENRY:  Why not?

CAROLINE:  Perhaps because I'm wasting my time on someone who doesn't deserve me.

HENRY:  How can you say that?

CAROLINE:  Any other man, especially Norfolk, would simply shower me with presents.

HENRY:  Norfolk is a peasant. I am a gentleman. In any case, you are a married woman. You shouldn't be receiving presents, much as I would like to give them to you.

CAROLINE:  A fine excuse! An intelligent man should know how to treat his mistress properly. And for someone about to ascend the throne, that ought to be no problem whatsoever. You can't be a king and not be generous. The two are synonymous.

HENRY:　　Then ask for whatever you want. If it's in my power, you can have it.

CAROLINE:　　That's much better. You have made me the happiest of women.

HENRY:　　What is it that you want?

CAROLINE:　　Not much. It's in your hands to give it. In fact, it's on your hand . . . the right one. I'd like to have that ring.

HENRY:　　I'm afraid not. It's quite impossible.

CAROLINE:　　You promised. You can't go back on your word.

HENRY:　　But you wouldn't be able to wear it. It's far too expensive. You couldn't explain it to your husband.

CAROLINE:　　That's my affair. Just give it to me.

HENRY:　　I'll give you something else. Quite frankly, I can't think why I have to give you anything.

CAROLINE:　　Perhaps because you are in my debt. And because you promised.

HENRY:　　It was a joke. I didn't really mean it.

CAROLINE:　　Well, isn't that fine! It was a joke, Caroline. When will I learn to understand men?

HENRY:　　Oh, don't start complaining!

CAROLINE:　　Why not? You only want me to amuse you and to keep you abreast of everything . . . my husband's affairs, for instance. But when it comes to something I want for myself!

HENRY:　　But why such interest in the ring? I have many others. Take whichever you want.

CAROLINE:　　This one is unique. I wanted it as soon as I saw it on your hand. You promised me that I could have what I want.

HENRY:　　But not this, Caroline. I'm sorry.

CAROLINE:　　So am I. Isn't it strange how the blindfold falls so suddenly from our eyes?

HENRY:　　Now you are being foolish.

CAROLINE:　　Very well, we'll put an end to foolishness . . . if you'll excuse me.

　　*She begins to dress.*

HENRY:　　It's far too early. You can't leave yet.

CAROLINE:    It *is* rather early. With a bit of luck Lord Norfolk won't have gone to bed. You know how men find me so amusing. It makes me feel that I'm being useful, as well as enjoying myself.

HENRY:    You were always very practical.

CAROLINE:    Precisely. And, as far as you are concerned, I know I've served my purpose. You know about my husband, as well as the young nobleman my stepson's brought from Spain . . . the one my husband thinks might be a spy. What further interest could I hold for you?

HENRY:    Caroline!

CAROLINE:    Perhaps such information isn't worth your precious ring. Neither is my body, or my love. Even so, I'm very discreet, as well you know. I wouldn't dream of telling Norfolk or anyone else that in Surrey, near a lake, in the castle owned by your first wife, you've got a woman hidden away . . . and some of the servants would swear, under oath, that you and she are married.

HENRY:    It's an absolute lie. She is merely my mistress. I plan to abandon her.

CAROLINE:    After she's had the child, no doubt. I hear she's four months' pregnant. All very strange and secretive! I must be on my way.

HENRY:    Wait! Tell me how you learned of it. Does your husband know? Does Norfolk or anyone else know?

CAROLINE:    You are hurting my wrist. No one knows. And no one need find out. Such a lovely ring would be my reward for keeping such a delicate secret.

HENRY:    Why does it have to be this ring?

CAROLINE:    Just a whim of mine.

HENRY:    More a foolish obstinacy.

CAROLINE:    Give it to me.

HENRY:    I cannot. It's a present from the Queen.

CAROLINE:    Oh, really? What a lame excuse!

HENRY:    It's the honest truth.

CAROLINE:    In which case, I like it even more. But don't be alarmed. I promise not to wear it in her presence. Place it on my finger. With this on my hand, I shall keep your secret. It shall be your talisman. It shall make me your slave. Or would you prefer that Norfolk pay me for my services, much more generously?

HENRY:    Do that, and I'll wring your neck!

CAROLINE:    The neck you should wring is this other woman's. Speaking of which, you became a widower very conveniently. It's almost as if the name of Henry guarantees the death of wives.

HENRY:    You good-for-nothing creature! I could break you in tiny pieces!

CAROLINE:    Anger always makes you more attractive. Oh, of course you could do it! There's nothing you'd like more. But you won't because you're a practical man. And extremely prudent too.

HENRY:    Your insight often surprises me.

*Caroline holds out her hand. Henry hesitates, then places the ring on her finger.*

CAROLINE:    I know you find it surprising. You used to think I was empty-headed and half-mad. At least, that's what you told someone else, who was so discreet he told me what you'd said.

HENRY:    I have never said any such a thing.

CAROLINE:    Perhaps you did, perhaps you didn't. In any case, you thought it. The way you treated me confirmed it. Recently, I think, you've changed your opinion.

HENRY:    True!

CAROLINE:    You see, I may be a little foolish, but I promise you that I'm not a fool.

HENRY:    I'm becoming aware of it.

CAROLINE:    The ring is certainly worthy of a queen. But we are being far too serious. I want to hear you laugh again: the laugh of someone soon to be a count, even a king. If this is the Queen's ring, I ought to behave like the Queen, don't you agree?

HENRY:    What do you mean, like the Queen?

CAROLINE:    You know exactly what I mean. Let's make love the Elizabethan way!

*Caroline and Henry laugh hysterically.*

## Scene Two

*Elizabeth, deep in thought. Enter Lord Moore.*

ELIZABETH:    Lord Moore. Where is your son?

MOORE:    He waits outside, your Majesty. I thought you'd want my information first.

ELIZABETH:    Indeed. The matter concerning my cousin . . . were you able to confirm it?

MOORE:    It appears that Queen Mary has indeed placed on her coat of arms the title of Queen of England.

ELIZABETH:    It's an outrageous insult.

MOORE:    Perhaps it's not as serious as you think. Monarchs tend to give themselves a list of titles, most of them pure fantasy. I doubt that Mary has in mind to seize the throne.

ELIZABETH:    To place that title on her coat of arms amounts to describing me as illegitimate. But let us consider other matters. I wish to see your son.

MOORE:    Your Majesty . . . the matter of Lord Henry. . . .

ELIZABETH:    I'd like your opinion.

MOORE:    The fact is that he's not at all liked. I can't be sure that my personal feelings do not affect my judgement, but I cannot say much in his favour. He was never a warm or pleasant man, but recently he's become extremely arrogant. Few at Court would agree with his ennoblement, least of all Lord Norfolk.

ELIZABETH:    Nor you, I imagine.

MOORE:    My personal feelings are irrelevant. If your Majesty likes him and thinks he is a man of worth. . . .

ELIZABETH:    It's very strange. I find that people are like landscapes. They change according to the time of day.

MOORE:    I am informed that there is a woman in his life. I don't mean Caroline. He uses my wife simply to keep me under surveillance. There is another woman. He keeps her hidden away in Surrey. A secret lover.

ELIZABETH:    He's never mentioned her.

HENRY:    He must have his reasons to keep her out of sight. I hope to have more details soon.

ELIZABETH:   Keep me informed of the matter.

MOORE:   Your Majesty.

ELIZABETH:   Much better to know the truth sooner than later. But now I'd like to see your son. Someone at least to brighten up the day. By the way, who is this Spaniard he's brought with him?

MOORE:   A cheerful young man. Too early to form a judgement yet, but I'm sure he isn't dangerous. He seems extremely pleasant.

ELIZABETH:   The most pleasant people are often the most dangerous.

MOORE:   Quite possibly.

ELIZABETH:   In any case I need to meet him. Tell your son to enter.

## Scene Three

*Elizabeth, Lord Moore, his son David Moore.*

ELIZABETH:   David Moore! I can't believe it! This is amazing!

DAVID MOORE:   Forgive me, your Majesty.

ELIZABETH:   And why should I forgive you? The change is for the better. Moore, you must be proud of him.

MOORE:   Of course, your Majesty. As well as somewhat concerned.

ELIZABETH:   He's grown so much! And such a wonderful complexion! As if he's brought the sunshine with him! I remember you, David, as a timid adolescent. I'd never have known you, least of all in this Spanish costume.

MOORE:   I told him you wouldn't like it.

ELIZABETH:   On the contrary, it's extremely elegant. I'm glad you came like this. A breath of fresh air on a very depressing day.

DAVID MOORE:   Having come so recently from Spain, I felt it would not be out of place.

ELIZABETH:   Of course not. It tells me something about the country.

DAVID MOORE:   Exactly, your Majesty.

ELIZABETH:   You like Spain, then?

DAVID MOORE:   Indeed I do. It's very beautiful.

MOORE:   Young people always like the exotic.

ELIZABETH:   No matter, Moore. One wearies of constantly praising one's own country.

MOORE:   Nevertheless, your Majesty, I feel quite sure he's glad to be back.

ELIZABETH:   Is that so?

DAVID MOORE:   Leaving Spain was a great sadness, but I am truly glad to be back in England.

ELIZABETH:   And what impression have you formed?

DAVID MOORE:   Oh, it's changed a great deal. Everything seems more cheerful. People seem more pleasant . . . friends, servants, everyone. Even Lady Caroline seems less argumentative. She was so pleased to see me, she convinced me she was sincere.

MOORE:   She was so delighted, she gave him a present.

ELIZABETH:   And what was that?

DAVID MOORE:   This ring. I really didn't want it . . . it's obviously very expensive. But she insisted, and so I accepted.

ELIZABETH:   It does indeed look rather expensive. Was it yours, Lord Moore?

MOORE:   Indeed, no. It belonged to Lady Caroline.

ELIZABETH:   Prior to your marriage?

MOORE:   I can't say, your Majesty. Lady Caroline has many secrets.

ELIZABETH:   We should all have secrets. Secrets are a source of strength, revealing them the means of our undoing.

MOORE:   Quite so.

ELIZABETH:   Moore, I'd like to speak to your son alone. A father's presence can be somewhat inhibiting. It prevents a child from speaking openly.

MOORE:   I understand. If you allow me, I shall withdraw. I wish to visit Wesley. He's recently sent me some wonderful horses. I need to thank him.

ELIZABETH:   Give him my best wishes.

MOORE:   Of course, your Majesty. I shall.

## Scene Four

*Elizabeth and David Moore. She pours out wine.*

ELIZABETH:   Lady Caroline seems to like you.

DAVID MOORE:   Oh, no, your Majesty. She's never liked me.

ELIZABETH:   But it *is* a rather curious present. Did she know you were coming to see me?

DAVID MOORE:   My father mentioned it in her presence.

*They toast each other.*

ELIZABETH:   I wish to speak to you. But no one must know the subject of our conversation, not even your father.

DAVID MOORE:   I understand.

ELIZABETH:   Your father is one of my very best men, perhaps the person I trust most of all. Anything that worries him concerns me too. Do I make myself clear?

DAVID MOORE:   Absolutely.

ELIZABETH:   He is not the luckiest of men. His marriage to Lady Caroline was a great mistake. Even so, he accepts it with an admirable calm and a sense of humour. But I hardly need to tell you that.

DAVID MOORE:   I know the problem, your Majesty.

ELIZABETH:   You are his only consolation, the only thing he has.

DAVID MOORE:   As well as your Majesty's confidence and the honour and respect which come with it.

ELIZABETH:   Respect counts for nothing. Nor do honour and wealth. When one is old, the only thing that matters is love.

DAVID MOORE:   Not being old, I cannot say.

ELIZABETH:   I am surrounded by old men. I observe them. I see their lives, empty, broken, destroyed. They cling to self-indulgence, wine, even hate, as though their lives depended on such things.

DAVID MOORE:   I never think about old age.

ELIZABETH:   Of course not. Why should it matter to you at all? But your father has to matter. His good and generous nature deserve it. Lately he's been extremely unhappy.

DAVID MOORE:   Perhaps Lady Caroline. . . .

ELIZABETH:   She doesn't concern him in the least. He's concerned about you. What's happened? What were you doing in Spain? Why should the news he received make him ask me to request you to return so promptly? I want the truth.

DAVID MOORE:   Your Majesty, why so many questions?

ELIZABETH:   It doesn't matter. Your expression provides the answer.

DAVID MOORE:   I don't understand.

ELIZABETH:   It's perfectly obvious. You aren't a child any longer. You've grown up. And you have a way of looking at things that I've never seen before . . . as if you carried within you a different kind of world . . . as if you'd seen a different kind of reality. It makes me realise that for a queen too much haste could be extremely dangerous.

DAVID MOORE:   I don't know what you mean.

ELIZABETH:   You do not need to.

DAVID MOORE:   In any case, I'll willingly answer your questions, whatever they are.

ELIZABETH:   Very well. What did you do in Spain?

DAVID MOORE:   I don't understand.

ELIZABETH:   I think you do. Answer the question as you understand it: what did you do in Spain?

DAVID MOORE:   Why, all kinds of interesting things. I discovered life.

ELIZABETH:   In Spain? In a country so given to death and mourning?

DAVID MOORE:   At the moment Spain is wonderful. So full of life!

ELIZABETH:   You do surprise me. How can anything flourish in Philip's miserable shadow? Madrid breeds intrigue.

DAVID MOORE:   Perhaps. But I was in Toledo. Everything is different there.

ELIZABETH:   Would you like to return? Be honest with me.

DAVID MOORE:   I'm not sure. I don't know what I really want.

ELIZABETH:   The young man who's come here with you. Who is he?

DAVID MOORE:   A good friend.

ELIZABETH:   A friend. . . . Of course! Such a lovely word! So in Spain you discovered life and . . . friendship.

DAVID MOORE:   In my opinion, friendship is life.

ELIZABETH:   I don't know if I understand what lies behind those words. But I do understand your father's concern. I think we did well to make you come back. You are safer here. Spain is a dangerous place.

DAVID MOORE:   My father wants to see me married, tied to a wife and a household.

ELIZABETH:   And you don't want to.

DAVID MOORE:   I'll never marry. I want to be free.

ELIZABETH:   And if I were to choose a wife for you, would you refuse?

DAVID MOORE:   Your Majesty, I have the greatest regard for you . . . a true regard. Don't make me lose it in favour of the false regard that comes from fear.

ELIZABETH:   You are a bold young man. What's more, you have character.

DAVID MOORE:   If honesty is character, perhaps I do.

ELIZABETH:   Today has been a dreadful day. Lots of disagreeable news. You've changed it for me, although in a sense you've also made me more unhappy. Next week we are going hunting. I'd like to see you join us . . . only if you wish to, of course.

DAVID MOORE:   I do, your Majesty.

ELIZABETH:   Agreed then. And now I'd like you to give me the ring.

DAVID MOORE:   Of course.

ELIZABETH:   I wish to conduct a little experiment. When that is done, you can have it back. I shan't keep it, not when it was given as a gift.

DAVID MOORE:   A Spanish friend once told me that a gift which is then returned as a gift is much more valuable.

ELIZABETH:   Even so, I shall return it. But until then say nothing.

DAVID MOORE:   My lips are sealed.

ELIZABETH:   You may go.

*He is about to leave. The Queen stops him.*

David. . . .

DAVID MOORE:   Your Majesty?

ELIZABETH:   You kissed me once . . . one night in the gardens. Have you forgotten?

DAVID MOORE:   I haven't, nor will I ever forget. The only time I have ever kissed a woman . . . sincerely.

ELIZABETH:   The only time!

DAVID MOORE:   From a kiss one can learn so much about oneself. There is something I'd like to tell you, your Majesty, although I don't know if I should.

ELIZABETH:   David Moore. . . .

DAVID MOORE:   Everything could have been so different!

ELIZABETH:   Completely different.

DAVID MOORE:   Now I have overcome all that, your Majesty. It's even possible that through that anguish I was able to discover my own truth and develop my own philosophy. But. . . .

ELIZABETH:   That great anguish. . . .

DAVID MOORE:   Indeed, your Majesty. And so strange. Life could have been much easier, simpler, much more comfortable. The path I follow now is much more exciting, richer, full of great emotion, but there are times when I feel so exhausted. Do I offend you, your Majesty?

ELIZABETH:   You move me greatly. Hearing all this makes me tremble. We can only live one way even though we long for what we have renounced. David Moore, we shall meet again at the hunt.

## Scene Five

*Elizabeth and Lord Henry.*

ELIZABETH:   Forgive me, Lord Henry. It took much longer than I thought.

HENRY:   Of course. Young Moore must have brought you lots of news from Spain.

ELIZABETH:   Nothing of great importance. He's far too young and not especially observant. Tell me, does he annoy you?

HENRY:   He is rather arrogant. How dare he appear before you dressed as a Spaniard! He lacks respect.

ELIZABETH:   He's young. You have to excuse him.

HENRY:     Youth is not an excuse for everything. He ought to be told.

ELIZABETH:     In any case, I'm sure he's not the reason why you've come.

HENRY:     Of course not.

ELIZABETH:     I don't have much time. . . . Where's the ring I gave you?

HENRY:     I don't wear it all the time. It's far too precious.

ELIZABETH:     I like to see it on your finger.

HENRY:     I prefer to keep it hidden away. It is, after all, our secret.

ELIZABETH:     But if you hide it, you cannot see it.

HENRY:     I see it every day. Before leaving this evening I looked at it.

ELIZABETH:     I want you to wear it.

HENRY:     Very well, I shall.

ELIZABETH:     I must be brief. I am dining with the Spanish Ambassador. At times like these I must have King Philip on my side.

HENRY:     What you need at your side is someone strong. We should get married.

ELIZABETH:     The time is not appropriate.

HENRY:     It never is. There are always obstacles. . . . Do you think the time is right to honour me? If that isn't done, we cannot be married.

ELIZABETH:     I am aware of that. I feel so ill at ease.

HENRY:     Elizabeth, marriage would give us peace of mind.

ELIZABETH:     That is what I long for most of all.

HENRY:     Though the marriage *is* to your advantage. Such acts demand sentence of death. I'd be risking my life.

ELIZABETH:     But I know you are brave.

HENRY:     It's because I love you. Much better for me not to marry . . . simply to enjoy your favours. But that would be unfair. I much prefer to share the risk. I'll come tonight.

ELIZABETH:     No, not tonight. I prefer tomorrow.

HENRY:     Tomorrow I shall be away. I leave early.

ELIZABETH:     Where are you going?

HENRY:     I told you earlier. To Surrey.

ELIZABETH:     Ah, yes.

HENRY: Some building work on the castle. I need to see what progress has been made.

ELIZABETH: How long will you be away?

HENRY: As long as I'm required. I will be back for the hunt.

ELIZABETH: I look forward to it.

HENRY: How can you be so cold? Have your feelings for me changed? You seem like ice. It's a week since I came to your bed.

ELIZABETH: But you have Lady Caroline.

HENRY: She means nothing. Other women mean nothing. I need the kisses, the embraces, the gentle, exquisite touch of someone else.

ELIZABETH: It's getting late.

HENRY: Very well, I shall go to my estate. When I return, you can tell me when you wish to see me. I am the servant who must jump when his master commands.

ELIZABETH: You might refuse.

HENRY: I will never refuse.

ELIZABETH: Why not?

HENRY: It would be cruel to deny you the body that you so desire.

ELIZABETH: It's late. You must go. I understand what you've said and I think I know the answer. The ring shall be our method of communication.

HENRY: In what way?

ELIZABETH: You must always wear it. On your left hand it will signify that you wish to make love; on your right that you do not.

HENRY: And if I am not wearing it?

ELIZABETH: It means that everything is ended. Agreed? I shall see you at the hunt. I shall look for the ring.


## Scene Six


*Lord Henry and Lady Caroline.*

HENRY: Where is the ring?

CAROLINE:   Which ring?

HENRY:   The ring you stole from me the last time I was here.

CAROLINE:   What do you mean 'stole'? You gave it to me.

HENRY:   I want it back. I need it.

CAROLINE:   It's mine. You can't have it.

HENRY:   I should never have agreed to it.

CAROLINE:   You gave me it of your own accord.

HENRY:   Only because you threatened to reveal my secret. But now I want the ring returned.

CAROLINE:   I don't have it. I seem to have lost it.

HENRY:   Then I think you'd better find it.

CAROLINE:   You are hurting me!

HENRY:   I could break every bone in your body.

CAROLINE:   Please!

HENRY:   Tell me what your game is.

CAROLINE:   There is no game. It's quite simple. I lost the ring.

HENRY:   Then someone could easily find it, and the Queen would get to know.

CAROLINE:   I don't think so. The fact is . . . I remember where I left it.

HENRY:   Where?

CAROLINE:   In my husband's hunting lodge. I can ride out there and get it tomorrow.

HENRY:   Tomorrow I have matters to attend to. I'll be back for the hunt. We'll meet the night before, and you'd better have the ring.

CAROLINE:   Are you going to Surrey?

HENRY:   Yes.

CAROLINE:   To see your wife?

HENRY:   No.

CAROLINE:   Then why are you going?

HENRY:   If you must know . . . to bury her.

## Scene Seven

*David Moore and Lady Caroline.*

DAVID MOORE:    Come in, Lady Caroline.

CAROLINE:    Were you reading?

DAVID MOORE:    Yes, I was.

CAROLINE:    Some men do the strangest things!

DAVID MOORE:    You think reading strange?

CAROLINE:    Yes, I do. What's the point of it? Oh, it's very fashionable. Do men in Spain read?

DAVID MOORE:    Of course.

CAROLINE:    Then the women must have a dreadful time.

DAVID MOORE:    There are also women who read. And some who study at the University.

CAROLINE:    Really? They must be extremely advanced. Why are you looking at me like that? What are you thinking?

DAVID MOORE:    Oh . . . just that a woman as practical as you doesn't use quite so much perfume simply to come and discuss reading.

CAROLINE:    No, of course not. Am I being a nuisance?

DAVID MOORE:    Just tell me what you want. I dislike prevarication.

CAROLINE:    I was just about to . . . but it *is* a rather delicate matter . . . to do with the ring I gave you.

DAVID MOORE:    What about the ring?

CAROLINE:    I see you aren't wearing it. Don't you like it?

DAVID MOORE:    Of course I do. It's very beautiful. But I rarely wear rings . . . or chains. Nothing that suggests the idea of being bound. I like to feel free.

CAROLINE:    Oh, yes, I understand. But you *do* like it?

DAVID MOORE:    I can't think why this ring is so important.

CAROLINE:    Then would you mind if I ask for it back?

DAVID MOORE:    Of course not. Why should I?

CAROLINE:    Are you quite sure?

DAVID MOORE:   If you want it, you can have it. I don't really mind.

CAROLINE:   I'll give you another that's worth even more.

DAVID MOORE:   There's really no need. You can have it back. Don't feel indebted.

CAROLINE:   In that case, could I have it?

DAVID MOORE:   Now?

CAROLINE:   If it's not too much trouble.

DAVID MOORE:   Impossible, I'm afraid.

CAROLINE:   But why? Don't tell me you've lost it, or had it stolen. You haven't given it to Don Alonso?

DAVID MOORE:   Nothing like that. But why this concern about the ring? You seem so nervous?

CAROLINE:   I'm so unhappy! No one likes me. . . . No one looks after me. . . . I feel so unprotected . . . so alone!

DAVID MOORE:   You have my father for a husband.

CAROLINE:   He ceased to be my husband long ago.

DAVID MOORE:   Lady Caroline!

CAROLINE:   Who can I tell if not you? But you are a man. What man can understand the bitterness of a woman vilified and cast aside?

DAVID MOORE:   You have lots of friends.

CAROLINE:   Don't insult me! I needed something else . . . love, tenderness . . . those things that exist within the family. What use are so-called friends and lovers? What can a lover give a married woman?

DAVID MOORE:   A ring perhaps?

CAROLINE:   You are just as bad as all the others. You despise me! You hate me too!

DAVID MOORE:   Lady Caroline!

CAROLINE:   Lady Caroline has her head in the clouds. She expects too much. Lady Caroline is a foolish, unhappy woman.

DAVID MOORE:   I'm sorry. I didn't mean to offend you. I was merely joking.

CAROLINE:   That's what I seem to be for you all: a joke. No one respects me. No one takes me seriously.

DAVID MOORE:   I promise you. I've never regarded you as a joke.

CAROLINE: No, you regarded me as worse than that. I wanted to be your friend, but your father saw it differently. That's why he sent you to Spain, to avoid a relationship between us.

DAVID MOORE: It isn't true.

CAROLINE: It's as true now as it was then. Your father saw guilt where there wasn't even desire. You rejected me before I had even made an advance.

DAVID MOORE: You must have been imagining things. You were spending too much time alone.

CAROLINE: Of course! The fantasies of a mad woman! Oh, I don't blame you for thinking that. But since you came back, I've tried to be your friend once more . . . to join in when you've gone walking or hunting with Don Alonso. But you've excluded me completely.

DAVID MOORE: But you're a woman.

CAROLINE: It's not because of that. It's not because I'm a woman. It's because I'm Lady Caroline. The two of you want to be alone. I can't think why. Perhaps I daren't think why.

DAVID MOORE: Lady Caroline . . . if my father. . . .

CAROLINE: Oh, your father isn't afraid of us anymore. He's quite happy in that respect. But I pray to God you aren't involved in a kind of love more culpable than mine could ever be.

DAVID MOORE: Madam!

CAROLINE: Like the love you feel for Don Alonso. Quite shameful!

DAVID MOORE: No love is shameful.

CAROLINE: I disagree. Some kinds of love are monstrous . . . so hideous and repulsive that those who practice them merit execution.

DAVID MOORE: Get out! Get out at once, before I throw you out!

CAROLINE: Admit that you hate me. No, not that you hate me . . . that you despise me. You look down on me. I'm not good enough to merit your hate. You despise me, all of you! But I swear to you I'll have revenge. I swear it! I'll have my revenge on all of you. I promise!

## Scene Eight

*The hunt. Elizabeth, the deaf-mute guard, Lady Caroline, Lord Henry, Lord*

*Moore, David Moore, the Ambassador of Spain, Norfolk.*

NORFOLK:    The Queen has wounded a boar. Long live the Queen!

ALL:    Long live the Queen!

*The Queen and the Spanish Ambassador.*

AMBASSADOR:    It's true what they say, your Majesty. You are a king and queen in one. There is no better horseman, and no one here could wound a boar with greater skill. You have the qualities of a man.

ELIZABETH:    Should there be war, I shall lead my soldiers into battle.

AMBASSADOR:    You'd acquit yourself well in battle, I'm sure. But the battlefield is no place for a woman.

ELIZABETH:    I am not a woman. I am the Queen.

*Elizabeth and Lord Moore.*

ELIZABETH:    Moore, my friend. What news?

MOORE:    Your Majesty. The woman is called Elizabeth. She is his wife and expects a child within four months. Their marriage has been kept a secret.

ELIZABETH:    For what reason?

MOORE:    The family is Catholic. They were stripped of their lands by your Majesty. Should I make further enquiry?

ELIZABETH:    There is no need. Lord Henry will not be my husband.

MOORE:    I am pleased to hear it.

ELIZABETH:    I thought you would be. Is your son here?

MOORE:    He is.

ELIZABETH:    I wish to speak to him.

*Lord Moore and Lord Henry.*

HENRY:    Lord Moore, why so alone? You bring your wife and your son to the hunt, and here you are completely alone. Why is that?

MOORE:    Children are uneasy in the presence of their father. As for Lady Caroline, Norfolk is her companion today. Have you hurt your hand?

HENRY:    I fell from my horse. It's nothing serious.

MOORE:    And you such an excellent horseman?

HENRY:    I wanted to arrive in time. I was rather careless.

MOORE:    From Surrey, I suppose?

HENRY:  Indeed.

MOORE:  Matters to attend to, or simply pleasure?

HENRY:  To be quite honest, a rather sad affair. I went to see what progress had been made on the castle and found myself attending a funeral.

MOORE:  Really?

HENRY:  No one of any importance. An unfortunate girl.

MOORE:  A friend of yours?

HENRY:  The daughter of some friends of mine.

MOORE:  Married?

HENRY:  No.

MOORE:  A great pity.

HENRY:  Who can say? Perhaps it was all for the best.

MOORE:  Do you mean the lady was with child?

HENRY:  I think so, yes.

MOORE:  I assume she was four or five months advanced.

HENRY:  Quite possibly.

MOORE:  Some deaths are extremely opportune.

HENRY:  Indeed they are.

MOORE:  I don't suppose it was a case of murder?

HENRY:  The doctor says not.

MOORE:  Then there is no problem.

HENRY:  No problem of any kind.

MOORE:  Except for the hand.

HENRY:  Not even with that. One hand is enough to corner my prey.

*Norfolk and Lady Caroline.*

NORFOLK:  Lady Caroline, where are you going?

CAROLINE:  I don't know.

NORFOLK:  Take care. The path is dangerous. What is it?

CAROLINE:  I feel so hot, as if I'm choking. My heart is beating so quickly.

NORFOLK:  Can I be of assistance?

CAROLINE:　Of course you can. The state I am in is all your fault.

NORFOLK:　I don't understand.

CAROLINE:　You abandoned me. If you'd come to see me more often, perhaps I wouldn't be like this. But you don't care any more.

NORFOLK:　How can you say that? I thought you didn't wish to see me. I thought you were well looked after.

CAROLINE:　I lost interest in Henry some time ago.

NORFOLK:　I didn't mean him. I meant young Moore, now that he's back.

CAROLINE:　My stepson doesn't need me. He's brought his amusement with him from Spain.

NORFOLK:　What does that mean?

CAROLINE:　Norfolk, if you were to visit me, I'd give you some useful information.

NORFOLK:　Regarding Moore?

CAROLINE:　And his son. Oh, this dress is so hot! And this hat so heavy!

NORFOLK:　Then why not remove it? You look more beautiful without it.

CAROLINE:　In the absence of other caresses, the wind shall stroke my hair.

NORFOLK:　Caroline!

CAROLINE:　Such interesting information! And since I've been on my own, I've even thought of a plan.

NORFOLK:　A plan for what?

CAROLINE:　I feel so tired! Do you see the hut, there by the river? Why not come with me? We can rest and talk. What do you say?

NORFOLK:　The path is dangerous.

CAROLINE:　We'll take great care. Are you coming?

NORFOLK:　I'm coming.

　　　*Elizabeth and David Moore.*

ELIZABETH:　For love one can pay a very high price.

DAVID MOORE:　Everything has its price. Death is the price of living.

ELIZABETH:　You are a bold young man.

DAVID MOORE:　I do my best not to be reckless. But I find it difficult to lie or pretend.

ELIZABETH:    Of course.

DAVID MOORE:    Life can only begin with the truth.

ELIZABETH:    And the truth often brings danger with it.

DAVID MOORE:    But constant fear destroys us. I shall never be ashamed of myself. I am proud of what I am.

ELIZABETH:    You enjoy taking risks?

DAVID MOORE:    With you I know there is no risk. I have kissed those lips.

ELIZABETH:    But now I am the Queen.

DAVID MOORE:    It is the Queen I wish to speak to. Your Majesty, a kiss should never be judged a crime.

ELIZABETH:    I did not make the laws.

DAVID MOORE:    But you can change them. Your Majesty, the whole world is changing. Even the evening light seems much brighter. All our laws are unnecessarily cruel.

ELIZABETH:    You are so young!

DAVID MOORE:    I shall always be young! You ought to know the world can be other than it is. The exercise of power need not be so despicable. There is a new kind of life, your Majesty. New men for whom love is their banner and their destiny.

ELIZABETH:    Lower your voice!

DAVID MOORE:    Your Majesty.

ELIZABETH:    You are in love, a kind of madness. But you must be prudent. I have no wish to know this friend of yours, but if he is so wonderful, if your feelings for him are so intense. . . .

DAVID MOORE:    You are wrong, your Majesty. Don Alonso is a friend. Nothing more.

ELIZABETH:    Nothing more?

DAVID MOORE:    I shall never belong to just one person. My love is a banquet, attended by many guests.

ELIZABETH:    I see!

DAVID MOORE:    And that is how it will always be.

ELIZABETH:    A bold attitude. And difficult to sustain.

DAVID MOORE:    It means accepting loneliness instead of freedom.

ELIZABETH:   It seems to me that the price of anything worthwhile is loneliness.

DAVID MOORE:   Perhaps inevitably.

ELIZABETH:   Perhaps not. David, don't you think the joy of such a banquet might be renounced in favour of something deeper and more important? A passion that justifies one's earthly existence? Wouldn't that be worth the effort?

DAVID MOORE:   I don't know, your Majesty. That would be to bring back old ghosts, the phantom I had renounced.

ELIZABETH:   Perhaps love and freedom can sometimes exist together. It might not be impossible.

DAVID MOORE:   If not impossible, it is extremely difficult.

ELIZABETH:   Loneliness is a high price to pay.

DAVID MOORE:   I am aware of that.

ELIZABETH:   (*taking his hand*) David Moore. . . .

DAVID MOORE:   In any case, you are a woman, though for me very different from the rest of them.

ELIZABETH:   I am the Queen.

DAVID MOORE:   You might be the only woman I could love, but still a woman. I have no wish to deceive either you or myself. I shall not allow myself such weakness. I shall not darken the brightness of my horizon. I would have to renounce so much!

ELIZABETH:   Perhaps not as much as you think.

DAVID MOORE:   What do you mean?

ELIZABETH:   Nothing. At least not for now. My moment of madness is over. It's time to think and be calm. But the possibility exists. I see it. I feel it.

DAVID MOORE:   Your Majesty.

ELIZABETH:   We shall speak again. But no more for now. Come, let's return. . . . What's this? A lady's hat!

DAVID MOORE:   It belongs to Lady Caroline. She must have lost it.

ELIZABETH:   Lady Caroline doesn't lose things. What is your relationship with her?

DAVID MOORE:   I hardly see her. But she did come to my room last night.

ELIZABETH:   Is she pursuing you?

DAVID MOORE:   I very much doubt that I'm the only one.

ELIZABETH:   I suppose not. But coming to your room. . . .

DAVID MOORE:   She wanted the ring returned, the one she gave me when I first arrived. I thought at first it was just an excuse, but when I said I didn't have it she became very angry.

ELIZABETH:   Then we must make sure she gets it back.

*Lady Caroline's hat has a jewelled clasp. Elizabeth places the ring over the feathers in such a way that it seems another clasp.*

We'll leave it there. Your father's coming.

*Elizabeth, David Moore and Lord Moore.*

ELIZABETH:   Lord Moore. . . .

MOORE:   Your Majesty.

ELIZABETH:   And Lady Caroline?

MOORE:   With Norfolk. I trust they have heard the call.

*Elizabeth, David Moore, Lord Moore, Lord Henry and the Spanish Ambassador.*

ELIZABETH:   How goes the hunt?

AMBASSADOR:   Extremely badly, your Majesty.

ELIZABETH:   Then let us hope your luck improves. As for you, Lord Henry, you cannot hope for success with a damaged hand, though, fortunately, it *is* the left.

HENRY:   Unfortunately for me, I'm afraid.

ELIZABETH:   Why is that?

HENRY:   I wanted to wear a ring on it today. Of course, it's quite impossible.

ELIZABETH:   Why worry about a ring? It won't be necessary for the task I have in mind for you.

HENRY:   What task, your Majesty?

ELIZABETH:   A trip to France. Our ambassador has fallen ill. Your presence there will be most opportune. You have shown us today you are a man of great resource.

AMBASSADOR:   Indeed, your Majesty. With just one hand he brought down a deer.

ELIZABETH:   Is that so?

HENRY:   In fact it proved to be a stag.

AMBASSADOR:   An arrow straight through its heart.

HENRY:   Sometimes, you see, a man can catch his prey with just one hand.

AMBASSADOR:   Ah, here are Norfolk and Lady Caroline.

*Elizabeth, David Moore, Lord Moore, Lord Henry, the Ambassador of Spain, Norfolk and Lady Caroline.*

CAROLINE:   Forgive us, your Majesty. We lost our way.

ELIZABETH:   No matter. Congratulations! A delightful costume!

CAROLINE:   You like it?

ELIZABETH:   The dress is superb and the hat most attractive. I love the clasp.

CAROLINE:   Would you care to have it, your Majesty?

ELIZABETH:   Indeed I would. Thank you.

*Lady Caroline gives her the clasp, but Elizabeth points to the other one.*

I prefer that one.

CAROLINE:   Why . . . yes . . . of course, your Majesty. Take it.

ELIZABETH:   Ah, it's really a ring! Only Lady Caroline, I think, has sufficient wit to use a ring as a clasp for a hat. How did the idea come to you?

CAROLINE:   I can't think, your Majesty. Who knows how things come to one?

ELIZABETH:   I fancy I shall use it as a ring. It fits my middle finger perfectly. But let the hunt continue.

HENRY:   Your Majesty.

ELIZABETH:   What is it, Lord Henry?

HENRY:   There's something I wanted to say.

ELIZABETH:   Isn't it a little late?

HENRY:   I think not.

ELIZABETH:   Very well, then. Go ahead of us, gentleman. Lord Henry will accompany me.

*Elizabeth and Lord Henry.*

I trust that, after all that's happened, your hand will quickly improve.

HENRY:   Why did you make me look such a fool?

ELIZABETH:   It's you who made a fool of me. You lied.

HENRY:    Lady Caroline must have stolen the ring. I told her I wouldn't see her again. It made her angry. A woman scorned. . . .

ELIZABETH:    It no longer matters. I have the ring. Tomorrow I shall name you Ambassador to France.

HENRY:    What you have to do is make me King of England.

ELIZABETH:    Our marriage was a foolish idea.

HENRY:    We've gone too far. We can't turn back.

ELIZABETH:    What we can't do is get married. You are married already.

HENRY:    My wife is dead. I have just come from her funeral.

ELIZABETH:    You don't mean to tell me. . . ?

HENRY:    You can think what you like. If you think I was responsible, it merely proves how serious I am. She was the only love of my life.

ELIZABETH:    You admit, then, that you don't love me?

HENRY:    What exists between the two of us is much, much stronger: something inadmissible.

ELIZABETH:    You have to go to France. Some time apart will help to cool our ardour.

HENRY:    My leaving England could prove dangerous.

ELIZABETH:    Because of what you might say? No one would believe you. As you said yourself, it's too incredible.

HENRY:    You could be accused of being an impostor, of having killed the real Queen in order to take her place. You know the penalty for regicide.

ELIZABETH:    Tell me, Lord Henry. Did you dream up these clever ideas on your own?

HENRY:    Do you wish to know if I've told someone else?

ELIZABETH:    I wish to know the extent of your imagination. I had always thought it much less inventive.

HENRY:    Which goes to prove, your Majesty, how much you underestimated me. I may not be quick or brilliant. But I know how to focus my mind when I'm obliged to. On the other hand, I did enjoy the game. Your secret is like a precious stone. It can be shaped in many ways. A real jewel.

ELIZABETH:    Which you intend to use as far as possible.

HENRY:    You think so?

ELIZABETH:   As the proverb goes: 'Reveal a secret to a friend, and his boot will soon press on your throat.' Isn't that the case?

HENRY:   I am not a scoundrel.

ELIZABETH:   You *are* a practical man.

HENRY:   Your Majesty has always recommended it.

ELIZABETH:   Indeed.

HENRY:   You see, I could go to France quite easily . . . forget the whole affair as a man of honour. But I doubt that your mind would be at ease. The thought that at any moment I could be indiscreet would make you feel uncomfortable, and any accident that might befall me more to be desired. Can't you see that? Your secret was a kind of trap that we both fell into. Our union is sealed. Our marriage is inevitable. And why not? Oh, I know young David Moore makes eyes at you and tells you wonderful stories about Spain. But Moore is just a dreamer. You need a different kind of man. Someone you can rely on. Someone to excite that body. A queen can't behave like Lady Caroline, least of all a queen like you. Nor can you marry a king. What would you do on your wedding-night? Be sensible. I have learned to renounce certain things and accept others. Life is a fact, not a fantasy. One has to accept one's limitations, as you yourself observed.

ELIZABETH:   It's true.

HENRY:   Will your actions therefore contradict your words?

ELIZABETH:   I am so confused. . . .

HENRY:   Give me the ring. Give me the ring, your Majesty!

*Elizabeth gives him the ring. He places it on his right hand.*


## Scene Nine


*Norfolk, Lord Moore, the Spanish Ambassador.*

NORFOLK:   The Queen is far too sensible to marry Lord Henry.

AMBASSADOR:   Even so, that is what I've heard.

NORFOLK:   No doubt he's spreading the story himself.

AMBASSADOR:   From what they say, it's not so much a story as a fact.

NORFOLK:   I don't believe it. I advise you not to believe it either.

AMBASSADOR:   What's your opinion, Lord Moore?

MOORE:   The Court is always full of rumours, some quite credible, others not.

NORFOLK:   You see?

AMBASSADOR:   Lord Moore has said nothing specific.

MOORE:   Because I know nothing. The Queen has told me nothing.

AMBASSADOR:   Would you be surprised if it were true?

MOORE:   I approve of whatever the Queen does.

AMBASSADOR:   Of course. Tomorrow I shall send messages to Spain.

NORFOLK:   I wouldn't do that. Forgive my daring to advise you. It seems to me rather premature.

AMBASSADOR:   But I wouldn't wish to speak to my King of events of which I had not already informed him in advance.

NORFOLK:   Anyone would think the wedding is about to take place.

AMBASSADOR:   That is my information.

NORFOLK:   Impossible! Even if the Queen had agreed to it, she'd have to wait. Who is Lord Henry, after all? He lacks sufficient nobility.

AMBASSADOR:   As I understand it, an English monarch can ennoble a subject. Isn't that the case, Lord Moore?

MOORE:   It is indeed. But that is not exclusive to the English. Nobility is a very vague concept, often just words on pieces of paper. Any king can ennoble whom he fancies.

AMBASSADOR:   You see, Lord Norfolk?

NORFOLK:   I repeat what I said before: Lord Moore has said nothing specific.

MOORE:   Gentlemen, why bother to speculate? Time will reveal all.

AMBASSADOR:   And in the meantime?

MOORE:   If you hear any rumours, let me know. And if they should ever become fact. . . .

NORFOLK:   Never!

MOORE:   You see? At least a part of the Court refuses to entertain them.

NORFOLK:   Absolutely!

## Scene Ten

*Elizabeth, Lord Henry, a scribe, an attendant, the Ambassador of Spain.*

ELIZABETH:   'The reasons aforementioned are more than sufficient to confer further nobility on someone who is shortly to become our husband. We therefore offer to Lord Henry. . . .' What noise is that? Find out what causes it.

ATTENDANT:   Your Majesty, the Spanish Ambassador wishes to be received. He says he has urgent business.

ELIZABETH:   Show him in.

AMBASSADOR:   Your Majesty.

ELIZABETH:   Has something happened?

AMBASSADOR:   Please excuse this interruption. But, in view of the serious nature of the matter, I very much doubt you will be surprised.

ELIZABETH:   On the contrary. I am very surprised indeed.

AMBASSADOR:   In matters of honour we Spaniards are extremely rigorous. King Philip. . . .

ELIZABETH:   Excuse me, your Excellency. I haven't the slightest idea what you are talking about.

AMBASSADOR:   As Spanish Ambassador here, I request custody of the prisoner Don Alonso and permission to send him back to Spain.

ELIZABETH:   What Don Alonso? Who is this person, and why is he a prisoner?

AMBASSADOR:   Your Majesty, the son of Lord Moore and Don Alonso were discovered this morning in circumstances I would rather not describe, but which leave no doubt as to the hideous and unnatural character of their crime. Consequently. . . .

ELIZABETH:   Where are they? What has happened to them?

AMBASSADOR:   I understand they have been arrested.

ELIZABETH:   Why wasn't I informed? Summon Norfolk. I wish to see him at once. Summon Norfolk!

AMBASSADOR:   Your Majesty. . . .

ELIZABETH:   Please forgive me. I cannot tell which is the greater: my anger or my sense of shock.

AMBASSADOR:    I understand, your Majesty. And I know you also understand my attitude. In Spain we have certain customs . . . a question of honour, do you know what I'm trying to say?

ELIZABETH:    Of course. A matter of honour.

AMBASSADOR:    In which case Don Alonso should return to Spain. Here he will have his head cut off. That should not be. He has to be burned at the stake. Unspeakable crimes are punished in Spain with fire. We burn them out. I wish to know if the prisoner is to be handed over.

ELIZABETH:    Of course. I wouldn't wish to deprive King Philip of the pleasure of seeing one of his nobles burn.

AMBASSADOR:    Do you disapprove, your Majesty?

ELIZABETH:    Not at all, Ambassador. I am happy for you. You seem to have come to life. Honour has put a spring in your step.

AMBASSADOR:    Thank you, your Majesty.

ELIZABETH:    Put your request on paper. I shall receive it tomorrow. Please leave me now. There is something else I have to attend to.

AMBASSADOR:    Good night, your Majesty. I am most grateful.

*Elizabeth and Lord Henry.*

HENRY:    May we continue?

ELIZABETH:    I think not. The news I have received does not allow me to devote myself to trivial matters.

HENRY:    You regard my ennoblement as trivial?

ELIZABETH:    Lord Moore's son is in the greatest danger. Anything might happen to him.

HENRY:    Nothing that he does not deserve. We know that he is guilty.

ELIZABETH:    I suppose you think that he ought to die? No doubt, you want him to die?

HENRY:    He should be put on trial. He is an extremely arrogant young man. He even boasts about his perversity. He is quite loathsome and depraved. Your personal liking for him should not blind you. He is an insult to us all. He dishonours the English Court.

ATTENDANT:    Lord Norfolk.

*Elizabeth, Lord Henry, Norfolk.*

NORFOLK:    Your Majesty.

ELIZABETH:   Welcome, Norfolk. Lord Henry. . . .

HENRY:   Perhaps I ought to leave.

ELIZABETH:   No, not at all, Lord Henry. We have to complete the document.

HENRY:   Do you think you can spare the time? Certain matters can always be postponed.

ELIZABETH:   Perhaps you are right. But why not dictate the wording yourself? Withdraw with my official. When the document is to your satisfaction, I shall sign it. Agreed?

HENRY:   Agreed, your Majesty.

*Exit Lord Henry. Elizabeth and Lord Norfolk.*

ELIZABETH:   Norfolk, what's happened? Why was I not told at once? I had to suffer the indignity of being informed by the Spanish Ambassador.

NORFOLK:   Lord Henry informed me that he'd tell you himself.

ELIZABETH:   You mean that he knew?

NORFOLK:   I'm sure he did, your Majesty.

ELIZABETH:   He'd only just arrived, of course, and we weren't alone. But what precisely is going on?

NORFOLK:   I have to say that I am concerned. I'm afraid the affair might affect relations with Spain. The news has spread like wildfire. Such a disgusting business.

ELIZABETH:   What do you mean?

NORFOLK:   It's the second time recently that something like this has occurred. And on both occasions with a foreigner. Everyone agrees that this sort of depravity always comes from foreign shores.

ELIZABETH:   Why must patriots always be so insensitive?

NORFOLK:   Your Majesty.

ELIZABETH:   Now hear me well. The same is to be done as in the case of Wesley's son.

NORFOLK:   It is being said that the outcome would be the same.

ELIZABETH:   I'm not concerned with what's being said. I will not have them put on trial.

NORFOLK:   Your Majesty. . . .

ELIZABETH:   Adultery is also a crime, Norfolk. And Lady Caroline talks too much. It would not be difficult to produce witnesses.

NORFOLK:    It might be a crime but it does not go against Nature.

ELIZABETH:    Norfolk, can I rely on you or not?

NORFOLK:    I am always at your Majesty's service.

ELIZABETH:    Proceed then. It has to be tonight. Inform Wesley. He will provide the horses. In the meantime I need to see Lord Moore. Summon him
yourself. Tell him to come at once.

NORFOLK:    Of course.

ELIZABETH:    And remind him . . . everything as before.

NORFOLK:    Good night, your Majesty.

ELIZABETH:    Good night.


## Scene Eleven


*Elizabeth and the ghost of Ann Boleyn. The deaf-mute guard.*

ANN BOLEYN:    Elizabeth, you have to take great care. You cannot continue to
take such risks. You've gone too far already. There is much more danger
than you imagine. Be prudent. Forget everything else. No one is worth it.
Nothing is worth it. Everything passes. Everything is forgotten. Nothing
is important, except to survive. Elizabeth, you have to take great care.

*Elizabeth tugs on the rope, and the deaf-mute guard descends from his
room, emerging from behind the tapestry. Elizabeth approaches him, and
he shows her the dagger which he has in his hand. Elizabeth pours some
wine and he drinks it. He kisses her hand and returns to the upper room.*

ELIZABETH:    One has to survive. It is all that matters.

ATTENDANT:    Lord Moore.


## Scene Twelve


*Elizabeth and Lord Moore.*

MOORE:    Your Majesty.

ELIZABETH:　My dear friend. . . . There is no time to lose. It has to be tonight. The same arrangement as for Wesley's son. You will see to it yourself. I must confess that I am frightened. It seems to me that someone amongst us has struck this blow. I suddenly feel the presence of traitors.

MOORE:　Your Majesty, I. . . .

ELIZABETH:　Go quickly. When the guards have made their second inspection: just as before, although I feel there is something different here. Take care, my friend. Take very great care. And God be with you.

## Scene Thirteen

*Elizabeth and Lord Henry. On the bed the body of David Moore.*

ELIZABETH:　It was you. It is written on your face. It was you.

HENRY:　It had to be done.

ELIZABETH:　Why? Why did it have to be done?

HENRY:　For your safety, as well as for mine.

ELIZABETH:　He was about to leave the country. How could he threaten us? A man who would never do anyone harm.

HENRY:　He was dangerous. Men of his kind always are. You have no idea.

ELIZABETH:　Both of us are of his kind!

HENRY:　Not both of us. Just you.

ELIZABETH:　You are right. Of course you are right. Just me.

HENRY:　You were obsessed by him. You'd have done anything, risked everything . . . I know you would. That's why I did it.

ELIZABETH:　A crime will always find some justification.

HENRY:　But I don't have to. I did what I had to, what any man of honour would have done. Men like him deserve that kind of treatment. In future we need to be merciless. We have to be if no one is to learn of our secret.

ELIZABETH:　No one shall. At least no one will suspect you, now that you aren't to be my husband.

HENRY:　I shall be your husband sooner than you think. I have taken steps. You are in my hands.

ELIZABETH:   I am the Queen.

HENRY:   *You* are a degenerate wretch and at my mercy. You can thank my sense of duty to my country for not attempting to help your sister. And, of course, the fact that there are nights when I desire you. Otherwise, your death would have been more painful by far than your mother's.

ELIZABETH:   At last you are being honest.

HENRY:   It is time.

ELIZABETH:   Not yet perhaps.

HENRY:   Don't be foolish. We'll get married at once. In fact, tomorrow. From now on I shall be at your side. I shall stay the night here. You are in my hands. You have to realise that I am the man, that I command. You are simply a tawdry imitation of a woman . . . even worse than that . . . the lowest of the low.

ELIZABETH:   You may be making a mistake.

HENRY:   I never make a mistake. Alone with me you are powerless, and we shall spend much time alone. You will do as I say . . . what pleases me, and when it pleases me.

ELIZABETH:   Ah!

HENRY:   And without complaint.

ELIZABETH:   You are hurting me!

HENRY:   I shall hurt you more than this . . . whenever I wish.

ELIZABETH:   Release me!

HENRY:   You will learn to enjoy pain. People like you . . . I know how much they enjoy it.

ELIZABETH:   You aren't as strong as you think, nor I as weak. (*Pressed back against the tapestry, she pulls the rope*) You see this neck? It seems so delicate, but if you were to try to squeeze it. . . .

HENRY:   Indeed I shall, so you understand your situation that much better. Let's see your neck and face go red! Only then shall I . . . Ahhhhhh!

*Lord Henry falls to the ground, stabbed by the deaf-mute guard who has appeared from behind the curtain.*

ELIZABETH:   David Moore, you are avenged! But what is vengeance now? It will not bring you back. We have lost the beauty of your person, the world is a sadder place on that account. You brought with you a light that shone on everything, and with your death it has been extinguished. Without you here, my reign will be the poorer. Fear shall cast its shadow over everything. You created truth and lived it. You discovered a door and opened it on to a different world, on to a path which led to other feelings. Who knows how many years will pass before your like is seen again. You discovered something so obvious and simple: that it is far better that two men kiss than kill each other. And because you thought and felt like that, they ended up by killing you. They are responsible who feel that the thrust of a sword is more noble, more beautiful, more manly than a kiss. Oh, may the day soon come when people like these are given their proper name: assassins!

# TRAGIC PRELUDE

# Alfonso Sastre

Born in Madrid in 1926, Alfonso Sastre was one of four children. His father worked as an engineer for the Madrid-based German company, Siemens. Ten years old at the time of Lorca's murder, Sastre spent his childhood in the lead-up to the Civil War. He experienced at first hand the bombing of the city, the ensuing food shortages and the political repression. The child of a middle-class family, Sastre was conventionally educated, completing his schooling at the Instituto Cardenal Cisneros. He subsequently made efforts to find work, notably in Customs and Excise but, having failed to do so in the harsh economic climate of the time, began a degree course in the Arts Faculty of the University of Madrid in 1947. He was not, however, a particularly assiduous student and did not complete his degree until 1953 at the University of Murcia.

Sastre's interest in theatre had been evident before he embarked on his academic studies. At the age of nineteen, he had already helped to form the Arte Nuevo (New Art) theatre group, whose interest in presenting new work was combined with a desire to revolutionize theatrical forms. Five years later, he became a member of a group with similar aims, Teatro de Agitación Social (Theatre of Social Agitation, or TAS). It was then that he encountered the kind of opposition he would experience for much of his career as a writer. In 1950, TAS's plans to present plays by Galsworthy and Toller — dramatists who embodied the ideological aims of the company — were thwarted by the censorship. Similarly, much of Sastre's own work fell foul of the regime. Although some plays had no problem in reaching the stage (*The Gag* in 1954, *The Blood of God* in 1955 and *Bread for Everyone* in 1957), others were either banned after a few performances or simply rejected out of hand by the censors. *The Condemned Squad* ran for only three performances in 1953, while *Death in the Neighbourhood* and *William Tell Has Sad Eyes* were both banned in the same year, as was *Tragic Prelude* in the following year. It was a pattern which affected the work of many writers and which would silence Sastre as a dramatist even more in the sixties than it had in the fifties.

In December 1955 Sastre married Eva Forest Tarrat, a graduate in medicine and psychiatry who would prove to be a constant companion in his opposition to the dictatorship. In 1953 Sastre had denounced censorship in a lecture in Santander and had repeated those views two years later in a manifesto signed by a group of writers in the same city. In his book of 1956, *Drama and Society*, he proposed that the true purpose of theatre should be to agitate and disturb. In the same year he was charged with participating in student demonstrations, and his theatre earnings were confiscated to pay his fine. Deprived of his income, without a roof over his head, and with a pregnant wife, Sastre left for Paris, where he remained for six months. Set-backs of this kind, however, did nothing to soften Sastre's aggressive stance towards the dictatorship. Indeed, his ability to absorb and survive constant persecution has helped to transform him into a heroic figure in his own personal drama.

The sixties represent a period in which Sastre was increasingly influenced by the 'epic' theatre of Brecht and in which his own work was effectively suppressed. *Night Assault*, written in 1959, was the first of a number of plays in which Sastre employed a looser structure and made use of direct address to the audience, as well as of slogans and titles. These two developments, coupled with a tendency for characters to step outside their roles in the action and with an overall attempt to distance the audience and encourage it to think about the meaning of the on-stage events, suggest a certain Brechtian influence. Although some of his plays did reach the stage (*Death Thrust* in 1960 and *Office of Darkness* in 1967), many were banned: *Blood and Ashes* and *The Banquet* in 1965, *The Fantastic Tavern* in 1966 and *Roman Chronicles* in 1968. In addition to the content of the plays themselves, Sastre's own political activities during these years undoubtedly had much to do with the banning. In 1961, for example, he had written a paper in which he advocated an amnesty for political prisoners. A year later he became a member of the Communist Party. In 1963 he joined other intellectuals in protesting against the treatment of miners in the province of Asturias and in 1966 he took part in the 'National Day Against Repression', an event held in the University of Madrid. For this he was fined 50,000 pesetas and, when he refused to pay, imprisoned in Carabanchel. Similar action was also taken against Sastre's wife, who, if anything, was an even more aggressive opponent of the regime. In 1962 she had been arrested for taking part in a political demonstration and was subsequently imprisoned. It was a pattern which would continue to be repeated for much of the seventies.

Despite the actions taken against him, Sastre frequently travelled abroad, sometimes to take part in conferences of various kinds, sometimes to attend productions of his plays. In 1972, however, his passport was temporarily withdrawn. In 1974 he was imprisoned on a charge of terrorism after protesting about the arrest and imprisonment of his wife who, earlier that year, had been accused of involvement with the Basque terrorist group, ETA. Released in 1975 on payment of a sum of 100,000 pesetas, he had to wait another two years for the release of his wife.

Even after Franco's death and with the new democracy imminent, Sastre continued to suffer the political repression he had endured during the dictatorship. Since 1977 he and his wife have lived in Fuenterrabia in the Basque country, and he has continued to write for the theatre. However, his more recent work contains neither the themes nor the driving motivation shown in his earlier plays.

# TRAGIC PRELUDE

a play by

**Alfonso Sastre**

# Characters

Beltrán

Antón

Oscar

Doña Julia

Pablo

The Mother

Laura

Newspaper Seller

Police Inspector

Doltz

Julio

# Scene One

*Beltrán's room in a modest pension. Beltrán, sitting at an upright piano, is playing a sad and evocative tune. Oscar is attempting to read a book. Antón is standing, looking from the window to the street. He begins to pace nervously around the room. The telephone rings suddenly, insistently. Beltrán stops playing. Antón goes to pick up the phone. Beltrán's voice stops him.*

BELTRAN:    No. Don't answer it.

ANTON:    Why not? It could be Pablo. We've waited long enough already. Or maybe it's one of the others. (*He moves away*) I see. So that's the signal. We aren't here. There's no one in your room, Beltrán. Not you, not me, not him. It's just as if we were shadows on a screen. Someone wants to tell us something, seems to be concerned. . . . But it doesn't really matter.

BELTRAN:    So what's wrong? (*Smiling*) You are putting on that voice again, the one you keep for big occasions. You always use that dramatic tone when something big is about to happen . . . like when, in a couple of hours' time, the moment comes to carry out a murder. What's wrong with you?

ANTON:    Nothing . . . I'm being stupid. . . . Whoever it was who phoned, I started thinking. . . . It's not important. . . . It set me off, that's all . . . gave me something to think about. . . . You know: a man or a woman at the other end of the phone . . . when no one answers, their hand begins to shake. . . . It might, after all, be a matter of life or death. . . . Or maybe it's someone who's feeling really down, who's afraid of the dark and wants to talk to someone. . . . But there's no one to listen, no one to take the call. . . . He's on his own. . . . Will he end it all tonight? (*Laughs nervously, addresses the phone*) There's no one here, my friend. There's no one here to take your call. (*He lights his pipe*) My God, how things have changed! It used to be I'd phone some girl, or one of my friends would phone me and we'd go and see some Shakespeare. Those days are gone forever.

*The piano again. Oscar takes a glass, fills it with water, swallows an aspirin.*

BELTRAN:    You're always taking aspirins, Oscar. You'll end up with an ulcer.

OSCAR:     I've got a splitting headache.

BELTRAN:     (*joking*) It's all that German philosophy. Too much for your poor brain.

OSCAR:     (*smiles*) I wish it were, Beltrán. But everything's getting too much for me, and yet it's all too little. I'm not myself these days. . . . I think I think too much.

BELTRAN:     You mean the girl.

OSCAR:     I can't seem to forget her.

BELTRAN:     (*begins to play a sentimental melody*) I think a little atmosphere. . . . Continue. . . .

OSCAR:     A woman arrives one afternoon . . . perhaps it's raining, we feel a little sad . . . or perhaps it's spring. . . .

BELTRAN:     (*continues playing*) Go on. . . .

OSCAR:     A woman with whom we'd planned to spend our entire lives, and now she's gone, abandoned us. The pain of it remains with us forever, despite the fact that with friends we go on smiling, or telling jokes or recalling the things we used to do. . . .

BELTRAN:     Like the wonderful day we spent in that bar, the place where we met the Americans . . . and greeted the dawn with sandwiches. . . . The day we met a girl on the bus and everything seemed easy. . . . The day a bomb fell on our hiding-place. . . . The day they threw us out of experimental psychology. . . . Your turn. . . .

OSCAR:     A man records his experiences . . . sleeps . . . some nights gets drunk. . . . He joins a political party . . . fights for the revolution . . . a very willing man. And after a time he begins to think that everything's turned out for the best.

BELTRAN:     He must be happy then.

OSCAR:     Of course.

BELTRAN:     But why?

OSCAR:     He decided to fight for others. He thinks he's got no future himself, but feels the lives of others can be improved. And when he fights on their behalf, he's suddenly surprised . . . he feels that his wounds begin to heal . . . though the sickness itself is still inside. Sometimes with friends you feel quite sad, you can't think of what to say . . . which means the sickness is still inside. (*Change of tone*) But since this story's about myself, I admit to being happy in spite of everything. I enjoy belonging to the party. I really believe it gives my life new meaning.

BELTRAN: You've got much more to cling to . . . family . . . mother . . . older brother . . . a sister soon to be married . . . a perfect family set-up.

OSCAR: True enough. But sometimes the family seems so far away. Sometimes I think it doesn't even exist. . . . But still, I go home at night, and there they are. I know I've got a lot to be thankful for.

BELTRAN: It's early days. You'll have nothing in the end.

OSCAR: What do you mean?

BELTRAN: The family of a revolutionary disappears. You'll be on your own. You'll see. (*Looks at his watch*) Pablo's late. He should be here by now. From what I've heard there's something lined up for tomorrow.

OSCAR: I think you're right. (*Quietly, as if he feels a chill of fear*) So easy to say: 'Something lined up for tomorrow.' And tomorrow a few more people dead.

ANTON: (*his voice is somewhat harsh*) Isn't that strange?

BELTRAN: What?

ANTON: I find it very strange. (*Pause. He laughs rather nervously*) 'A few more people dead.' Don't you think it strange to think that *someone*'s going to die, and we don't know *who*? Of course you do, even if they tell you it doesn't matter. We never know who it's going to be. It could be all of them out there.

BELTRAN: Don't be a bloody fool! What's got into you tonight?

*Pause, as if Antón doesn't dare continue. At last he does so nervously.*

ANTON: I can only kill a man of flesh and blood. Put a bomb in the street, and it's all too vague, too random. It scares me, like the dark used to do when I was a kid. . . . The thing is . . . I've got to say it . . . the kind of acts we carry out are far too indiscriminate. . . . I want to be responsible for something more specific, more concrete, even if it means the death of a child.

BELTRAN: Oh, do shut up, Antón. You are getting on our nerves.

ANTON: The anarchists claim such an act must be gratuitous. But for me it's completely sickening, inhuman. They demand much more of us than of anyone else.

BELTRAN: What I find strange is hearing you saying this . . . you know exactly what is going on. . . . We have to be patient, Antón. We have to keep our powder dry until the moment's right, until we know exactly who we are aiming at. It's early days. The dictator isn't yet within our sights. Even so, the party asks us to act with some precision.

ANTON:       Oh, yes. . . . Someone dies because he has to, because he's guilty. But others die with him too. Others who had no cause to die. Do you understand? Innocent people sacrificed. Completely pointless bloodshed.

BELTRAN:       Oh, don't be stupid. Just shut up!

OSCAR:       No, let him speak. We shouldn't be afraid to air things face to face. . . . You are right. Others do get killed, but for me it's not completely pointless. We have to regard the thing as a whole . . . innocent victims as well. . . . It's the only way to move this structure we call the State, and we have to destroy it, whatever the cost.

ANTON:       When I think of the State, I think of its people. You want to destroy the people.

OSCAR:       We've had all this before, Antón. It's up to us to create a mood of fear and distrust throughout the country. We have to weaken the Government's hold, discredit it, and bring the entire political edifice crashing down. We need to show it doesn't have control.

ANTON:       Of course, but the way we do things is still not specific enough.

BELTRAN:       Ah, so you mean it's not specific enough to cause a train to crash . . . despite the fact it might be carrying some high government official, or a chief of police?

ANTON:       All right. But what about the other passengers? What are they? Ghosts? Faceless men and women? Who do you think are laughing, chatting away in every compartment? I suppose you think they don't matter! Can't you see? It could be a girl I spent the night with. It could be my own mother.

BELTRAN:       We stick to our methods. That's all there is to it.

ANTON:       You know what they call us, don't you? They call us 'terrorists'.

BELTRAN:       (*coldly*) Believe me, Antón. You are starting to skate on very thin ice.

ANTON:       Oh, yes? Who says so?

BELTRAN:       There's nothing more to discuss. If you're scared, of course, you shouldn't be here . . . there's nothing worse than some gutless coward. . . .

ANTON:       (*extremely angry*) Beltrán! (*Pause*) I'm not a coward. I'm not afraid. Being scared is a thing of the past. Like the rest of you, I've overcome the simple feelings. . . . It's not a question of fear. . . . For us, it's become a question of love and hate. It's not that I'm afraid to kill, but to kill a man I need to hate him, and to love the rest at the same time, because they are good and unfortunate people, and they need to have me put an end to the cause of their suffering and hunger. . . . Those poor people deserve that someone should die and that we should kill them with genuine hate. . . . But when the party requires me to do it, I don't know why . . . I can't feel hate. . . . I feel so alone, frozen. . . .

BELTRAN:     You think too much. Don't you agree, Oscar?

ANTON:     Whenever I go on a mission, I feel exposed, vulnerable, like a frightened child made to stand in front of the class. It makes me feel, well, dirty. Maybe I shouldn't belong to any party.

BELTRAN:     Then just get out . . . if you think you can manage that. (*Pause*) Anyway, don't mention it to Pablo. He hates this sort of thing.

ANTON:     I'll tell him what I want. I've felt like this since the time they tortured me. I've given the party everything. He'll have to listen, though he won't take any notice.

BELTRAN:     He won't take kindly to it, that's for sure.

OSCAR:     It's still raining. What a wretched night it is! Let's hope nothing's happened to Pablo.

*A knock at the door.*

BELTRAN:     That'll be Doña Julia. Come in, Doña Julia.

*Doña Julia enters with some coffee.*

DOÑA JULIA:     Sorry the coffee's taken so long. We had no gas. I've brought some sugar for you.

*A clock chimes.*

Is it nine o'clock already?

OSCAR:     It's a quarter to.

DOÑA JULIA:     Are you expecting your friend?

BELTRAN:     Yes. Please let him in straight away.

DOÑA JULIA:     Of course I shall. I'll leave you to drink your coffee.

*She leaves. Antón begins to laugh.*

BELTRAN:     So what's wrong now?

ANTON:     (*still laughing*) I was just thinking. . . .

BELTRAN:    You're off your head.

ANTON:    I don't know if you've cottoned on, but in my opinion we'll never go back to the University. For us, it's a thing of the past. All the others will go back, books under their arms, nine o'clock lectures. . . . For them the strike is just a holiday, but it's all finished for us. Remember how the lecturers were nice to us? How they gave us good marks . . . or maybe even sometimes failed us? Can't you see how absurd it is? We'd register in September, save some money to spend in the bar, sing some student songs, some of them silly, some sad. It seems so long ago when really it was just the other day.

OSCAR:    (*recalling*) The songs weren't always silly or sad, Antón. There were some about the girl-friend we always dreamed of, or marching songs, or songs of the revolution.

BELTRAN:    I remember last November very clearly . . . before we became involved in the revolution. Killing was a vague, forbidden dream for us . . . the revolution a few secret notes we used to pass to each other, or the odd confrontation with someone in the corridor. . . . Do you remember, Oscar? We went out with girls we always fell in love with. Antón used to go to Mass once a week.

*Silence.*

ANTON:    (*harshly*) Yes, and what's become of it all?

BELTRAN:    It's finished. That's exactly what's become of it. The situation demanded our involvement . . . and, more than that, that we follow a certain programme. We're on our own, yes, but in the end we have to stick to it.

ANTON:    (*darkly*) I suppose you think that that is what redeems us. The flash of our explosions makes us pure.

BELTRAN:    I'd prefer a different kind of fight as well, you know. The flash of a gun would make me feel much better. But I do what I'm told. My job is to obey.

ANTON:    There are times when doing that just isn't enough.

BELTRAN:    You pay too much attention to the papers. They make it all as bloody as they can.

ANTON:    I know all that. But it's not the blood affects me, it's the anguish.

OSCAR:    Antón, there's nothing romantic about our struggle. In the past, a revolution was a very romantic thing. A 'coup d'etat' barely needed any preparation. But times are different now. We have to prepare the ground and everyone has his job to do.

ANTON: Oh, yes . . . and who else in the background but the people who spout theory, decked out in their uniforms, getting all the credit, and not a single mention of us? We'll be left to our own devices.

*Pablo enters just in time to hear Antón's last words.*

PABLO: (*softly*) What was that, Antón?

ANTON: I said we'll be left to our own devices.

PABLO: Just admit it . . . you're a coward. Oh, yes, I know about your damaged back and spitting blood when the police picked you up because of your own stupidity. You were a coward then, and you are still a coward now. But in this party you follow orders. It's not a bloody game. You've signed on for a difficult course, Antón. We aren't messing about.

ANTON: (*defiantly*) We'll be left to our own devices. That's what I said, and that's what I believe.

PABLO: Then why not go back to your classes? Save your pity for the down-and-outs outside the University. Feel sorry for people who owe you money and let them feel sorry for you. Be satisfied with that. It's much more up your street.

ANTON: Pablo, their hands will be clean, and we'll be left to pick up the pieces.

PABLO: 'They'? I'd like to know who 'they' are. Tell me who 'they' are. In the party, there is only 'us'.

ANTON: I mean the demagogues. There's too much blood being spilled by far, and all of it will be blamed on us because we are the ones who actually spilled it. They'll see us all as extremists, traitors . . . out of control, only concerned with terrorist acts. They'll disown us, claim they've got nothing to do with us. It's a filthy, rotten game, Pablo. We wanted a revolution, and what we've got is this bloody mess.

*Pablo hits out at Antón, who falls to the ground. Beltrán, in case someone should hear, plays the piano furiously.*

PABLO: Stop that bloody noise! It's pathetic enough without bloody background music!

*Beltrán stops playing.*

Oscar, a job for you tomorrow. You place a bomb, designed to explode when a certain car arrives, at 7 p.m. precisely. It will coincide with trouble at the University. But not to worry, everything's arranged. In the morning, you'll buy a portable typewriter from Hartman's. Everything's inside it, including the instructions. The car will be carrying the Minister of War. Is everything clear? 7 p.m. precisely.

## Scene Two

*A room in Oscar's house. Oscar's mother. Oscar enters.*

OSCAR:     Hello, mother.

*He kisses her.*

MOTHER:     It's half past ten. Where have you been? I can see you've been buying books again . . . wasting your money!

OSCAR:     I'll take the exams one day, you'll see. That's why I bought them. . . . I feel so hot.

*He puts the radio on. Music.*

MOTHER:     You must be going down with something.

OSCAR:     No, I'm all right. (*Pause*) Where's Julio?

MOTHER:     He's not home yet.

OSCAR:     Has he phoned?

MOTHER:     No.

*Pause.*

OSCAR:     Where's Laura?

MOTHER:     She went to the cinema.

OSCAR:     What? With Jaime?

MOTHER:     Yes.

*Pause.*

OSCAR:     I don't like her being out so late, not with the way things are.

MOTHER:     She won't be long. (*Pause*) Is it still raining?

OSCAR:     Just a bit.

MOTHER:     You ought to get a new mac for next winter.

OSCAR:     The one I've got is fine.

*Pause.*

MOTHER:    Any more news of the University?

OSCAR:    The students are still on strike.

MOTHER:    I'm quite convinced they've all gone mad. . . . Are you sure you're all right? You look so pale.

OSCAR:    I'm fine, mother.

MOTHER:    You seem to be on edge. Your hand is shaking.

OSCAR:    But it always shakes. You know that. (*Attempting a joke*) Maybe I'd better stop drinking. It's not as if I really enjoy it.

MOTHER:    Anyway, going back to the students . . . what exactly are they trying to do? I can't imagine. I suppose it must be about student matters, but I think they've gone too far this time.

OSCAR:    These aren't just student matters. The workers are with them too. The factories are just as empty as the University. These aren't just student matters anymore. That's all in the past.

MOTHER:    I'm not so sure. The workers will do what they want in the end, they won't want to know about students. And if one day the killing starts, they'll start with you. (*Pause*) Just you wait and see.

*Pause. She gets up, goes to the window, closes the blinds.*

OSCAR:    What's the matter?

MOTHER:    Nothing.

OSCAR:    Why are you crying?

MOTHER:    I've lived all my life in this house. This house is my whole world. I've always made sure you had clothes for the winter, food on the table, that the house was warm and cheerful. My children have been my whole existence.

OSCAR:    (*wanting her to be quiet*) Mother!

MOTHER:    (*smiling*) We've always been very happy here . . . there's always been lots of laughter . . . birthdays . . . and even though your father's gone, we remember him every year, and so he's still with us. It's all I really care about . . . I'm telling you this because I've known for a while that something's going on . . . something no one will talk about, that worries me and I can't say why.

OSCAR:    You see it in the newspapers. This whole situation . . . it's going to explode, that's all.

MOTHER:     Your brother doesn't tell me a thing. I get the impression there's something he's seen that he doesn't want to talk about. He comes home with some secret he keeps to himself, as if it were unrepeatable.

OSCAR:     A woman's collapsed in the street from hunger, her head split open as it hits the pavement. Her little girl, a sad little thing, stares at her, not daring to cry. Thousands of men are constantly being humiliated in offices, workshops and hospitals. They are the slaves of the times we live in, accustomed to humility, to averting their eyes, to having no rights, to accepting what they get as if it were an act of charity. They have the expression of obedient dogs, they expect nothing, they die of pneumonia, tubercolosis, hunger, lack of shelter. That's what Julio sees, and that's what he doesn't want to tell you.

*Pause. The clock chimes.*

Julio's late.

MOTHER:     Listen. The lift. It could be him. Or it might be Laura.

OSCAR:     It hasn't stopped. Laura shouldn't be out so late.

MOTHER:     I'll get Paula to lay the table. Paula!

OSCAR:     I'm not hungry.

MOTHER:     You aren't feeling well. I knew it.

OSCAR:     I'm perfectly all right. Listen. The front door.

*Paula enters.*

PAULA:     Did you call?

MOTHER:     Would you lay the table, please.

PAULA:     Of course, señora.

*As she goes out, she meets Laura coming in.*

LAURA:     Hello, mother. Oscar.

OSCAR:     Laura!

LAURA:     Such a horrible night!

MOTHER:     Is it still raining?

LAURA:     Yes, it is. Where's Julio?

MOTHER:     He's not back yet. I'm worried about him.

OSCAR:     He'll have gone to see some friend. So what was the film like?

LAURA:     All right, I suppose. A bit boring really. Anyone seen the scissors? (*Oscar hands her the scissors. She seems engrossed in her thoughts, a little distant*) It started well and then it seemed to lose its way. But the acting was extremely good.

MOTHER: (*watching her*) What are you thinking about?

LAURA: Nothing, mother. What should I be thinking about? I've got a bit of a headache.

MOTHER: I want you to tell me, Laura.

LAURA: But, mother, there's nothing to tell.

MOTHER: I could tell as soon as you came in . . . the same as when Julio comes in. What did you see?

LAURA: Nothing, mother. Why are you asking?

MOTHER: (*changing her tone*) I only want you to tell me the truth, instead of hiding things.

*Pause.*

LAURA: (*wearily*) Yes, mother. There was something this evening. I didn't see it myself but Jaime did . . . he looked as white as a sheet. He said he'd sensed it even before it happened. I knew at once what he meant . . . you suddenly feel a kind of tension . . . passers-by exchange glances . . . someone stops . . . others stare at a given point . . . 'Something's happening or about to happen.' Haven't you ever had that feeling? It's just for a moment and then it's gone, like when you think a film is about to break and the cinema lights will suddenly come on, but luckily . . . or unluckily. . . .

MOTHER: What is it, Laura? Tell me what happened.

LAURA: Something awful.

MOTHER: An accident?

LAURA: About seven, in the Avenida de las Acacias. A bomb exploded under a bus.

MOTHER: A bomb?

LAURA: Yes. Some people on the bus were killed and others injured. Jaime saw a dead woman, lying in the road in a pool of blood. Someone was shouting to cover her up. The horror of it all was in his eyes. I've never seen him so distraught, such hatred in his face. He wanted to describe it all. I had to stop him.

MOTHER: We live in desperate times. It's safer to stay at home and never go out. Anyway, let's eat . . . I feel so tired. Too much reading, I expect. It's given me a headache. You know how tired it makes my eyes. . . . We ought to spend some time in the country, in grandfather's house. It's nice there. Getting old here is becoming painful, shut in the house, and seeing my children aren't very happy. It's as if there's no one happy anymore.

LAURA:     Mother. . . . (*The telephone rings. The Mother answers it*)

MOTHER:     It's probably Julio. Hello? Ah, Juan. He's not home yet. What? Half past six? No. He must have called on someone. Yes, try later. (*She puts the phone down*).

OSCAR:     Was that Uncle Juan?

MOTHER:     He said that Julio left his house at half past six, to come home.

OSCAR:     That's ages ago.

LAURA:     Something must have happened.

OSCAR:     Oh, don't be silly. Julio never looks for trouble.

LAURA:     But tonight there were people killed.

MOTHER:     What are you saying, Laura? Are you mad?

LAURA:     (*in a slow, monotonous tone*) We mustn't get frightened. Let's consider calmly. At seven o'clock Julio could well have been coming through the Avenida de las Acacias. Consider, mother. It's very strange that he hasn't yet come home . . . or let us know. I feel as if we are all alone tonight. We shouldn't get frightened but let's consider calmly. To get here from Uncle Juan's house you have to come down the Avenida de las Acacias. It's the obvious route, the one you'd take every day. Help me, mother! Help me, mother! Help me to stop thinking it!

MOTHER:     You must be mad! You must be mad!

LAURA:     Mother, I'm frightened. I'm so afraid!

OSCAR:     The lift's coming up! Quiet! Listen! (*Silence. They listen*) It hasn't stopped. It's gone past.

LAURA:     (*weeping*) I'm frightened, mother.

OSCAR:     Shut up, you fool! (*He switches off the radio*) Nothing's happened. Nothing.

## Scene Three

*The street outside Oscar's house. Oscar is leaving just as Beltrán arrives.*

BELTRAN:     Oscar. Your phone's been engaged for ages. I thought I'd better come myself.

OSCAR:     We've been trying to phone the police and all the hospitals. It's two in the morning and my brother hasn't come home.

BELTRAN:     There's been a tip-off. There's not a moment to lose. They'll be looking for you.

OSCAR:     Looking for me? Who do you mean?

BELTRAN:     The police. Someone's tipped them off. You have to disappear for a while.

OSCAR:     I'm on my way to the General Hospital.

BELTRAN:     What for?

OSCAR:     We couldn't get through on the phone. We've been trying for hours. They must be rushed off their feet.

BELTRAN:     But Oscar, they'll pick you up. You're in great danger . . . both of us are. What happened tonight was big. . . They are really pleased with you . . . but you've got to get away. If they pick you up, we've had it . . . all of us.

*A newspaper vendor passes.*

NEWSPAPER VENDOR:     Paper! Paper!

OSCAR:     Hey, wait!

NEWSPAPER VENDOR:     Paper, sir?

OSCAR:     Yes. Keep the change.

BELTRAN:     Oscar, stay away from the light.

OSCAR:     I want to see what it says.

BELTRAN:     But this is stupid. You know what I said.

OSCAR:     Just leave me alone.

BELTRAN:     Oscar, listen!

OSCAR:     Go away! I've told you. Leave me alone!

BELTRAN:     But what's in the paper that's so important? What are you looking for? You'll ruin everything. Forget it. What does it matter what it says? 'Three dead in bomb attack'. There! See? So what the hell is wrong with you?

OSCAR:     Beltrán, I need you with me tonight. Three dead. (*He reads on*) 'This evening in the Avenida de las Acacias. . . . The Minister's car escaped the explosion. . . . The bombers. . . .'

BELTRAN:     (*snatches the paper from him*) Stop it, for God's sake! Control yourself, Oscar. Have you lost your senses?

OSCAR:     Beltrán, I want you to read me the names. Read them. I have to know the names.

BELTRAN:     What names? What the hell are you talking about?

OSCAR:     I have to know who the people were. I can never cope with the deaths of nameless ghosts. The people I killed had real names and I need to know what they are.

BELTRAN:     The paper doesn't say who they are. No doubt you'll know tomorrow. But now you have to come with me. By dawn they'll have got you out of the city. What is it?

OSCAR:     Look, there's someone out there.

INSPECTOR:     This is the police. We've got the street surrounded. Don't move. Drop the gun. You'd best come quietly.

*Beltrán fires and makes a dash for it. Oscar doesn't move. He allows himself to be handcuffed.*

INSPECTOR:     Oscar Marto, correct?

OSCAR:     Yes.

INSPECTOR:     Take him away.

*The Inspector speaks into his walkie-talkie.*

ZX2081. Castro speaking. We've arrested Oscar Marto. No problems . . . though the other one's tried to make a run for it. Make the necessary preparations. I'm going over to the house. Over and out.

## Scene Four

*A cell at the police station. Outside, a policeman walks up and down. Oscar has been beaten and lies on the floor of the cell, groaning. He struggles to a sitting position.*

OSCAR:　　Hey, you! I need a drink of water. Do you hear me? Water! I need a drink. I'm dying of thirst. Listen! Do you hear me? Listen!

*The policeman watches him in silence.*

What do you think you are looking at? What are you doing staring at me?

*He tries to move, groans with pain.*

What have you done to me? Bastards! I can hardly move.

*Pulls himself to his knees.*

The one who hit me while my arms were being held. He enjoyed doing that, the bastard!

*Struggling to his feet.*

I can barely stand. What time of day is it? I feel sick. My God, I'm going to be sick. My God!

*He falls to the floor, groaning and vomiting. After a while he is calmer.*

I want to see my family. Do you hear me? I need to see my family at once. How long have I been here? My brother could be dead, don't you see? I need to speak to my family. Do you have a phone? There must be a phone in this God-forsaken place. All I want to do is make a phone-call.

*Silence. After a little while.*

The pain seems to have gone. It's suddenly disappeared. I feel much better. . . . But that makes this more difficult to bear. . . . I can't afford to feel no pain . . . I need to feel it in my chest, my back, my legs, my face . . . the emptiness in the pit of my stomach, my heart missing a beat, in order to resist it! . . . But it seems to have gone. I can't explain it. I feel so different . . . as if I were somehow floating . . . outside myself . . . it's difficult to put into words. . . .

*He cries out.*

I want to know what's happened. I don't know what I've done. I need to know where my brother is. I feel so helpless . . . no news of anything out there . . . not a single word . . . nothing . . . in this God-forsaken cell. They've got no right to keep anyone here. . . . A human being needs to see his fellow human beings . . . what's going on in the outside world . . . or else go mad . . . and be quite useless even to the police. (*His tone becomes monotonous*) Whatever someone does, he has a right to speak to his family. . . . It's the only thing they can't deprive him of, even if he's killed a child, or poisoned someone. . . . He has a right to speak to his brother or his sister, to tell them there's nothing to worry about, that everything will turn out fine and soon he'll be back home. He ought to be able to know that his family are free to sleep, to listen to the radio, to read a book. . . . He ought to be sure of all those things before he answers any questions . . . it will help to stop him going mad . . . from losing his senses completely. . . .

*Silence. The Inspector and another man appear. The policeman unlocks the cell door. The Inspector and the other man enter and the door is locked behind them.*

INSPECTOR:    Well then, lad. Maybe we can make some progress. Leave it, Doltz. It won't be necessary this time. He's going to talk, aren't you, lad? (*Pause*) If you only knew how much I hate all this. It's a case of seeing too much, you see. It gets you down in the end. I often wish I'd chosen another profession. What I'd really like best, of course, would be you giving me some information, so I wouldn't be obliged to make you suffer. What do you say? You tell me who's in charge of your group and the names of some of your friends . . . do you really think that would make me happy? I very much doubt it. In fact, I'm not that interested. I'm just a chap who has a job to do. I mean to say, if my wife's sick or my eldest son goes down with something, and I get uptight about it, does it make it better to know your boss's name? Of course it doesn't. It doesn't change it at all. . . . On the other hand, if you were to give me such information, it would make my job a little easier . . . and save you a good deal of pain. . . . In my opinion, lad, it's definitely worth it. My job's become very hard, you know. You insist on making it hard for us. . . . All right, I'm listening. I'm waiting to hear what you've got to say.

*Silence.*

All right, if that's the way you want it. You see, Doltz? He won't see reason.

*Doltz approaches Oscar and hits him to the floor. He pulls him up again and hits him once more. As Oscar lies on the floor, Doltz kicks him in the face.*

No, that's enough. He seems to be unconscious. Throw some water over him.

*Doltz throws a bucket of water in Oscar's face. He comes round.*

I think you should know I've been to your house. I spent some time with your mother, poor woman. . . . I didn't really want to mention it . . . I'd rather have you speak of your own accord than take advantage of your situation. . . . But you've given me no choice . . . I'll have to tell you, I'm afraid, exactly what has happened . . . the full extent of what you've done . . . I hardly know where to start. . . . The awful thing is that such things happen at all. Who would have thought that your exploits would make such a mark or move people to tears? I think you know what I'm talking about. (*Pause*) You've killed your own brother. He was on the bus when the bomb went off. From the moment he got on the bus, his fate was sealed, and even then he may, of course, have been thinking of you, because he was really fond of you, as brothers are. . . . (*He produces a photograph*) You'd better take a look. It's a photograph that ought to make you die of shame and horror . . . one for the School of Medicine's records . . . neatly filed away. But maybe you'd like to have it for your own records. . . . You needn't be scared. . . . The face is blown to bits, it's true, but it won't be the first or the last. . . . You see, you can just about tell who it is, despite the damage. (*Oscar begins to moan*) Maybe you'd better think it over. I'll come back later, in half an hour . . . we'll have a little talk. . . . My God, I'm feeling tired! You see, despite what you think, I find all this extremely painful. I'll see you later then.

*The Inspector leaves. Doltz drags Oscar into a sitting position. As he does so, he whispers to him.*

DOLTZ:      Listen to me, lad. Pay attention. I'm a Party member. You'll be out of here in forty-eight hours.

## Scene Five

*Beltrán's room in a modest pension. Beltrán is playing the piano absentmindedly. Pablo is working at some papers.*

PABLO:   Beltrán.

BELTRAN:   What?

PABLO:   The news looks good. It seems that things are going well in the provinces. The foreign press refers to various acts of sabotage . . . the agencies seem to want to give us maximum publicity. The outside world knows that something big is going on, though it's only the left-wing press, of course, that draws attention to it. It seems an armaments factory has been blown up . . . must be the work of Group 28. The police threw a cordon around the area and caught no one. Their information is completely out of date, at least fifteen years old. They don't seem to realize that this is all new. It does mean, though, that thirty to forty of our people are being tortured to no purpose. Do you have the stuff for the newspaper?

BELTRAN:   Here.

PABLO:   Most of it is pure rubbish. Here's Oscar's piece . . . you know, the one the Committee rejected the last time around. 'In Defence of Terrorism'. Not a bad title.

BELTRAN:   He's never been afraid of words.

PABLO:   The Committee was right. 'Terrorism' is nothing but a concept invented by the bourgeoisie that has nothing to do with us. They call everything that. They wave their arms in the air and call us 'terrorists'. Why should we play along with them?

BELTRAN:   Why be scared of a word they use to discredit us? Oscar wasn't scared. Wherever they've got him now, he's putting his seal on this article . . . by telling them nothing. What Oscar says is important, because he's not a theorist. A theorist can change his mind and never run the risk of dying. Oscar puts his life up front, not just his views. What information have we got?

PABLO:   Apparently, he told them nothing. That's all it says. Maybe it isn't complete.

BELTRAN:     But he told them nothing. That's what matters. A theorist would have told them everything.

PABLO:     Even so, the article was a mistake. It's too intellectual. Listen: 'In given circumstances terrorism is a necessary evil.' That's what it says.

BELTRAN:     You can't dispute the fact that Oscar's got plenty of guts.

PABLO:     It's just that I dislike statements of that kind, especially when they appear in black and white. (*Reading another piece of paper*) It seems we are getting arms into the country.

BELTRAN:     Who's doing it?

PABLO:     Certain specialized groups.

BELTRAN:     Do you mean from abroad?

PABLO:     No, technical personnel. They don't have any country. They simply service machines, handle weapons, in this case machine guns.

BELTRAN:     I've heard it said there are foreign agents amongst us.

PABLO:     It isn't true. The revolution is ours and ours alone. We haven't even considered asking for help. Oh, don't worry: I'm always in touch with our command. I know their orders. . . . The metal workers are still on strike in spite of threats. There've been some scuffles with people trying to go back to work. . . . Some blood, of course, but the workers haven't been upset. They've suffered too much to be upset by blood. . . . The miners down South have blown up a dynamite depot. There are frequent clashes everywhere, inspired and controlled by the Party.

BELTRAN:     It's a great opportunity. I hope our leaders make the most of it.

PABLO:     That's out of our hands. The boss has the last word.

BELTRAN:     Yes, he could light the fuse all right. . . . It would be terrific . . . like a sudden, strangulated hernia, and no one knows what's going to happen. You have to be a real leader to give the final order and not have any qualms. It's the moment when you suddenly age but also become invincible, forever remembered by the people.

*He stops speaking. Oscar enters. He says nothing.*

BELTRAN:     Oscar!

OSCAR:     You seem surprised.

PABLO:     We barely had any information.

OSCAR:     I managed to escape. It wasn't difficult. It was almost as if they showed me the door. Obviously, the Party takes care of even its most humble members. It's clear things are going well and we are all extremely brave.

PABLO: Why are you speaking like this?

OSCAR: Like what?

PABLO: I don't know. I thought. . . .

OSCAR: Maybe you thought I wouldn't come? At least I can see I'm not exactly warmly welcomed. The faces of people I thought old friends seem quite unmoved, if not completely cold . . . not the slightest sign of emotion. All this despite the fact I could be six feet under or lying in some corner like a piece of rubbish. Why so surprised that I've turned up?

BELTRAN: But it isn't true. I don't know what you mean. You are safe here . . . if no one's followed you.

OSCAR: The entire police force are after me, but no one's followed me. I mean I managed to shake them off. I found a car in the street, almost as if it were just for me. I'm quite convinced it was. I don't know why but that's what I thought immediately. The car was there for me and that's when everything started moving again.

BELTRAN: Moving again? I don't follow.

OSCAR: The whole business, tracking me down, like a great machine. You can hear it ticking over. It won't stop until the day they get me.

PABLO: There's nothing to be afraid of. The Party will look after you.

BELTRAN: Of course, Oscar. There's nothing to fear. But you need to rest. You don't look well. How bad was it? I've heard they beat some prisoners so much they drive them mad. Most of us have no idea what goes on there. What did you see?

OSCAR: They beat me senseless, that's all. They almost killed me.

BELTRAN: If they'd made you talk, most of us would have been picked up.

PABLO: Of course we wouldn't. The Party would have got us out of the city. It has great influence. If it didn't, you wouldn't be here now.

OSCAR: Never mind all that. The one thing I know is that I *am* here and I told them nothing. Not a word, Beltrán. That's the plain truth. . . . I can't explain it . . . it's almost as if it happened to someone else . . . as if it were nothing to do with me. I was . . . well, kind of watching myself, observing my own silence, as if it were some objective fact that had nothing to do with me. I simply accepted it. It never even occurred to me that I might tell them anything.

PABLO:     Oscar, you have to stop all this. If you prefer, I order you to stop. I can see you've started to think too much. It isn't good for you. The Party needs men of action. Thinking too much is a luxury we can do without for now. Later on, maybe, our actions can be justified. We'll always find some intellectual or some fool to explain our cause.

OSCAR:     (*angrily*) Shut up! For God's sake, shut up!

*Pablo is silent. Pause. Oscar continues.*

I've come to talk to you, Pablo. I don't give a damn about the Party any more. I've come back to take charge of our group.

PABLO:     What *are* you talking about?

OSCAR:     I've come to take over. I shall give the orders. We shall do exactly what I say. I don't agree with the Party's tactics.

PABLO:     (*astonished*) I think you need a complete break. All this has really got to you. You've lost control. You don't know what you are saying. Remember, I'm studying medicine. . . . Although I doubt I can give you a diagnosis. . . . Poor Oscar. It's been too much for you. There's not much point relying on you until you are fully recovered.

OSCAR:     Don't be so stupid! I intend to take charge of our group.

PABLO:     You can't be serious.

OSCAR:     I plan to reform it as I see fit and have it work in the way I want. Only important people will die. Specific targets, not just anyone. Only those who need to die, and we'll know who they are in advance. A precise and accurate shot, aimed at someone we've targeted.

PABLO:     That's quite enough. I'm telling you, don't say another word. Don't you see? I have to take note of your attitude towards our own command. All this is very painful, especially for me. (*Oscar has buried his face in his hands*) Oscar, what's wrong?

BELTRAN:   Oscar, why are you acting like this?

*Pause.*

OSCAR:     (*harshly*) My brother's dead.

BELTRAN:   Did you say 'dead'?

OSCAR:     Yes.

PABLO:     (*after a moment*) Oscar, you're obviously very upset. Your life's been turned upside down. You are thrashing about in a vacuum. But you are only one individual, and from that point of view you don't really matter.

You'll be set aside if you've gone mad, and trying to wreck the revolution is just the same as going mad.

OSCAR: (*not really listening, his eyes closed*) He died in the Avenida de las Acacias, and when he died lots of things became very clear. When I was small, he used to take me across that street to go to school. Lately he was a bit depressed. He knew about my commitment to the Cause . . . but pretended he didn't know. He really understood me. He was good and honourable. . . . In the past he'd thought about joining the Revolution. He took part in the coup on the twenty-third. He saw what was going on but he got disillusioned. He was never a happy person but he had respect for everyone else. . . . And now he's dead! I can't describe what I'm feeling. I can only tell you I'm suffering. Do you understand? I'm suffering. (*He sees his article lying on the table*) This piece I wrote: 'In Defence of. . . .' The real terror is what I'm going through now. The terrorist isn't someone who lives outside terror. He lives at its very heart. . . . Pablo, I've come to talk to you. I promise you I'm not mad. This business with my brother . . . it's very difficult, as you can imagine. But at least I'm not to blame. If I were, I couldn't stand it. But I'm not to blame. That's why I've come. I've come to tell you to your face that you are to blame because you gave the order. I know you couldn't care less. I know it doesn't bother you. My brother is just another victim. Isn't that right?

PABLO: I don't know what you are talking about.

OSCAR: I'm looking for the person to blame and that is you. I know you don't regard it as important. . . . It wouldn't matter who it was, provided the job was carried out. You gave the order and that's the only thing that matters, right? The Party has to triumph over everything. We have to follow through a predetermined plan, correct?

PABLO: Of course we do! Your brother's dead. All right. As far as I'm concerned, it's not important.

OSCAR: It's not only that it's not important . . . you are also the only person responsible for his death. You are the boss. Everything's down to you. Whether someone lives or dies. Everything! I carried out your order. I only obey . . . only obey. . . .

PABLO: Oscar, take a look at yourself. You've come apart at the seams. You're a pitiful, disgusting sight! What is all this . . . this sickening self-pity, this wallowing in your own grief? No, you aren't deranged. You are just a stupid fool!

OSCAR: Pablo!

PABLO: I'll show you what a fool you are. You talk about blame. I promise you that no one's to blame. Or to put it a rather different way: we are all to blame. When you carry out an order and someone dies, every single member of the Party is to blame.

OSCAR:    I don't agree. You can't blame everyone just like that.

PABLO:    You aren't one of us anymore, Oscar. You've gone soft. You're only concerned with yourself. It's pathetic.

OSCAR:    All right, Pablo. I've changed my mind. I don't agree with the rest of you. (*Pablo laughs*) Don't laugh at me. Why are you laughing?

PABLO:    Because I find you so ridiculous.

OSCAR:    You're a murderer, Pablo. We made a big mistake. You are to blame for my brother's death, as well as the fear that everyone in the city has to endure. We made a big mistake in letting you go on. But now I'm going to take your place, which means you have to die. You can't be one of us. I realize now why I haven't exposed you before. I want you dead, but not in the way that they would do it. If you were to die at their hands, I'd feel the despair I feel now for not having killed you already.

PABLO:    Why don't you just shut up!

OSCAR:    It's finished, Pablo. From now on our group shall work properly for the Revolution. Our actions will be specific and effective. Our bullets shall be targeted, the general terror of the past forgotten. I know I can rely on Antón. He'll support me. He knew the truth already. Where is he? (*The others are silent*) I want to know. Where is he?

BELTRAN:    Anton's dead. Yesterday. He shot himself.

PABLO:    He'd changed his mind . . . just like you. He couldn't face it. So what are you waiting for?

*Oscar cries out in anguish, seizes a knife which Beltrán has left on the table, and drives it into Pablo's throat.*

BELTRAN:    Oscar! What the hell have you done? You've killed him.

OSCAR:    It's what I came to do. It's over . . . or maybe it's the beginning of something else . . . who knows? . . . Beltrán, I think I'd best be getting home . . . I need to get back home tonight.

## Scene Six

*A room in Oscar's house. Oscar enters. His brother, Julio, is sitting in an armchair.*

OSCAR:   Julio! . . . I can't believe it! . . . You're alive! . . . I thought you were dead . . . I thought I'd killed you . . . Julio! . . . You've no idea . . . it's been awful . . . Hell on earth, believe me. . . . And here you are . . . alive . . . I can't help crying. . . .

JULIO:   How did you get out?

OSCAR:   I can scarcely believe that you aren't really dead. They showed me a photo . . . a photo of your body. A photograph of you. . . . And you were dead.

JULIO:   It was someone else . . . killed in a car crash, maybe.

OSCAR:   It was your face . . . your blood-stained face.

JULIO:   They must have set you up . . . can't you see how they did it? Whatever photo you saw, you'd think it was me. You must have been willing already . . . to be convinced.

OSCAR:   That's hideous.

JULIO:   That's the police, as simple as that.

OSCAR:   And they call us terrorists.

JULIO:   Yes.

OSCAR:   When that's what they are.

JULIO:   Calm down.

OSCAR:   Where were you that night? What stopped you coming home?

JULIO:   I was late, that's all, as I often am. No one seems bothered most of the time. When I arrived, the police had already been here. Afterwards they picked you up and showed you the photograph. It was all so easy.

OSCAR:   You had to be late on that particular night. That's why things happened as they did. Why?

JULIO:   What's the point of asking?

OSCAR:     There is no point . . . but just because you arrived home late, I lost everything . . . everything.

*Pause.*

JULIO:     They let you go.

OSCAR:     No.

JULIO:     You mean you escaped?

OSCAR:     Yes.

JULIO:     Then why come here? It's the worst thing you could do.

OSCAR:     I don't know.

JULIO:     You are putting your head in the noose.

OSCAR:     I know . . . they've set me up . . . they'll be here at any moment. . . .

JULIO:     Oscar. . . .

OSCAR:     Leave me alone!

JULIO:     It's very dangerous.

OSCAR:     What?

JULIO:     If they catch you.

OSCAR:     I suppose so.

JULIO:     You killed the Minister of War.

OSCAR:     The attempt failed.

JULIO:     Of course it didn't!

OSCAR:     What are you saying?

JULIO:     The newspapers kept it quiet. They were told to hush it up. The public learned of his death later . . . without any reference to the ambush.

OSCAR:     (*excited*) You mean he's really dead?

JULIO:     When the bomb exploded, the Minister's car continued, but a piece of shrapnel had pierced his skull.

OSCAR:     I didn't know. Pablo and Beltrán didn't say a word. Maybe I didn't give them a chance. . . . So he's dead! How did the people react? What do they think of us?

JULIO:     The people support the Revolution. . . . There was a big funeral . . . a public show of mourning . . . without a public. . . . No one went. The streets were empty. . . . When the coffin passed, there were only groups of casual observers. A black day for our dictatorship.

OSCAR:   An even blacker one for me! (*Speaking more quietly*) You see, if you had died . . . I know it's a terrible thought . . . but if you had died, I'd have felt completely justified instead of feeling lost. You see, I killed a man tonight . . . because I thought you were dead . . . in order to avenge your death. . . . Do you see how absurd it is? He's lying there, a knife in his throat, and I did it for you. If I'd done it for other, pointless deaths, I'd be justified in theory, but in your case . . . in your case . . . it was all too much. . . .

JULIO:   (*deeply moved*) Oscar, don't upset yourself. Try not to think . . . you need to rest . . . there's plenty of time. . . .

OSCAR:   I murdered Pablo! It's as if someone's playing a game with me . . . a cruel, heartless trick . . . as if I were a helpless child . . . it frightens me!

JULIO:   Calm yourself!

OSCAR:   I murdered Pablo! Do you know what kind of man he was? A man who knew no fear. A man who knew the truth. He believed in the Revolution. He fought for it with all his soul until some worthless, frightened creature . . . until I. . . . He looked at me with scorn . . . he didn't lift a finger . . . he despised me to the end. . . . There's nothing left for me, Julio. No need for you to waste your time. . . .

JULIO:   For God's sake, Oscar. You sound like someone condemned to die.

OSCAR:   That's what I am. I serve no purpose. If I was strong enough, I could go on . . . despite feeling sick and useless. But now I've lost the will to fight . . . I serve no purpose . . . I know that I am finished . . . I feel so tainted, as if I'm fatally wounded. . . . The Revolution needs other people, like Pablo. I know he loved his fellow men, although he hated admitting it. . . . The Revolution will go on, and they ought to throw me aside, like rubbish. . . . It makes me happy, gives me a little dignity. . . . I don't feel quite so wretched. . . . They are fighting for justice, Julio, for a life worthy of all men. . . . If they achieve it, a few innocent victims don't really matter.

JULIO:   Of course not.

OSCAR:   Then they ought to carry on. Why shouldn't there be a little bloodshed? I'm cold, Julio. Look after me, as if I were seriously ill. . . . There's just one thing. Don't tell a soul what happened. . . . No one must know what happened to me . . . in case it makes them realize that they, like me, can suddenly do something dreadful. If they know what happened to me, they might not think it was a pure accident . . . more that it had some significance . . . that I was being punished, I don't know by whom, so that others shall know that they, like me, can experience this black night, this desolation. And if they reach that conclusion, they'll abandon the struggle, begin to tremble and, when the crucial moment comes, turn white with fear, start to weep, serve no useful purpose, be withdrawn, and be swept aside by their companions. No one must know, Julio. . . . No one.

JULIO:     No one shall know. I promise.

OSCAR:     (*a little relieved*) Thank you. . . . While the fight goes on, what's to become of me? The coward, the traitor, the black sheep of the Party . . . what's left for him to do? . . . Perhaps I can find something not too demanding . . . something I can cope with. . . .

JULIO:     Oscar . . . I remember, when we were children, they used to say to us. . . .

OSCAR:     What?

JULIO:     Not that I believe there's anything beyond this life. It's not so much that.

OSCAR:     Tell me.

JULIO:     It's just that some of the stories we used to hear were about people showing love for each other. If that were the case, there'd be no need for the revolution . . . and you wouldn't have come to this.

OSCAR:     'People showing love for each other.' Go on.

JULIO:     That's all there is. I believe it's true, but then there's just a void.

OSCAR:     (*desperately*) Which we are in! Which we are falling into!

JULIO:     You need to rest. Are you feeling any better?

OSCAR:     A little.

JULIO:     Close your eyes. . . . Rest. . . . It's been too much for you. . . . Who knows? Perhaps it's just the beginning . . . and afterwards. . . .

OSCAR:     You really think so? The tragic prelude to a long and happy day. Why not? I almost feel as if someone somewhere is offering me a reconciliation. . . . (*distracted*) Pablo! Pablo!

JULIO:     Oscar, what are you doing?

OSCAR:     (*pause*) It's quite all right. I feel much better now. Don't leave me, Julio. I feel much better. Nothing bothers me. I hope for nothing. . . . Or maybe it's now that I really hope for something . . . I don't know. . . .

*A noise outside in the street. Julio goes to the window.*

OSCAR:      Oscar, it's the police. They are coming in. You have to hide. I'll try my best to delay them.

OSCAR:      No. . . . What for. . . ? It doesn't matter. . . . It really doesn't matter. . . . There is something I can still do for our cause . . . a way in which I can still be useful. . . . I can learn to suffer . . . to endure whatever pain they inflict in that filthy cellar until they say: 'It's useless. This Party is invincible. Its members can't be made to tell us anything.' My place is in that cellar, so let them come and take me, let them beat me up and burn my hands! I'll shout at them: 'Long live the Revolution!' until they beat my face to pulp . . . but what is left of me will be a man again. . . . (*smiling*) Julio, what's the matter? Do you remember when we were kids? You used to take me across the road to go to school. I liked that. Nine o'clock in the morning, cold, you telling me to keep my scarf across my mouth. When spring arrived, the daffodils were always a great surprise. . . .

JULIO:     The police are coming up the stairs!

OSCAR:      Every spring . . . they'll always be a great surprise . . . the girls will always look attractive . . . the children will always play their games. . . .

JULIO:     The police, Oscar!

OSCAR:      Julio, something has happened tonight. . . . A strange kind of peace. . . .

JULIO:     The police!

OSCAR:      Every spring the flowers . . . the girls so pretty . . . the children always playing their games. . . .

# TWO SIDES TO DR VALMY'S STORY

# Antonio Buero Vallejo

Antonio Buero Vallejo was born on September 29, 1916, in Guadalajara, the son of an army captain. In school he revealed a talent for writing as well as an interest in such foreign dramatists as Ibsen and Bernard Shaw. However, Buero's real interest at that time was in painting. At the age of eighteen he left Guadalajara and went to Madrid where, between 1934 and 1936, he studied painting at the prestigious Escuela de Bellas Artes de San Fernando. Exposure to the cultural life of Madrid at a time when it was flourishing under a Republican government helped to broaden Buero's knowledge considerably. Although he still had no plans to become a dramatist, Buero was in the capital when some of the greatest Spanish plays of the twentieth century received their première.

The Civil War brought Buero's studies to an end. Anxious to enlist immediately as a volunteer on the Republican side, Buero served as a medical orderly on both the Jarama and the Aragon fronts. The last months of 1936, however, proved deeply tragic for Buero's father, Francisco. A right-wing liberal, he believed that, as a professional soldier, he should obey the orders of the left-wing government in power. Stationed in Madrid when Franco's Nationalists were attacking the city, he was detained by Republic supporters on suspicion of collaboration with the enemy. Although Buero was convinced that his father would not come to any harm, Francisco was never seen again nor were the circumstances of his death clarified.In 1939 Buero was himself arrested for his Republican sympathies, put on trial and condemned to death. Eight months later the death-sentence was commuted to imprisonment and, over the next seven years, the original term was reduced until he was conditionally released in 1946. The experience explains the centrality in Buero's theatre of themes connected with the War and its aftermath.

Back in civilian life, Buero attempted to take up painting again but found it much more difficult than he had anticipated. He therefore turned to writing and in 1946 completed the first version of *In the Burning Darkness*, which received its première four years later. In the following year, he wrote *Story of A Stairway* which premièred in Madrid in 1949 and is now usually regarded as a turning point in post-war Spanish theatre. The play's commercial success, — it ran for 187 performances — anticipated the next twenty-five years in which Buero would triumph on the commercial stage, becoming the most frequently performed dramatist of the dictatorship.

*Story of A Stairway*, like many of Buero's plays of the fifties, is strongly naturalistic and reveals the influence of a Spanish tradition centuries old. It is also true, however, that Buero was much affected by Ibsen and the kind of symbolic realism evident throughout his theatre. Thus, the stairway of the tenement building is symbolic of the characters' soaring dreams and aspirations and of their inevitable failure. The same mixture of naturalism and symbolism characterizes many other plays written and produced during the decade: *The Weaver of Dreams* (1952), *Almost a Fairy Tale* (1953), *Today's a Holiday* (1956), *Cards Face Down* (1957) and *Dreamer for a People* (1958). *Today's a Holiday*, in particular, repeated the success of *Story of a Stairway*, running in Madrid for 149 performances.

In 1959 Buero married the actress, Victoria Rodríguez, by whom he would have two children. As far as his writing is concerned, the sixties would be a period of continued success, theatre awards and successful productions. In 1960, for example, his play on Velázquez, *Las meninas*, ran at the Teatro Español in Madrid for 260 performances, while in 1967 *The Basement Window*, produced at the Teatro Bellas Artes, exceeded 500. There were other notable productions, including *Concert at Saint Ovide* in 1962 and Buero's 1966 version of Brecht's *Mother Courage*.

As far as ideas on the purpose and function of theatre are concerned, the early sixties also saw an important difference of opinion between Buero and Alfonso Sastre. While Sastre's position was confrontational and uncompromising, increasingly causing him to fall foul of the dictatorship, Buero largely accepted the constraints of the regime, preferring to achieve what was possible within the limitations it imposed. His success was achieved because he was largely content to make oblique rather than direct attacks upon it. However, in the case of *Two Sides to Dr Valmy's Story*, Buero suffered precisely the same fate as Sastre in having the work banned because of his refusal to make cuts.

Although Buero achieved further successes in the seventies (the play on Goya, *The Sleep of Reason*, in 1970; *The Foundation* in 1974; and *The Shot* in 1977), the end of the dictatorship undoubtedly saw a falling away in Buero's writing. Although advancing years may have also played their part, Buero's case, like Sastre's, illustrates how a dramatist whose work was defined by the circumstances of the Franco dictatorship has subsequently found himself in a creative vacuum.

# TWO SIDES TO DR VALMY'S STORY

A Play by

**Antonio Buero Vallejo**

# Characters

Man in Dinner-Jacket

Woman in Evening Gown

Secretary

Dr Valmy

Mary Barnes

The grandmother

Daniel Barnes

Marsan

Paulus

Pozner

Luigi

Hannibal Marty

Lucila Marty

Male Nurse

The action takes place in Surrelia: a far-off country.
The time is the present.

# A Note on the Set

A simple set, without a ceiling and in two sections, against a neutral background. The downstage section consists of a rectangular platform which almost reaches the proscenium arch and extends from the wings, stage-left, to a point two-thirds of the way across the stage. This represents the Barnes' house. The only complete wall is to the left of the stage, and in the wall a curtained door with a chair to either side of it. The back-wall is of the same height for only a short distance; from left to right a radiator, with a reproduction of some modern painting above it, and another curtained door. Then a standard lamp and a sofa against the wall. Half-way along the back of the sofa the wall disappears, running along behind it, no more than a metre high, and ending at the back right-hand corner of the platform. To the right of the sofa and up to the corner of the platform, a low bookcase the same height as the wall, with a drinks cupboard in the centre of it. In front of the sofa a low glass table with an empty vase. Close to the front right-hand corner of the platform, an armchair and a small table with a telephone to its left. In the centre of the room a chromium-plated cradle with wheels. One of the chairs stage-left is to the left of the cradle.

The upstage section represents an office in the Secret Police, at the height of the wall that adjoins the bookcase in the Barnes' house. It takes the form of a large, wide L, one part of which begins where the back-wall of the Barnes' house is broken, extending to the right-hand side of the stage; the second part advances towards the proscenium arch, ending half-way along the right-hand edge of the first platform. A strip of wall, the same height as the bookcase, fronts it. There are two entrances to the office: the first stage-left where there is no wall and where there is an invisible staircase situated behind the back-wall of the Barnes' living-room. The second entrance is a stairway located between the right-hand edge of the first platform and the projection of the second. It extends therefore from a point at the top of it close to the bookcase. The triangle formed by the left-hand side of this stairway, at right angles to the bookcase, forms part of the wall in the Barnes' house. The office is schematically suggested: at the back of the door to the right-hand side. The back-wall of the office is like the back-wall of the Barnes' house but in reverse, for it runs from the rear left-hand corner of the platform at a low height to a point half-way across the back of the stage where it becomes a complete wall, extending to the back right-hand corner. The right-hand side wall is also incomplete, for close to the back right-hand corner it begins to descend until it reaches the front right-hand corner at floor-level. Placed in the centre of the

L-shape, an office table with files, papers, a telephone with several lines, a chair behind it. To the left, another chair. Against the strip of wall at the back, a broken-down sofa. To the left of this, a hatstand. Where the back and the side-wall meet, a small table with a typewriter and a chair.

The set consists, therefore, of two rooms which are joined and at a different height but which, in the action of the play, are far apart. The general effect of the first should be smart and pleasing; that of the second, cold and impersonal. Down-stage at either side of the stage there should be room for entrances and exits.

Down-stage left and in front of the Barnes' house, a stone bench in a park.

In the rectangular space stage-right, a comfortable winged-chair with another chair to its left. This is Dr Valmy's consulting-room.

# Part One

*'The Twist' played loudly on a piano. The curtain is still down. Stage-left a woman enters, wearing an evening gown and bedecked with jewels. A moment later a man enters downstage right, wearing a dinner-jacket. The woman is fair and is still quite young. The man is elegant. They both smile. In a pleasant and assured manner they speak over the music, which is now less loud.*

MAN:     My dear friends. . . .

WOMAN:     We know the story you're about to be told.

MAN:     They've told it to us already.

WOMAN:     It's quite untrue.

MAN:     Precisely, or, at least, an exaggeration.

WOMAN:     And you haven't come here to be convinced of anything: simply to enjoy yourselves.

MAN:     You know how: enjoy what you hear but don't believe it. We'd like you to bear it in mind, if only because there is always someone naïve enough to believe the most fantastic things.

WOMAN:     Or those who cling to a quite ridiculous love of melodrama.

*The curtain rises to reveal the stage in half-light. To the right, a winged-chair in which Dr Valmy sits, wrapped in his own thoughts. In another chair, close to him, his secretary, with notebook and pencil, looks at him and waits. In the Barnes' household a child, a few months old, in a cradle. Seated next to it, the grandmother watching him.*

MAN:     If there are such people here, we'd like to remind you of a well-known fact: when someone tells a story, he embroiders it.

WOMAN:     And tries to make it relevant: it's always as if it had taken place next-door to us.

MAN:     We want you to understand that point. If something like this happened, it wasn't here. If these things ever happen, they happen in backward countries.

WOMAN:    In far-off places.

MAN:    So rest assured. Not only is the story false; it comes from foreign parts and is, therefore, irrelevant.

WOMAN:    Above all, you must always smile. The world is full of problems; always has been. But in spite of it, we have learned to smile.

MAN:    And the smile remains man's greatest discovery. Never lose the habit.

WOMAN:    Always keep on smiling.

*During these exchanges the man and woman have drawn closer.*

MAN:    But now it's time to listen.

*They bow, the man takes the woman's arm and they exit stage-left. The piano music moves without interruption from 'The Twist' to Chopin's 'Nocturne in B Flat Major'. Lights up slowly on Dr Valmy and his secretary. He is a man of about forty. He wears a simple but respectable suit and looks tired. The Secretary is a pleasant-looking woman, a little younger.*

SECRETARY:    Did you want to stop, Doctor?

DR VALMY:    No. It's just that I was thinking. Read it back to me.

SECRETARY:    (*deciphering her marks*) 'End of first case-history.'

DR VALMY:    Thank you. (*Dictating*) End of case number one. We'll begin number two. But before we do . . . (*He stops, thinks, gets up*) it occurs to me that . . . (*He steps forward, stops*) when doctors decide to publish case-histories, they prefer to include, like second-rate novelists, those with a happy ending. But the ones that found their expertise inadequate are often more revealing. (*He looks at her*)

SECRETARY:    Revealing.

DR VALMY:    Like our patients, we'd like to ignore our weaknesses. But one day they consult us and one day we decide to write a book. We aren't as indifferent to suffering as we are sometimes thought to be; the memory of those poor people we failed to help pursues us all our lives. Including the doctor who tries to forget. It pursues him in another way, but it still pursues him.

SECRETARY:    Pursues him.

DR VALMY:    Such books are also our confessions. I must admit that . . . in this second case . . . I behaved rather badly. In the presence of a patient, a doctor should always keep his feelings to himself. I failed to do so sufficiently. If I did wrong, the reader will judge. (*He is silent*)

SECRETARY:     Will judge.

DR VALMY:     For the most part, human beings are rather ordinary. That's why we can achieve some modest success. The circumstances which make them ill are things they can mostly deal with. But what about an ordinary man confronted by an extraordinary situation? My patient was such a man.

SECRETARY:     Such a man.

DR VALMY:     Not so much through lack of feeling as lack of courage. But I cannot help thinking that, in his situation, few would have had that courage. I know I probably wouldn't.

SECRETARY:     I probably wouldn't.

DR VALMY:     (*sighs*) I'd been practicing in the capital for quite some time, and D.B. lived quite near my consulting rooms.

SECRETARY:     Sorry, Doctor. Could you repeat that?

DR VALMY:     Capital D, stop. Capital B, stop.

SECRETARY:     Ah, I'm sorry.

DR VALMY:     A friendly, outgoing person; at first sight the complete opposite to a patient. His wife, not so young anymore, worshipped him. (*He has moved stage-left and sits on a bench which is now lit*) I had treated her once, when she was still single, for nervous problems that responded to drugs . . . and marriage. From time to time we'd meet again in the street or as we crossed the park.

*Mary Barnes enters stage-right. She crosses the stage, smiling, and stops in front of the doctor. She is a slim, mature, attractive woman, simply but elegantly dressed. She carries a shopping-bag and some flowers. The Secretary goes on writing.*

DR VALMY:     Good morning. (*He gets up, shakes hands*) I see you've been shopping.

MARY:     I've no choice. Mother-in-law's not up to rushing around the shops anymore, poor thing! Aren't the flowers lovely? Would you like one?

DR VALMY:     I'm sure they suit you rather better.

MARY:     I saw you from over there. I said to myself: can that be the Doctor sitting on the seat?

DR VALMY:     I sit for a while now and again. It's rather pleasant here.

MARY:     You don't understand, Doctor. It's the seat, you see.

DR VALMY:     The seat?

MARY:     (*laughing*) It's a rather romantic story. It's the seat where I met my husband.

DR VALMY:     Really?

MARY:     (*softly*) Yes . . . just there. Don't get up, please! (*She holds out her hand*)

DR VALMY:     (*taking her hand*) I think I better had. I wouldn't dream of spoiling it. (*He looks at her professionally*) You've never looked better.

MARY:     I'm fine.

DR VALMY:     That's good. I know I haven't met him yet, but give my regards to your husband.

MARY:     I shall. One day I'll introduce him to you. He's . . . always so busy.

DR VALMY:     (*looks at her with interest*) Of course.

MARY:     Perhaps you could come to dinner sometime?

DR VALMY:     That's very kind of you.

MARY:     I could give you a ring.

DR VALMY:     Excellent.

MARY:     Goodbye, then.

DR VALMY:     Goodbye.

*Mary Barnes leaves stage-left, observed by the doctor.*

A pleasant enough woman, but rather distant. She never did phone. At bottom she was always rather neurotic. They had a child a few months old, and the husband's mother was getting on in years and almost deaf, though I never actually met her.

*Lights up on the cradle and the grandmother. Piano music: Brahms's 'Cradle Song'. Dr Valmy sighs and moves stage-right.*

We psychiatrists know very well that every case, however sad, longed to be one of love and beauty. This second case longed to be that too, and on that account, instead of hushing it up, it's better to show exactly how, though grossly distorted, the love and beauty we all seek lay at its very heart.

SECRETARY: In that case, then.

DR VALMY: What?

SECRETARY: Sorry.

DR VALMY: No. Say what you think.

SECRETARY: It could well be, in spite of everything. . . .

DR VALMY: What?

SECRETARY: A story of love and beauty. . . .

*Dr Valmy looks at her but doesn't reply. He looks down and exits stage-right. The Secretary gets up and follows him. Brahms's 'Cradle Song' over.*

GRANDMOTHER: You know your Gran, of course you do! You want me to tell you a story. Let's see you smile, then. Your Daddy used to smile when he wanted a story. And he understood them, just like you. Oh, I know you understand them. Here we go, then. . . . Once upon a time there was a little boy, more handsome than the sun, whose name was . . . Daniel! (*She laughs*) You little rascal, you know your name already, but it might not be you I mean. I used to tell it to your father! (*She sighs, her tone changes*) Dear God! Here we go. And Daniel's mother worshipped him, I mean his grandmother. And the mother used to say: 'My Daniel will be as big and strong as a captain.' And Daniel used to smile. 'And because he's so good-looking all the girls will fall in love with him. And because he's so good, people will want to be his friend.' (*She sighs*) Oh, God! 'And because he's so clever, later on, when he has a big moustache, he'll be his mother's pride and joy, and they'll go off together and visit all the countries of this lovely world, and everyone will welcome them and cry aloud: 'Long live Daniel the great!' And Daniel used to smile. . . .

*The piano stops. The grandmother looks up.*

I thought I heard the door. . . .

*She gets up. Mary enters with the shopping-bag, the flowers and a folded newspaper.*

MARY: (*speaking loudly*) Hello, Gran. I brought the paper.

GRANDMOTHER: Thanks.

*She takes the paper and searches in her apron for her spectacle-case. Mary puts the flowers in a vase on the table. She leaves the shopping-bag on the chair near the cradle.*

MARY: Has he been a nuisance?

GRANDMOTHER:  Oh, no. He's only just woken up.

*The grandmother sits on a chair next to the telephone and puts on her glasses.*

MARY:  (*caressing the child*) So what do you say, my sweet? Glad to have Mummy back? Let's see that little botty. I expect it's soaking wet.

*She puts her hand under the blanket and feels. The grandmother looks at her.*

GRANDMOTHER:  I've changed him already. (*She begins reading again*)

MARY:  (*to the child*) I think she likes to see that little thing of yours. I'd better take a look myself before I eat. (*Looks at her watch*) When you see your bottle, it's just like turning the tap on. (*She straightens up*) Did Daniel phone?

GRANDMOTHER:  What?

MARY:  Did Daniel phone?

GRANDMOTHER:  No.

MARY:  (*to the child*) Don't look at me like that. I know very well what you want.

*She fusses him and picks up the shopping-bag.*

GRANDMOTHER:  The paper gets worse every day.

MARY:  (*she stops*) Oh, I don't know.

GRANDMOTHER:  What?

MARY:  (*going towards her*) Look at the front page. We've launched another space station.

GRANDMOTHER:  I only read the other pages.

MARY:  (*shakes her head, smiles*) I'll get his bottle ready.

*She moves stage-left.*

GRANDMOTHER:  (*annoyed*) They've even changed the television programmes. There's nothing on tonight.

MARY:  (*stops, smiles*) I am sorry.

GRANDMOTHER:  (*she puts the paper on the small table and gets up, removing her glasses*) You ought to give him his bottle.

*She goes to the chair next to the cradle and moves it to a corner of the room.*

MARY:      I've just told you, I'm going to do it. Why don't you wear your hearing-aid?

GRANDMOTHER:      I can hear perfectly well.

MARY:      (*smiling*) And I can see it's one of your bad days. (*She moves to go out of the room*)

GRANDMOTHER:      When does your leave end?

MARY:      I can take as much as I like.

GRANDMOTHER:      (*moving towards her*) Don't you want to go back to the school?

MARY:      (*quietly*) Oh yes, you'd like that, wouldn't you?

GRANDMOTHER:      What? You'd have something else to think about. You hardly ever go out.

MARY:      (*quietly, smiling*) You'd like to have your son and your grandson all to yourself. I can't say that I blame you.

*The grandmother, struggling to hear, moves forward.*

GRANDMOTHER:      (*annoyed*) You'll have to speak up!

MARY:      (*going up to her*) I said I'm perfectly happy. (*She kisses her*)

GRANDMOTHER:      (*curtly*) It's time to get the dinner started.

MARY:      (*laughing*) And his milk. (*She takes her by the arm, and they move stage-left*)

GRANDMOTHER:      (*stopping her*) Listen. . . . Is Daniel all right?

MARY:      (*seriously*) What do you mean?

GRANDMOTHER:      You're always whispering.

MARY:      (*disturbed*) It's just that he's tired. They've so much work.

GRANDMOTHER:      (*thoughtful*) I find it strange.

MARY:      (*without looking at her*) You're imagining things.

*She leads the grandmother. Her face lights up and she stops.*

GRANDMOTHER:      Did someone knock?

MARY:      (*gives her the shopping-bag*) I heard the key.

*She runs to the back of the stage as Daniel enters. He is a good-looking man, something of the sportsman about him. Mary embraces him.*

DANIEL:    Hello, darling. (*They kiss*)

MARY:    Are you eating with us?

DANIEL:    If they don't call me out.

MARY:    Fine. (*She kisses him again. The grandmother watches them, ill at ease*)

DANIEL:    Mother. (*He goes to her. Mary follows, holding on to his arm*)

GRANDMOTHER:    My boy. (*They exchange kisses*)

MARY:    Would you like crème-caramel. We've plenty of eggs.

DANIEL:    Yes, great. So how's the little one?

*He goes to the cradle. Mary follows him.*

MARY:    Bright as a button. Look who's come to see you, cheeky!

*They sit either side of the cradle.*

DANIEL:    Now then, handsome. (*He bends to kiss the child*) How about a little smile? There we go! (*They both laugh. The grandmother goes over, smiling. She feels out of place*) By the way, Mother, Paulus sends his regards.

*He goes to the bookcase. Mary follows him.*

GRANDMOTHER:    Always such a charming fellow.

DANIEL:    Of course he is! He's always sending his regards.

*He removes a revolver from a shoulder-holster, checks the safety-catch and places it on the bookcase.*

When did you see him last?

GRANDMOTHER:    When the child grows up, I hope you'll keep that somewhere else.

DANIEL:    Of course I shall.

MARY:    (*putting her arm around his waist*) Do you think Mr Paulus was one of her old flames?

DANIEL:    (*passing his arm over her shoulders*) Who knows? But like she says, he is a charming fellow. (*He goes to the cradle*) The image of correctness and duty. (*He snaps his fingers at the child*) What do you say, rascal?

*He laughs. Mary takes his arm again.*

GRANDMOTHER:    Are you staying to dinner?

DANIEL:    (*agreeing*) Yes. It's been a good day. (*He goes to the armchair and sits on the arm as he looks at the paper*) Have you seen the news?

MARY:     (*moving towards him*) It's wonderful.

DANIEL:     It really makes people feel good. The work we do plays a part in such successes.

MARY:     So you do feel . . . better, then?

DANIEL:     (*looking straight at her*) Of course I do.

GRANDMOTHER:     (*still watching them*) I'll get his bottle ready.

*She moves stage-left with the shopping-bag.*

MARY:     (*quickly*) She's a tiny bit jealous. Say something.

DANIEL:     Any phone-calls, Mother? (*He moves towards her*)

GRANDMOTHER:     Someone came on a bike, for the piece you were writing.

DANIEL:     (*clicking his tongue, annoyed*) When do I get any time?

GRANDMOTHER:     I told him you'd be in touch.

DANIEL:     (*kissing her*) Quite right too.

GRANDMOTHER:     I must do the bottle. He's waited long enough.

*She exits stage-left.*

MARY:     She's annoyed because I haven't done it. But I needed to talk. She says you aren't yourself. (*He looks at her, then walks slowly to the chair by the telephone*) She's not as daft as you think.

DANIEL:     It's not that. She always fussed over me. She doesn't need a reason. (*He sighs and sits down*)

MARY:     (*going up to him, sitting on the arm of the chair*) But you do really feel better? (*She strokes his neck*)

DANIEL:     (*closing his eyes*) I don't know.

MARY:     You said you do.

DANIEL:     For her benefit . . . maybe to convince myself.

*A short pause. The grandmother enters, stage-left, carrying a pair of slippers.*

GRANDMOTHER:     (*approaching him*) If you aren't going out, you'd better take your shoes off.

MARY:     (*quietly*) She's put her hearing-aid in.

*The grandmother has, in fact, inserted her hearing-aid. Daniel removes his shoes.*

GRANDMOTHER:     (*facing him*) You don't look well. Have you got a head-
    ache?

DANIEL:     No. (*He tries to smile*) I'm perfectly all right.

*He puts the slippers on. The grandmother takes his shoes, goes to the
cradle and starts to rock it.*

GRANDMOTHER:     I'll give you your bottle, my lovely. No one wants us here.

*She sings.*

>   If your nose is blocked and you're feeling down,
>
>   And your head is spinning round and round. . . .

DANIEL:     (*exchange glances with his wife*) What on earth is that, Mother?

GRANDMOTHER:     What? Nothing. (*She goes on singing, rocking the cradle*)

>   Try 'Clear Head', it stops the pain,
>
>   You'll soon be feeling right as rain. . . .

MARY:     It's the T.V. commercial. The one for headaches.

*The grandmother takes the cradle out, stage-left. Her voice fades. Daniel
puts his head in his hands. Mary goes to the armchair.*

It's just a phase. You'll see.

*She leans over and kisses him warmly.*

DANIEL:     I feel ashamed.

MARY:     Don't be silly. You need to be coaxed, that's all.

DANIEL:     It's no joking matter.

MARY:     But it's not important. It's simply because you are over-tired.

DANIEL:     I've been tired before. It didn't happen then. (*Suddenly annoyed, he
    gets up and paces about*) I can't understand it.

MARY:     (*somewhat impatiently*) We said we wouldn't panic. It's probably
    quite common. (*She goes across to him*) Daniel. (*She embraces him. He
    kisses her hair*)

DANIEL:     Mary, if it doesn't stop. . . .

MARY:     It will!

DANIEL:     You couldn't stand it.

MARY:     I'm your wife.

DANIEL:     (*moves away, agitated*) And it's driving me mad!

MARY:     (*sadly*) You have to be patient.

*A lengthy pause. A noise is heard. the grandmother enters, stirring a glass of water with a spoon. Mary goes to look at the paper.*

GRANDMOTHER:     Take this.

DANIEL:     What?

GRANDMOTHER:     I thought you had a headache.

DANIEL:     But it won't. . . .

MARY:     (*quietly*) Take it.

DANIEL:     Thanks.

GRANDMOTHER:     (*to Mary as he drinks*) I'll see to the dinner.

MARY:     I'll be there in a minute.

*The grandmother picks up the glass, looks at them and goes out.*

DANIEL:     Go and help her. Talking about it gets us nowhere.

MARY:     (*about to go out, hesitates, turns*) Why don't you see Dr Valmy?

DANIEL:     What would be the point? Psychiatrists explain nothing. They only confuse you more.

MARY:     I found him . . . very helpful.

*Lights up on the office area. Marsan enters by the door back-stage. A man of about thirty-five, he goes to the phone and starts to dial.*

DANIEL:     (*smiling sadly*) Marriage helped *you* get better.

MARY:     If you like, I'll make an appointment. We could go together.

DANIEL:     Forget it. That's one thing I couldn't stand.

*He sits down in the armchair.*

MARY:     (*sighing*) I'll go and help your mother.

*She moves stage-left. Marsan has finished dialing. The telephone rings. Daniel watches it but doesn't move.*

MARY:     I'll answer it. (*She picks up the phone*) Yes?

MARSAN:     (*smiling*) Mrs Barnes?

MARY:     Yes. Who is it?

MARSAN:     Marsan. Is your husband there?

MARY:     (*covering the mouthpiece*) Marsan. Shall I tell him you're out?

DANIEL:     No, of course you can't.

MARSAN:     Is your husband there, Mrs Barnes?

MARY:     I'll put him on.

MARSAN:     Sorry to drag him away again. . . . Are you there, Mrs Barnes?

MARY:     Yes.

> *Daniel reaches for the phone. She gestures to him to wait.*

MARSAN:     There are times when I'm glad I'm single. I'm sure he doesn't enjoy leaving such an attractive woman on her own so often.

MARY:     You *do* have a sense of humour.

MARSAN:     (*seriously*) I promise you, I'm not joking.

MARY:     Here's my husband. (*She gives the phone to Daniel*)

DANIEL:     What did he say?

MARY:     Nothing that made any sense.

DANIEL:     (*into the phone*) What is it, Marsan?

MARSAN:     I'm bringing the car round.

DANIEL:     What for?

MARSAN:     Boss's orders.

DANIEL:     Come on! He gave me the evening off.

MARSAN:     They've just been on the phone to him. We have to collect our little friend.

DANIEL:     (*pursing his lips*) Why can't you take Dalton? Or Pozner? I'm supposed to see the doctor.

> *Mary's eyes light up as she hears this.*

MARSAN:     (*laughing*) Don't be stupid. We've got a doctor here. There's nothing wrong with you. Work getting you down, is it?

DANIEL:     Don't be a fool.

MARSAN:     (*laughing*) In any case, you've still got plenty of time. The party's not till tonight. I've got to go.

> *He hangs up, as does Daniel. Lights down on the office. Marsan goes down the invisible stairs, stage-left.*

MARY:     Shall I come to the doctor's with you?

DANIEL:   (*dismissive*) I had to tell him something. Bring me my shoes.

MARY:     I might have known!

> *She exits stage-left. Daniel walks up and down, confused. He goes to the small table, looks for a phone number in the book. The phone rings. He looks at in annoyance, picks it up.*

DANIEL:   Yes? (*Mary comes back with Daniel's shoes*) Yes, that's right. Just a moment. (*He hands the phone to Mary*) A friend of yours.

MARY:     Really? (*She takes the phone. Daniel takes his shoes and begins to put them on*) Who is it? (*Delighted*) Of course! It's just that you sound different. You used to have plaits. What a nice surprise! You must be quite grown up. Oh, yes, I got married too. Why not come this evening? (*She laughs*) I'll see. (*She covers the mouthpiece*) She'd rather not come if you are here. She was always shy when I taught her.

DANIEL:   Tell her to come. It'll do you good.

MARY:     Yes, that's fine . . . come at six and we'll have some tea. Don't forget now, will you!. . . Take care. See you. (*She hangs up*) She's really nice. You'll see for yourself.

DANIEL:   (*giving her his slippers*) Some other time. . . . Look, I've got to make a phone-call and then I'll have to go. Give Mother a hand, but don't tell her yet I had to leave. She was hoping I'd. . . .

MARY:     Yes, all right. (*Gives him a kiss*) Just think of what I said. And don't worry. (*She moves stage-left, turns*) Will you be home tonight?

DANIEL:   Probably not.

MARY:     You and your job!

> *She blows him a kiss. Daniel returns it, watches her go out and quickly consults the telephone directory. He nervously looks for a number, dials it. Pause, during which he looks stage-left.*

DANIEL:   Could the doctor possibly see me today? . . . the thing is . . . I'm always so tied-up, but I'm free this afternoon. . . . Yes, I'll wait. (*Pause*) yes . . . fine. Four o'clock. Thanks. . . . What? . . . Barnes. . . . Bye.

> *He hangs up, takes a deep breath and is lost in thought for a moment. Finally he walks up-stage. The grandmother enters stage-left, followed by Mary. He turns.*

MARY:     You know what she's like. She'd guessed already.

GRANDMOTHER:     You're going then?

DANIEL:     (*goes over and kisses her*) I've got no choice. We'll eat together tomorrow. (*He turns to go*)

GRANDMOTHER:     (*indicating the revolver*) Aren't you taking that?

DANIEL:     Oh, yes. (*He takes the revolver and places it in the holster*) Cheerio.

*He goes out. Mary goes out stage-left.*

GRANDMOTHER:     (*sighing*) God help us!

*She goes off stage-left. The lights go down on the Barnes household and up stage-right on Dr Valmy. Chopin's 'Nocturne' can be heard. The Secretary, with notebook and pencil, is to one side.*

DR VALMY:     My colleagues say I'm a bad psychiatrist. I laugh and give them as good as I get. I admit I'm not a specialist, but here we have to cover everything. Of course I studied psychotherapy, and I work in the mornings at a psychiatric clinic. In the afternoons I also see patients here. As a doctor I frequently make mistakes, but I've had my successes too, trusting to intuition. They spend their entire lives discussing complexes or transferences, which this book doesn't do at all because it's aimed at the average person. And if a sociologist were ever to read it, he won't find here an account of those general factors that, in his opinion, explain everything. I'm really just a family practitioner. The psychiatrist and the sociologist have much more scientific knowledge, but it's also colder. In the face of their perfect analysis, pain itself is unimportant, whereas I can never forget it. What matters most to me is the human being who comes to me in tears, with a troubled heart.

SECRETARY:     With a troubled heart.

DR VALMY:     I prefer to reveal pain in a way that people can understand, which doesn't explain much but awakens our dulled sensibilities. Our aim should be, after all, not only the improvement of the world through science, but also through our sense of shame.

SECRETARY:     Of shame. (*The piano stops*)

DR VALMY:     This case was, in spite of everything, one of my great successes. I say it without boasting because I believe it was really straightforward.

*He turns to the Secretary who steps forward with a medical card.*

SECRETARY:     The appointment for four o'clock, Doctor.

DR VALMY:     (*takes the card, reads it*) Daniel Barnes. Government employee . . . (*He hands back the card*) Send him in.

*The Secretary leaves. Daniel enters.*

DANIEL:     Afternoon, Doctor.

DR VALMY:     (*advancing, shaking hands*) How do you do, Mr Barnes. If I'm not mistaken, I know your wife. How is she?

DANIEL:     She's very well, doctor. I've come about myself.

DR VALMY:     Please, take a seat. (*He offers him a cigarette*) Care for one of these?

DANIEL:     (*sits in the armchair, smiles*) Thank you. (*He smiles a little as Dr Valmy gives him a light*) Forgive me smiling. It's because you are doing for me what I often do for others.

DR VALMY:     What? Lighting a cigarette?

DANIEL:     Yes . . . I'll try to explain.

DR VALMY:     (*sitting on a chair, lighting his cigarette*) In your own time.

DANIEL:     You'll see. It's not so easy. . . .

DR VALMY:     I'm here to help. Relax. Start where you wish. It doesn't matter.

DANIEL:     (*with a sigh*) It's best if I get to the point. For the last three weeks, Doctor . . . I haven't been able to carry out my marital obligations.

DR VALMY:     Are you afraid of the word?

DANIEL:     Word?

DR VALMY:     Do you mean to say you are impotent?

DANIEL:     (*looking down*) Yes. And really scared.

DR VALMY:     Let's see if I've got it right. Do you mean that you try and don't succeed, or that you just don't try?

DANIEL:     I try and I fail. I'm not really sure if I want to. My wife does her best to excite me, arouse me . . . and it's all completely useless. Sometimes nothing happens, but sometimes . . . before the moment's right . . . I reach a climax unexpectedly.

DR VALMY:     For the moment try not to worry. These things are much more common than you think.

DANIEL:     I'm glad to hear it. (*He stubs out his cigarette in the ashtray fixed to the arm of the chair*)

DR VALMY:     Has this ever happened before?

DANIEL:     Sometimes I haven't felt like it. I suppose that's normal.

DR VALMY:      This premature ejaculation . . . have you ever had that before?

DANIEL:     Never.

DR VALMY:      Are you an excitable person, Mr Barnes?

DANIEL:     Well . . . yes. Or, at least, I was.

DR VALMY:      Do you find your wife attractive?

DANIEL:     More than any other woman.

DR VALMY:      Even so, you tire of her at times.

DANIEL:     No, Doctor. That's what I thought at first. I told myself I needed a change. Since the day I was married I've never been with another woman, but now I would. For her . . . for things to be normal with her. And believing that I went with a woman I really fancied. It was humiliating! And that's when I started to be afraid.

DR VALMY:      How many hours a day do you work?

DANIEL:     Quite a lot. But I always felt fine. No, I don't feel tired. I don't drink; I hardly smoke. As well as that, they've started me on a hormone treatment. I saw the doctor at work, told him I was having an affair, but didn't want to neglect my wife. . . . It hasn't done a thing.

DR VALMY:      (*shrugging his shoulders*) Sexually you seem quite normal. Nevertheless . . . you must be honest with me. It's far better.

DANIEL:     Of course.

DR VALMY:      During your adult life, have you ever experienced the slightest homosexual inclination?

DANIEL:     Never.

DR VALMY:      And before that?

DANIEL:     Not that I can recall.

DR VALMY:      What about other ways of making love. I mean with women?

DANIEL:     That . . . depends on what you mean. . . .

DR VALMY:      Have you ever indulged in abnormal sexual practices to achieve satisfaction?

DANIEL:     No. It's always been perfectly normal.

DR VALMY:      You seem abnormally normal, Mr Barnes. (*He smiles*) This could take rather a long time. But we'll do our best. What kind of work do you do?

DANIEL:     I'm a . . . government employee.

DR VALMY:     Of course. What kind of employee?

DANIEL:     (*smiling*) We try not to talk about it too much. There's a lot of prejudice. But I can't see what it's got to do with. . . .

DR VALMY:     (*observing him closely*) Are you a policeman, Mr Barnes?

DANIEL:     (*a moment's pause*) I belong to the Political Section of the National Security Force.

DR VALMY:     (*unable to conceal his surprise*) You belong to the Secret Police?

DANIEL:     I do. (*Pause. Dr Valmy gets up slowly, walks around the room, thoughtful. Daniel's voice hardens*) I'm sorry to see you share that prejudice.

DR VALMY:     I haven't said a thing, Mr Barnes. It must have been Doctor Clemens who prescribed the hormone treatment.

DANIEL:     Yes. Do you know him?

DR VALMY:     Just a little. Did you discuss your problem with him?

DANIEL:     I don't want them to know.

DR VALMY:     Of course. How did you come to join the police force?

DANIEL:     (*restraining a gesture of impatience*) Do I need to go through all that?

DR VALMY:     It could be important.

DANIEL:     I've been in the Political Section for the last three years, in the police force for ten. My father died when I was still a child and I went to work in a shop. I wanted to study, to write. (*He smiles*) As a matter of fact, I still do some writing for our magazine.

DR VALMY:     Excellent.

DANIEL:     My current boss was a friend of the family and he told my mother I should think of signing on. That's how I started. And three years ago he took me into the Section, when he thought I'd matured politically.

DR VALMY:     Can you think of any possible cause for your problem? The patient sometimes has some idea. . . .

DANIEL:     I . . . don't know.

DR VALMY:     Think about it. Something in your childhood, of a sexual nature, or the sex-life of your parents . . . or your friends. . . .

DANIEL:     (*shakes his head*) I've thought about all that.

DR VALMY:     Can you think of any recent dreams?

DANIEL:     No.

DR VALMY:     You said it began three weeks ago.

DANIEL:     Yes.

DR VALMY:     (*sits down again*) Was there anything in the days leading up to that, anything to do with sex? Even something you may have read?

DANIEL:     (*pauses, looks away*) No.

DR VALMY:     Why do you look away?

DANIEL:     (*looking at him*) I've told you, Doctor: no.

DR VALMY:     In spite of which, I think there probably was. The question made you hesitate.

DANIEL:     It was unintentional.

DR VALMY:     It was not. You're a policeman. You know it wasn't, just as you know that giving a prisoner a cigarette will put him off his guard. I'm a policeman too . . . in my way. You have to tell me.

DANIEL:     It's nothing to do with it.

DR VALMY:     Don't be so sure. Tell me. Even if it doesn't seem important.

DANIEL:     It's not that it's not important. I've told you, it's quite irrelevant. In any case, my work is confidential.

DR VALMY:     And so is mine, Mr Barnes. People come here to tell me their secrets.

DANIEL:     That may be so . . . but I can't.

DR VALMY:     You are very good at hiding things. Which means that I can't help. (*He gets up*)

DANIEL:     (*getting up*) All right. If you insist. But it really has nothing to do with it. . . .

DR VALMY:     (*strongly*) Tell me, Mr Barnes. That's why you are here.

DANIEL:     There are things that people don't understand, but that have to be done.

DR VALMY:     Please begin. (*He sits and points to the armchair*)

DANIEL:     (*without sitting*) It's absurd. You ought to be looking somewhere else.

DR VALMY:    (*insisting*) Tell me!

DANIEL:    And you have no right to judge what I've done.

DR VALMY:    I judge nothing. You are the one who will judge.

*A greenish and unreal light fills the office.*

DANIEL:    Everyone who goes there lies, Doctor. You must bear that in mind. It must have been a month ago . . . we had to get tough with someone we'd arrested. (*He laughs nervously*) And the Boss, that's what we call him, gave me the difficult bit.

*As these words are spoken Paulus enters the office by means of the up-stage door and sits behind the table. He is an old man with grey hair and a tough-looking appearance.*

DR VALMY:    The Boss?

DANIEL:    The head of our section. An amazing person.

DR VALMY:    Did you give him the nickname?

DANIEL:    I don't recall.

DR VALMY:    But he is the old family friend?

DANIEL:    Yes.

DR VALMY:    Continue, please.

DANIEL:    (*goes towards the stairs*) As you know, the country faces serious problems. Because of the recent disturbances, we've detained more than sixty men. (*He turns to look at Dr Valmy*) It's a tough job, Doctor. But without us the country would be lost. You must understand that.

DR VALMY:    Continue.

*Daniel draws breath, turns, goes up the stairs. Paulus looks at him. Dr Valmy's office is in shadow.*

DANIEL:    He's confessed, sir. Dalton's taking his statement.

PAULUS:    (*looks at his watch*) In two hours flat?

DANIEL:    He just couldn't take it.

PAULUS:    Well done, lad. If Marsan breaks his, we'll have it all tied up. Smoke?

DANIEL:    (*takes a cigarette*) What about Marty?

PAULUS:    They're bringing him up. That's why I want you here. We have to make him talk, whatever it takes.

DANIEL:      (*shrugging his shoulders*) After what they've done to him already. . . .

PAULUS:      I've been thinking. (*The telephone rings. He picks it up*) Yes? (*His
tone changes*) Whatever you say, sir.

*Up the unseen stairs, stage-left, come Luigi and Pozner, leading Marty,
who is handcuffed. Paulus gestures to them to wait while he goes on
speaking into the phone. Luigi is slight, almost always smiling, and there
is something odd about his movements. Pozner is a heavily-built, calm
character. The prisoner, Hannibal Marty, is no older than 35. He is in his
shirtsleeves, wearing old trousers and sandals. He has not shaved for
several days, his appearance grotesque, reminiscent of a corpse.*

Yes, sir, they've almost all confessed. Couple of days. . . . Whatever you
say. (*He puts the phone down*) Pozner, take the handcuffs off.

*Pozner removes the handcuffs. Marty rubs his wrists with trembling fin-
gers. Luigi sits on the sofa. Paulus gets up and approaches the prisoner.
Daniel leans against the table.*

Bit tight, were they?

POZNER:      Not so much that, sir. Any kind of rubbing kills him. It's the burn
marks.

PAULUS:      Ah, the burn marks! (*He takes Marty's wrists and looks at them*) Just
a few sparks from metal to skin. The method isn't perfect yet. How many
shocks, Luigi?

LUIGI:      Not many, sir. Maybe six.

PAULUS:      Let's see your fingernails. (*He takes Marty's left hand and lightly
applies some pressure. Marty stifles a cry*) Don't make a fuss, lad. We've
left the ones on your other hand, to allow you to sign your name.

*Marsan enters from up-stage. He is in shirtsleeves. He places two sheets
of paper on the table.*

MARSAN:      They've both confessed.

PAULUS:      (*to Marty*) You see, fool? They all confess and sign. Come here.
It's not a trick. (*Pozner pushes Marty towards the table. He cannot avoid
an uneasy glance at the papers*) You'd like to read them, eh? Take a look!
(*He pushes the papers towards him. Marty reads them. Luigi laughs.
Paulus walks around the table and, as he passes Marty, takes him by the
shoulders and forces him into the chair*) Sit down! You are going to need
it. (*He snatches the papers from him and reads them quickly*) Good
work, Marsan.

MARSAN:       Thank you, sir. (*He moves away and leans against the wall next to the sofa*)

PAULUS:       Sit down, Pozner. You too, Daniel. (*Pozner goes to the sofa, Daniel sits next to the typewriter*) So . . . you're on your own, lad. You are going to talk.

MARTY:       I've told you all I know.

MARSAN:       Hear that, Luigi? He's told us all he knows.

LUIGI:       (*laughing*) I *do* feel touched.

PAULUS:       Shut up! Daniel, give him a cigarette. We are going to have a little chat.

*Paulus lights a cigarette. Daniel gives the prisoner a cigarette, places it in his mouth and lights it. He sits down again.*

Marty, we know you were just the link-man. The second of last month you had a visit from a stranger from abroad. And you don't know who he is. He gave you a letter to deliver to a certain place, and you don't know what was in it. All right, that's fair enough. But the place you went to, the person you gave the letter to . . . of course you know!

MARTY:       I've told you once. It was a café.

PAULUS:       It was a house! (*He picks up the confessions*) They all agree on it.

MARTY:       They might have said it under. . . .

MARSAN:       (*harshly*) Under what? (*Marty looks at him, afraid. Marsan approaches him*) Come on! Speak!

PAULUS:       Marty, they've done the dirty on you, lad. They're just a bunch of cowards. They don't deserve your silence. Why not protect yourself by saying who's responsible? (*Pause*) You were right, you know. Your friends have all betrayed you, saying you're in charge. As you can see, they've put their names to it. So why should you be braver? (*Pause*) You speak the truth, you have my word, (*Marty looks at him*) we shan't be tough on you. You were just a link-man after all, completely in the dark, which is why they wanted you. You'll get a three or four year stretch, that's all. Gone in a flash, and then you can start afresh. Of course you want to tell the truth! If you don't, you see, we'll make you say exactly what we want. You know yourself there's no way out. It's entirely up to you. (*Pause*)

MARSAN:       Do you want your wife brought in again?

*Marty looks at him in horror.*

PAULUS:     That would be very unpleasant, eh? You really love that girl. And yet, when she was here, you still refused to speak. Relax. We shan't bring her in again. Too many groups concerned with human rights. Too many lawyers sticking their noses in. And we don't want to bother with those we'd have to release. How long have you been married?

POZNER:     Eighteen months, sir.

PAULUS:     Still on your honeymoon then. So why get so involved in this kind of thing? If you get out of this, you'd like to have kids, yes? Answer me!

MARTY:     I don't know.

PAULUS:     Of course you would. And she would too. They say you're a pair of cooing doves. (*Very softly*) It's really a great pity . . . you not having them, I mean. (*Marty looks at him, puzzled*) I don't mean you're going to die, or spend your life inside. All things considered, I really prefer a shortish sentence, so that you are back with her in a couple of years.

*The policemen look at each other.*

MARSAN:     That's much too good for him, sir.

PAULUS:     You think so? But the truth of the matter is he'll need persuading. And because he will have made us use too much persuasion, maybe there'll be no kids. (*Marty looks at him, terrified. Daniel gets up. They all stare at each other*) But would he want to spend the rest of his life treating his wife like his sister? It's far too great a price to pay for adolescent whims.

LUIGI:     (*whistles softly*) That's really good!

PAULUS:     (*brutally, to Marty*) I hope you understand! I mean what I say and we've had it up to here. Are you going to confess?

*Luigi stands up and steps forward. Marsan leans forward.*

MARTY:     (*gets up, loses control*) I don't know. I don't know anything!

PAULUS:     Right! If that's how you want it. Take him inside. Get him undressed. Daniel, stay with me.

*Pozner and Marsan drag the prisoner upstage. Luigi opens the door.*

MARTY:     I don't know anything.

POZNER:     More like you don't remember. So now we'll help you remember.

*Marty looks at them in desperation. They go out.*

LUIGI:     Shall we make a start?

PAULUS:     I'll be with you in a minute.

*Luigi nods, goes out and closes the door. Paulus looks at Daniel.*

DANIEL:     I'm sure he'll talk. The threat has finished him.

PAULUS:     I promise you, it's not a threat.

DANIEL:     But. . . .

PAULUS:     He'll still refuse. He won't confess until we make a start. But then you'll see how loose his tongue becomes. I've seen it all before. I've much more faith in it than in these fancy, modern methods. What breaks a man is pain applied to vital parts. It never fails.

DANIEL:     And if . . . he doesn't talk?

PAULUS:     (*annoyed, rises*) He has to talk! (*Paces up and dow.*)

DANIEL:     Is there a risk that . . . he might die?

PAULUS:     We'll take good care. (*Turns, looks at Daniel*) I want you to do the job, son.

DANIEL:     (*with a start*) What? Me?

PAULUS:     The others can't be trusted. It gets them too excited. That's why I want you to do it. (*He places a hand on Daniel's shoulder*) Daniel, you mustn't feel sorry for them. These people are vermin to be stamped on!

DANIEL:     But . . . I wouldn't know how. . . .

PAULUS:     I'll show you what to do. (*He moves towards the door*) Let's go.

*Paulus opens the door. The light begins to fade up-stage. Lights up down-stage. Paulus goes out and shuts the door behind him. Daniel begins to descend the stairs. The up-stage area is in darkness.*

DANIEL:     (*coming down the stairs*) I had to go through with it.

DR VALMY:     (*without looking at him*) How did you do it?

DANIEL:     (*disturbed*) I'd rather not go into detail.

DR VALMY:     It's enough for now to see that it upsets you. Did the prisoner confess?

DANIEL:     (*coldly*) He blacked out. They had to take him to a hospital. He's back in his cell from today.

DR VALMY:     Ah! (*Daniel sits down once more*) So he's recovered?

DANIEL:     Almost completely, but he'll never be a normal man again.

DR VALMY:     How can you be sure?

DANIEL:     It's what the doctor said. (*Long pause*)

DR VALMY:     Do you regret doing it?

DANIEL:     I did my duty.

DR VALMY:     I don't know if you are fully aware of how you recounted the scene.

DANIEL:     Such things aren't very nice. But they have to be done. (*Pause*) Well, I've told you everything. I hope you are convinced.

DR VALMY:     Of what?

DANIEL:     That there's another explanation.

DR VALMY:     On the contrary. It's perfectly clear.

DANIEL:     Perfectly clear?

DR VALMY:     You say you don't regret it. . . .

DANIEL:     I've nothing to regret.

DR VALMY:     Much better if you did.

DANIEL:     I don't know what you mean.

DR VALMY:     It's very simple: you choose to express your guilt by becoming ill, precisely because you do not admit to guilt.

DANIEL:     Listen, doctor; I've read about these things. I'm sorry but they don't convince me.

DR VALMY:     Mr Barnes, you ought to feel relieved. There are cases that require years to solve, and it's taken us minutes to find an answer to yours. On the other hand, I doubt you'll feel relieved if, as I suspect, you may not wish to recover.

DANIEL:     But that's why I'm here.

DR VALMY:     In spite of being here. Something tells you you shouldn't have done what you did, although you insist it has to be done. In order to be cured, you'd have to admit to having performed a terrible and unjustified act. And even if you did, I doubt it would help. Or you'd have to believe, and be completely convinced, that this and similar acts were savage, but just and fully deserved. . . . And I do not believe that anyone, in his heart of hearts, can convince himself of that. You, I know, are not convinced.

DANIEL:     If that were the cause, it would only mean that my nerve had gone, that I'm still not mature enough. But I know I can deal with that.

DR VALMY:     Then you'd better try, if you think you can.

DANIEL:      I know I can. Maybe I haven't the strength myself. But others have.

DR VALMY:      You mean your colleagues?

DANIEL:      I know they aren't going through this.

DR VALMY:      How do you know? They could have other problems. From what you've said, I'd say they are sick as well. I'd like to know what they did with the prisoner's wife?

DANIEL:      That was some time before. I was in the South, arresting suspects.

DR VALMY:      You haven't answered my question. Did they beat her up? (*Pause*) Don't answer if you don't want to. It could well be that you punish yourself for what they did to her. (*Daniel looks at him*)

DANIEL:      I've never done that. (*Dr Valmy shrugs*) If it ever happens, it shows. . . .

DR VALMY:      That your colleagues have fewer qualms than you. Not that they aren't sick.

DANIEL:      There's one, at least, who isn't.

DR VALMY:      Your boss.      .

DANIEL:      Exactly.

DR VALMY:      Maybe he doesn't sleep too well, or his stomach plays him up.

DANIEL:      It doesn't!

DR VALMY:      Fine. Let's drop the subject. When was the first occasion you abused a prisoner?

DANIEL:      (*put out*) Several years ago.

DR VALMY:      Do you remember him?

DANIEL:      Yes. And I don't regret it. The bastard had abused a child.

DR VALMY:      Of course. It must be easy to learn to hate. Drunks, degenerates, con-men . . . and then they move you to another section, and you have to torture political prisoners, for which you must be politically mature.

DANIEL:      Troublemakers, Doctor. Worse than common criminals!

DR VALMY:      (*dryly*) Maybe so. But there is another possibility you ought to consider. Your political maturity, as you describe it, may well be due to the fact that you knew you'd be moved one day to the Political Section; and you felt you wouldn't be up to doing certain things without a reason that, at least in part, would make you feel rather better.

DANIEL:      (*sharply*) All this psychology's a waste of time.

DR VALMY:     As you wish. But I think you gave it some serious thought before you struck your very first blow. That's what it amounts to in the end, Mr Barnes. The first blow conceals much more than meets the eye. (*Pause*)

DANIEL:      (*quietly*) Why did you say you don't believe I can be cured, even if I admit that what I did was wrong?

DR VALMY:     Because you can't repair the damage. You can't restore the poor victim's manhood; therefore you've destroyed your own. A nice paradox: your cure is your illness. It has to be said, it does you some credit. But even so . . . (*He is silent*)

DANIEL:      What?

DR VALMY:     Nothing. I can't take on your case.

DANIEL:      But you're a doctor!

DR VALMY:     You know very well what's wrong with you. If anyone can cure you, it's you, not me. Even though . . . I don't believe you can.

DANIEL:      Why not? Why can't I?

DR VALMY:     (*rises. Daniel gets up slowly*) For what you've done you have to pay a considerable price, which is what you are doing now. In order to stop paying, you'd have to pay another price just as high.

DANIEL:      What price?

DR VALMY:     Who knows? You'd need to change. Perhaps give up your job. Seek some kind of pardon that wouldn't be easy, at a cost . . . I can barely imagine. You aren't a child anymore, and I think it most unlikely you'd go as far as to sacrifice your livelihood or your personality. . . .

DANIEL:      I want to get better.

DR VALMY:     What you want is to pay in the way you've chosen. I'm an honest man, Mr Barnes. To see you again and again would be dishonest. I have no wish to take your money.

DANIEL:      (*after a moment*) No. You want me out because you detest me. But do you know why you detest me? . . . Come on, confess the truth. Admit you've been blaming me to make me join the other side, your side.

DR VALMY:     You sound like a policeman, Mr Barnes. You haven't come here to cross-examine me.

DANIEL:      (*laughs nervously*) Do you mean to say you'd be just as hard on the other side if they were now in power?

DR VALMY: That's nothing to do with you. But if you insist, the answer's yes. I would.

DANIEL: (*after a moment, darkly*) It's easily said. Goodbye.

*He moves stage-right.*

DR VALMY: Mr Barnes. . . . (*Daniel turns*) One other thing. The day may come when you'll think yourself recovered, from having taken a decision that, at the time, seemed adequate. Don't be deceived. I repeat, the price to be paid is very high. The fact is that such recoveries are never permanent.

DANIEL: (*bitterly*) What do I owe you?

DR VALMY: Nothing at all. Goodbye. (*Daniel goes out. The Secretary reappears discreetly*) I know I wasn't exactly prudent. For days I thought I'd be taken away by the Secret Police, tortured to confess some lie. When you place such power in a patient's hands, anything can happen. But he was right in a way: I didn't behave as a doctor should because I suddenly despised him. It was only later that I also felt pity, perhaps as much as for the unfortunate man whose life he'd ruined.

SECRETARY: Ruined.

*A few moments previously lights up on the Barnes' household. Now the door bell rings. Mary enters stage-left, looking at her watch, followed by the grandmother who is carrying a tablecloth and serviettes. She gestures to Mary to answer the door while she goes to the small table. She puts down the serviettes and the tablecloth, picks up the vase and exits quickly stage-left.*

DR VALMY: I propose to avoid commenting on the political struggle, the subversive processes mentioned earlier. The reader unfamiliar with these events is free to imagine that the rebels were in the right, as well as the opposite. For many, I know my approach avoids examination of the problem, which only close study will help us understand. For me the opposite holds true: only by avoiding it can we hope to pose in all their

starkness the pressing questions that lie at the heart of our story and which all of us must think about, if we aren't too cowardly to face the answers.

*Dr Valmy and the Secretary exit stage-right. The grandmother enters again quickly and spreads the tablecloth over the table. Mary's voice is heard.*

MARY: (*off-stage*) My goodness, you do look attractive! (*Mary enters, followed by Lucila*) Though you are a bit pale, I must say. It's not good news, is it?

LUCILA:    No, not yet.

*Lucila is a very young woman, with attractive features but a shy manner. She dresses smartly but modestly.*

MARY:    It won't be long, you'll see. Gran, this is Lucila. I used to teach her.

LUCILA:    (*shakes hands*) How do you do?

GRANDMOTHER:    Pleased to meet you. Won't you sit down? Excuse me a moment.

MARY:    (*stopping her*) Let me go, Gran.

GRANDMOTHER:    You stay there. (*She moves stage-left*)

MARY:    Sit down, Lucila. (*The grandmother goes out*)

LUCILA:    Thank you. (*She sits on the sofa, and Mary sits next to her*)

MARY:    So, you are married already! I can hardly believe it. Though I couldn't believe it about myself either and here I am. What does your husband do?

LUCILA:    He . . . well, he works in a bookshop, and . . . I *am* making a mess of it!

MARY:    (*laughs*) You are still as shy as ever.

LUCILA:    He's . . . he's very nice.

MARY:    (*laughs, kisses her*) I'm glad to see you happy. So how are things going? Are you managing so far?

LUCILA:    Just about. I'm a nanny . . . I mean, I was. It's not always easy to find that kind of work. I'm about to start work in a store.

*The grandmother enters, bringing some tea on a tray. Lucila gets up.*

GRANDMOTHER:    Sit down, sit down, please.

LUCILA:    Thanks. (*She sits*) You shouldn't have bothered, really, Miss.

MARY:    Don't call me 'Miss'. It makes me sound so ancient.

*The grandmother leaves the tray and takes a few hesitant steps.*

GRANDMOTHER:    I'll leave you then. You've lots to talk about.

*She smiles and goes out.*

MARY:    She's rather deaf, you know. She much prefers to drink her milk in front of the television. (*Pouring*) Coffee?

LUCILA:    That's fine, thanks. (*Mary pours the milk*) Two sugars, please.

*Mary puts the sugar in and cuts some sponge cake.*

MARY:      Try some cake. It's delicious. Or would you prefer biscuits?

LUCILA:    I'll have some cake. (*Mary passes it*) Thanks. (*They begin to eat*)

MARY:      You should have told me about the wedding. Were you too embar-
           rassed?

LUCILA:    You didn't tell me about yours.

MARY:      That's because I *was* embarrassed. Compared to all of you, I seemed
           so old.

LUCILA:    So old?

MARY:      If you only knew. To tell you the truth. . . .

LUCILA:    (*strongly*) Please, Miss!

MARY:      You said it again.

LUCILA:    I'm just not used to it.

MARY:      You'll soon learn. Come along, eat something. (*Lucila eats some of
           the cake and leaves it*) We aren't teacher and pupil anymore; simply two
           good friends. Do you see, Lucila? No, of course you don't. For you,
           everything's happened naturally. But as for me. . . . Did you know I was
           engaged years ago?

LUCILA:    No.

MARY:      Of course not. You were only a child. And I was so old in comparison.
           The years I suffered, my dear! And the way you girls made me suffer!

LUCILA:    I don't understand.

MARY:      I'd watch you and think to myself: they'll all grow up, get married . . .
           and I'll go on being 'Miss'. You'll never know what it was like. My fiancé
           had been killed in the war. And I had such a thirst for life! I applied for the
           job at the school, believing the children would be mine. But I couldn't
           accept what had happened. The years slipped by and I spent them with my
           father. And when he died, I felt so completely alone. I'd go to the park
           with a book, or maybe to a café. I met him on a seat in a park.

LUCILA:    Your husband?

MARY:      He saw I was crying so he came over to me. He was lucky with
           women, it seems, but he married me out of pity. 'You aren't at all well',
           he'd say, 'but I shall make you better.' What I said to myself was: 'You
           shall love me.' (*She gets up and walks up and down, tears in her eyes*)
           Nowadays we sometimes sit on the same seat and he says: 'Well, did I
           make you better?' And we laugh. You'll see what a lovely child we have.

Of course, we have our problems, but nothing serious. There's nothing I wouldn't do to make him happy. (*She looks at her*) You haven't eaten a thing.

LUCILA:    (*her eyes lowered*) I'm not hungry.

MARY:    (*approaching her, curious*) Is there something wrong? You seem upset. (*Lucila looks at her and looks away again, disturbed*) It's not because of what I've told you, is it?

LUCILA:    (*unable to speak*) I . . . came to ask a favour.

MARY:    (*sits beside her*) What sort of favour?

LUCILA:    I don't know where to turn . . . I went to see a solicitor, but he says I shouldn't do anything. (*She looks at Mary, deeply troubled*)

MARY:    What is it?

LUCILA:    You were always so good to us.

MARY:    Tell me.

LUCILA:    (*after a pause*) Is it true . . . your husband's a member of the Secret Police?

MARY:    (*taken aback*) Why do you ask?

LUCILA:    They've arrested my husband. (*Mary looks at her in amazement*) Perhaps you've heard your husband mention him: Hannibal Marty.

WOMAN:    He never speaks about his work.

LUCILA:    He's been held for forty two days. And his case still hasn't gone to court.

MARY:    Lucila, I can't believe your husband is one of those . . . dissidents. . . .

LUCILA:    (*stiffening*) It depends what you mean by dissidents.

MARY:    What has he done?

LUCILA:    I don't know. They want him to tell them something they say he knows.

MARY:    What do you want of me? Do you want me to ask my husband to get the case to court?

LUCILA:    (*smiling sadly*) It would be just, but I knew it's pointless asking. I only wanted. . . . (*Weeping*) They had to take him to hospital three weeks ago!

MARY:    Lucila! Child! (*She takes her hands*)

LUCILA:    Don't ask me how I know. I can't say. But I know too that tomorrow, or maybe even today, they are taking him back to the Secret Police. (*She weeps uncontrollably.*)

MARY:    Don't cry.

LUCILA:    I only ask that . . . they aren't too hard on him. That they don't torture him anymore.

*She buries her head against Mary.*

MARY:    (*moved and astonished, stroking her head*) Come along now, calm yourself.

LUCILA:    (*trying to pull herself together*) I'm sorry. (*She pulls away*)

MARY:    I understand. It's perfectly natural. (*Pause*) Did you say torture?

LUCILA:    Yes. (*Weeping*)

MARY:    Don't cry, please! Do you mean they've made him stand for hours on end, or placed him under a bright light in order to question him? (*Lucila looks at her in amazement*)

LUCILA:    Do you think doing that would have put him in hospital?

MARY:    What?

LUCILA:    Of course it wouldn't!

*Mary gets up and paces around nervously.*

MARY:    (*turning*) Lucila, I know you mean well, but I don't know if you realize quite what you are doing. (*Gently*) Don't you see you've come here to tell me that my husband tortures people?

LUCILA:    I didn't say that.

MARY:    Of course you did! I can forgive you that because you are still so young and you are having a bad time. But take my advice, my dear: don't believe these lies. I expect your husband was ill; that's why they put him in hospital.

LUCILA:    (*totally amazed*) You mean you don't know what goes on there?

MARY:    Why go on with this?

LUCILA:    (*her expression hardens. She gets up*) I imagine you're a truthful person. . . .

MARY:    You are going to make me angry, my dear. I know my husband, and he doesn't lie to me.

LUCILA:     You said just now he doesn't talk about his work.

MARY:     Not in detail, no. But it's not what you think. (*Smiling*) Perhaps they overstep the mark sometimes; maybe the odd blow. . . .

LUCILA:     (*stubbornly*) They destroy people.

MARY:     Don't exaggerate. They subject them to a certain degree of physical pressure, agreed. But most of the time it's psychological.

LUCILA:     Is that what you call electric shock?

*Mary turns and looks at her. She approaches her, takes her by the arms and shakes her in a vigorous but friendly manner.*

MARY:     You are going too far.

LUCILA:     They put them in a bath and almost drown them, time and time again. . . .

MARY:     (*forces her to sit*) Sit down. (*Moves away, upset*) I'm sorry. I find it hard to believe that you too are one of these people spreading lies. What can you gain from saying such things?

LUCILA:     What can I gain? You know how dangerous it is. Which means that if we speak in spite of that, there must be a reason.

MARY:     (*goes quickly to sit beside her*) No, no! There are laws! Courts! If it were true, people would know.

LUCILA:     Not when others prevent it . . . and many more close their eyes to the truth. (*She looks away*) Like you.

MARY:     (*after a brief pause*) Lucila, you ought to see a doctor.

LUCILA:     (*gets up*) Be quiet! I didn't want to mention it, but now you force me to. They arrested me too, you know. (*Mary gets up. Lucila takes a few steps. She is extremely agitated*) They beat me horribly. (*She cries out, in tears*) They abused me in front of my husband. (*She weeps convulsively*)

MARY:     (*slowly*) You are making it up.

LUCILA:     (*staring at her*) I should never have come. (*She goes to pick up her handbag*)

MARY:     (*moving towards her*) Wait. (*Harshly.*) Are you implying that my husband would . . . abuse a prisoner?

LUCILA:     (*coldly*) Your husband wasn't there. They mentioned him, and when I heard the name I thought you might be his wife. He hasn't touched me. But I don't know what he might have done to others. (*Mary strikes her*) That's nothing in comparison. . . . (*Mary holds the hand which struck the blow and starts to cry)* You're a teacher, trained in your subject. And what's that? Ignorance? *(Mary looks at her, upset)* Who is the adult, and who is the child now?

MARY:    I never struck a pupil. I'm sorry, even if you are a liar. I shall forget you ever came. Please go.

LUCILA:    *(takes her handbag)* I'll make quite sure you never forget.

MARY:    Quiet. Someone's coming. *(She looks up-stage)* He said he wouldn't be back. . . .

*Daniel enters.*

DANIEL:    Sorry to interrupt. I'll go in the other room. Good evening.

LUCILA:    It's quite all right. I was just going.

DANIEL:    You must be the girl my wife used to teach.

*He holds out his hand. She takes it timidly.*

LUCILA:    Yes.

DANIEL:    No need to go on my account. I'll make myself scarce.

MARY:    She was about to leave, Daniel.

DANIEL:    What a pity! Call whenever you can. My wife would appreciate that.

LUCILA:    Goodbye. *(She walks up-stage)*

MARY:    I'll come with you.

*The two women exit. Daniel watches them, intrigued. He removes his revolver, checks the safety-catch and places it on the bookshelf. The grandmother enters stage-left.*

GRANDMOTHER:    It's you.

DANIEL:    Yes, Mother.

GRANDMOTHER:    *(goes up to him)* Where's the visitor?

DANIEL:    She's gone. *(He kisses her)*

GRANDMOTHER:    That was short. *(Mary enters up-stage)* Would you like something to eat? The cake's very nice.

DANIEL:    Thanks. I'm not hungry.

GRANDMOTHER:    I don't know! *(She places everything on the tray)*

MARY:    *(goes to take it)* Let me do it, Gran.

GRANDMOTHER:     What for?

MARY:     You go and watch television.

GRANDMOTHER:     There's nothing on at this time of night. (*She picks up the tray and stands in front of her son*) You don't look well. (*Mary removes the cloth and the serviettes*)

DANIEL:     (*taking his mother by the arms*) I'm fine, Mother. Don't you go bringing me a tablet I don't need.

GRANDMOTHER:     Do you want your slippers?

MARY:     I'll get them. (*She moves stage-left.*)

GRANDMOTHER:     (*looking at her*) What? . . . Ah!

*She follows her. Mary goes out. From the doorway, the grandmother looks back at her son, then exits. Daniel sits on the sofa, thoughtful, and begins to take his shoes off. He stops, looks up-stage, recalling Lucila. Mary enters with his slippers, puts them down, picks up his shoes and starts to leave.*

DANIEL:     That girl's face seemed familiar.

MARY:     (*looking at him*) I'm sure you've never met her.

DANIEL:     (*putting on his slippers*) Any phone-calls?

MARY:     Only for me. Pozner's wife, insisting we visit them.

DANIEL:     We should.

MARY:     I don't like her.

*The grandmother enters and tries to take the shoes from Mary.*

GRANDMOTHER:     Give them to me.

MARY:     (*resisting*) I'll see to them, Gran.

GRANDMOTHER:     (*insistent*) Give them to me . . . (*She takes the shoes and goes out.*)

DANIEL:     What else did Mrs Pozner say?

MARY:     (*looking directly at him*) She says her husband isn't well.

DANIEL:     Isn't well?

MARY:     He wakes up in the middle of the night, screaming. (*Daniel averts his eyes*) There's something wrong with all of you.

DANIEL:     (*startled*) What?

MARY:     The work seems to wear you out.

*Daniel looks away again. Mary hesitates: she wishes to speak but decides against it. The grandmother enters with some knitting.*

GRANDMOTHER:     He's sleeping like a little angel. Aren't you going to see him?

DANIEL:     In a minute.

*The grandmother sits on the sofa, takes out her glasses-case, puts on her glasses and begins to knit. From time to time she glances at the others.*

MARY:     (*leaning against the bookcase*) You never talk about your work in detail.

DANIEL:     It's not very pleasant.

MARY:     (*casually*) Do you have to beat the prisoners?

DANIEL:     Sometimes a little force is needed.

MARY:     Yes, of course. (*Daniel gets up, makes to leave*) Where are you going?

DANIEL:     To do some writing . . . the piece for the journal.

GRANDMOTHER:     Where are you going?

*Daniel smiles without answering and moves stage-left. When he is about to go out, he turns.*

DANIEL:     Mary. (*She looks at him. He takes a few steps towards her. The grandmother watches them*) Why did the girl come here?

MARY:     She wanted to see me after all these years.

DANIEL:     I know where I've seen her. A photograph in the police records. (*Mary looks away, moves down-stage*) Mary, don't ask her here again. (*Mary sits, deflated, on the chair by the telephone*)

MARY:     I don't intend to.

DANIEL:     (*advancing*) She spoke about the way that prisoners are dealt with, didn't she?

MARY:     I didn't believe her.

DANIEL:     Who did she talk about? Her husband?

MARY:     Herself too.

DANIEL:     But not about me. I was in the South when they took her in.

MARY:     Yes. She said you weren't there when your colleagues raped her.

DANIEL:     She said that?

MARY:     (*smiling nervously*) Yes! (*Daniel moves away. Mary's voice hardens*) Do you interrogate women as well?

DANIEL:     (*turning angrily*) I don't do that, Mary!

MARY:     (*gets up*) What about the others? (*The grandmother watches them*)

DANIEL:     Some of them . . . are very stupid.

MARY:     So she wasn't lying?

DANIEL:     (*disturbed*) I'll try to explain.

MARY:     (*approaches, takes him by the arm*) Tell me the truth. She seemed quite genuine. She came to beg . . . that you stop torturing her husband.

DANIEL:     (*with the grandmother in mind*) Be quiet. (*He moves away, disturbed. They look at each other. The grandmother gets up and, without glancing at them, goes out stage-left. Concerned, they watch her go out*) Do you think she heard? (*He goes to the door and checks*)

MARY:     (*quietly*) Can you do something for him?

DANIEL:     Only he can do something. He refuses to talk.

MARY:     What do you do to them?

DANIEL:     (*comes back*) They are criminals. They have to confess.

MARY:     (*horrified*) It's true, then.

DANIEL:     (*takes a step towards her*) Mary, it's not as bad as all that.

MARY:     (*approaching him*) Have you done something to him?

DANIEL:     (*edgily*) His wife knows nothing. Everything she's told you is a lie or an exaggeration. (*Not looking at her*) Mary, it's your husband you must believe. If she said that they raped her. . . .

MARY:     She said they abused her.

DANIEL:     That's not the same thing. Someone must have gone a bit too far. Did she tell you that I did something to him?

MARY:     No.

DANIEL:     You see?

MARY:     (*throwing herself in his arms, weeping*) I believe you. I believe you.

*The door bell rings. Daniel moves away from her, uneasy. She looks at him and goes up-stage.*

DANIEL: Mary . . . (*She stops*) I doubt it's from headquarters, but if it is, tell them I'm having a sleep. I went to the doctor's, and I'm not very well.

*She looks at him in surprise. He moves stage-left and goes out. Mary goes out up-stage. Another ring. In a moment, Mary enters again, followed by Marsan, who is wearing an overcoat and carrying a hat.*

MARY: I'm sorry, Mr Marsan. He was shivering, so he went to bed.

MARSAN: (*looking around, smiling*) Yes, I know. He said he wouldn't be in tonight. No doubt he'll get a visit from our doctor. Can I have a word?

MARY: He's asleep.

MARSAN: (*laughs*) Lucky him! (*He goes to the sofa*) I'd appreciate a drink, you know. I really need one. (*He sits down, completely at ease*)

MARY: (*coldly*) I was just about to go out.

MARSAN: (*getting up*) Fine. Mind if I come?

MARY: (*taken aback*) Do you think that would be wise?

MARSAN: (*approaching her*) Why not? It doesn't bother me.

MARY: It does me.

MARSAN: How much does it bother you, Mrs Barnes?

MARY: What do you mean?

MARSAN: (*coming closer*) I wish it didn't bother you so much.

MARY: (*moves away*) I don't understand.

MARSAN: You understood the very first time I came here.

MARY: Marsan, would you mind leaving?

MARSAN: (*his voice shaking*) There aren't many pleasures in life, Mary. Don't tell me you are happy with your husband. You can't be. (*He moves forward*)

MARY: (*moving away from him*) Get out!

MARSAN: There's something irresistible about you. Something other women don't have.

MARY: Must I put up with this in my own house! How dare you!

MARSAN: (*strongly*) I'm very persistent, Mary. You'll find that out.

MARY: Get out of here at once!

*Daniel enters, looks at him hard.*

DANIEL:    Wait. I'll come with you. (*An embarrassed silence*)

MARSAN:    You weren't asleep then?

DANIEL:    I'm feeling better.

MARSAN:    (*laughing suddenly*) Don't look like that, man . . . I was having a bit of a joke. I knew you were listening, and you'd come out. I'm sorry, Mrs Barnes.

DANIEL:    Marsan, you know we can't fight over this. The Boss will have to deal with it.

MARSAN:    (*coldly*) You'd better keep your mouth shut, or I'll tell him you were skiving. I don't want to get you into trouble. I only wanted to get you to work. That's all I came for.

*Lights up on the office of the Secret Police.*

DANIEL:    (*angrily taking a step towards him*) You're a liar.

*Above Paulus enters from up-stage and waits, leaning against the table.*

MARSAN:    Oh, yes? Then we'd better tell Paulus everything. Let's see who he believes.

DANIEL:    (*controls himself, goes to the book shelf and takes his revolver*) Let's get to the Station. (*He walks to the hall.*)

MARY:    He really isn't well, Mr Marsan.

MARSAN:    Of course he isn't, Mrs Barnes. I'll say cheerio. I'm sorry.

*He goes ahead of Daniel and leaves. Mary runs anxiously to her husband and kisses him.*

DANIEL:    Bye.

*Daniel goes out. Mary comes down-stage, her expression full of concern. Absent-mindedly she leans against the sofa. Pozner and Luigi come up the stairs stage-left, leading Marty, who has difficulty in walking. He now wears a jacket. His appearance is a little improved but his expression one of complete hopelessness. Pozner begins to remove the handcuffs.*

PAULUS:    Leave them on.

LUIGI:    Listen, Boss. The bath and the electric shock together. He wouldn't withstand it.

PAULUS:    (*approaching Marty*) So what do you think, fool? That there can't be anything worse? Don't fool yourself! You're only a piece of straw, easily broken and thrown away. Are you going to talk?

*The prisoner doesn't move. Although she cannot hear it, it is as if Mary knows what is happening elsewhere. With a sudden movement she attempts to obliterate these obsessive thoughts. She moves to the centre of the room, stops once more, disturbed.*

POZNER:     We'll start whenever you want, Boss.

PAULUS:     (*looks at his watch*) Marsan's late.

LUIGI:    He's coming.

*Marsan and Daniel climb the stairs, stage-left.*

MARSAN:     Better late than never. (*He places his hat and coat on a peg. The prisoner looks at Daniel who looks away*)

PAULUS:     Both of you take him in. (*Pozner and Luigi take Marty out up-stage and close the door. Daniel puts his hat on a peg*) What's the matter, Daniel? (*Daniel turns, hesitates*)

MARSAN:     (*stepping forward, quickly*) He felt depressed. But then he said he was better and insisted on coming.

*Mary goes out stage-left. Lights down in the Barnes household.*

PAULUS:     Doctor Clemens had better take a look at you. Let's go. (*They move up-stage. The telephone rings. Paulus answers it*) Yes? . . . Yes, doctor. I've just brought Marty up. . . . Don't you think that's my affair? Don't worry, we'll take care. . . . Of course, I know you are telling me for my own good.

*Dr Valmy enters down-stage left, and the Secretary down-stage right with her notepad and pencil. Dr Valmy is holding an unbound book with which he plays absent-mindedly.*

PAULUS:     Fine; thanks. Bye. (*Paulus hangs up and rubs his eyes. He looks at Daniel*) How is your mother?

DANIEL:     She's fine, thanks. She sends her regards.

PAULUS:     Thank you. (*He opens the door up-stage and goes out, followed by Marsan and Daniel. The door closes and remains softly lit while the lights fade on the rest of the office. Lights up down-stage*)

DR VALMY:     Behind the door of that small room screams would be heard during the night; and maybe now, at this very moment, some other unfortunate man is crying out in there. But ignorance of these things means that, like my patient's mother, we cannot hear them. (*He moves stage-right*) Her son heard them, of course, throughout the entire night, since he was one of those responsible. The hours went by. . . . (*He stops for a moment, looking at the door)* Then, in the early hours of the morning, something happened.

*Lights up in the office. The door bursts open, and Paulus rushes to the phone. While he dials a number, Luigi appears.*

LUIGI:     It's no good, Boss.

*Marsan and Pozner enter, bringing Daniel with them. He is in a state of collapse. All of them are in shirtsleeves, their hair ruffled, all of them exhausted.*

PAULUS:     Doctor Clemens? Well, wake him up! It's Paulus. (*He looks at the others*) Has he recovered?

MARSAN:     He's just a wimp.

PAULUS:     (*annoyed*) I don't want any criticisms. When I place my confidence in someone, I know what I'm doing, understand? Take him out of here.

MARSAN:     (*muttering*) You'll see I'm right, Boss.

*Marsan and Pozner take Daniel down the stairs stage-left.*

PAULUS:     Listen, Clemens. Get up here right away. Bring a cardiac stimulant. There's been an accident. . . . Yes, yes, with the prisoner. No sign of a pulse . . . I know you told me. Just get a move on.

*He puts the phone down, looks at Luigi and tells him to follow him. They both exit up-stage, closing the door behind them. Lights down on the office.*

DR VALMY:     I've already said that the patients in the previous case were told of this one without a single detail being spared. We know the outcome of that. I told them too to read the book my client's wife received one day. (*He flicks over the pages of the book he is holding*) That was a crucial day. After the accident at headquarters, they allowed my patient a week's leave. The book arrived two days before it ended.

*Lights up on the Barnes household. Dr Valmy and the Secretary sit in a corner in shadow. Daniel is sitting on the chair by the telephone, absent-mindedly reading a paper. The grandmother enters stage-left and puts some nappies on the radiator. She looks at Daniel, who hasn't moved.*

GRANDMOTHER:     You can't see.

DANIEL:     What? . . . I wasn't reading.

GRANDMOTHER:     It's getting dark.

*She switches on the light. She puts on her glasses and takes from her overall a piece of brown paper, torn and crumpled, which she holds up to the light.*

DANIEL: (*looking at his watch*) Ten past eight. (*He throws the newspaper on the table in annoyance. The grandmother picks it up. Daniel gets up and begins to pace up and down impatiently*) What time did she go out?

GRANDMOTHER: (*cupping her hand to her ear*) I've told you once: as soon as you went to lie down. She's gone to buy you some shirts.

*She goes to the sofa, puts aside the newspaper and studies the piece of brown paper under the light.*

DANIEL: We'd arranged to go out this evening as we always do. (*He goes to the shelves to look for a book*) What are you looking at?

GRANDMOTHER: (*shaking her head slowly*) This book wasn't for you, then. (*She looks at him*)

DANIEL: (*stops looking through the shelves*) What book?

GRANDMOTHER: The one that came this morning.

DANIEL: This morning?

GRANDMOTHER: You were asleep. I thought Mary said it was for you.

DANIEL: She said nothing to me. (*Looks through the shelves again*) There's nothing new here.

GRANDMOTHER: (*quietly*) She must have taken it with her.

DANIEL: (*confused*) But why?

GRANDMOTHER: You know she does some very funny things.

DANIEL: (*going to her*) What book was it?

GRANDMOTHER: What? I didn't get a good look. She threw the wrapping away at once. I didn't see the book again. (*Holds up the paper*) It was wrapped in this.

*Daniel takes the paper and sits beneath the light to look at it. Suddenly he looks up towards the up-stage area, listening. He quickly hides the paper behind his back. Mary enters up-stage. She has a bag and a cardboard box. The grandmother takes the newspaper and walks around the table to sit next to Daniel.*

MARY: I'm sorry, Daniel. I know I'm late. (*She puts the box on the table and goes across to put the bag on the bookcase*) Hello, Gran. (*She goes to the box*) Would you like to see the shirts?

DANIEL:     In a minute. Why were you so long?

MARY:     I bumped into an old friend.

DANIEL:     Who?

MARY:     You wouldn't know her. She asked me to tea, and the time just flew. I'm going to see the baby.

*She takes the box and exits stage-left. Daniel raises the brown paper to the light.*

GRANDMOTHER:     (*quietly*) Doesn't it say, 'Mrs Barnes'?

DANIEL:     Yes. I can't make out the sender's name. (*He smiles nervously*) How strange! (*He crumples the paper thoughtfully and gives it to his mother*)

GRANDMOTHER:     Shall I put it in the bin?

*Daniel nods. The grandmother conceals the paper in her clothing, gets up and begins to go towards the door.*

DANIEL:     Mother.

GRANDMOTHER:     What? Did you say something?

*Daniel gets up, goes across to her and whispers to her.*

DANIEL:     It's not important, obviously. That's why she didn't mention it. (*Without looking at her*) Do me a favour: tell her to come in here and you go into the other room. All right?

GRANDMOTHER:     (*smiling*) Of course.

*She leaves. Daniel moves up-stage. He touches the bag and thinks about opening it. Finally he sits on the sofa and picks up the newspaper. Mary enters.*

MARY:     What is it?

DANIEL:     How's the baby?

MARY:     Quiet as a lamb. We can go out, if you want.

DANIEL:     What for? Going out hasn't helped at all.

MARY:     (*going to the bookcase*) That's because you think too much.

*She picks up the bag and turns to go out.*

DANIEL:     Why don't you stay with me, woman?

MARY:     I. . . .

DANIEL:     Can't you bear being with me?

MARY:     Don't be silly. (*She sighs, puts the bag down again and picks out a book. She sits by her husband and opens the book*)

DANIEL:     What book's that? (*Mary shows him the cover*) You've read that before. Why not read the one you got this morning? (*She looks at him, her face pale*) Or didn't you get a book? (*She looks away*) Well?

MARY:     Yes. There was a book.

DANIEL:     (*sweetly*) What's happening to us, Mary? There's nothing special about a book, unless. . . .

MARY:     What?

DANIEL:     It's a present. From an admirer. (*Mary looks at him in astonishment*) Don't look at me like that. In my position . . . we ought to consider even that possibility calmly. (*Mary cannot avoid a nervous laugh. She raises her hand to her face*) It's nothing to laugh about, Mary.

MARY:     The book is in the bag.

DANIEL:     (*curtly*) Thank you. (*He gets up, goes across to the shelves*)

MARY:     I sat in a café and read it from cover to cover. That's why I was late.

DANIEL:     (*opens the bag*) Who sent it to you?

MARY:     I don't know.

DANIEL:     You have to tell me. (*He takes the book from the bag, reads the title*) 'A Short History' . . . (*He looks at her*) I don't believe it!

MARY:     'A Short History of Torture' The author's foreign. (*Daniel is flicking through the book quickly*) As you can see, it's got lots of illustrations. And it's horribly complete. It brings us up to the present day.

DANIEL:     (*beside himself*) Who sent it?

MARY:     Can't you guess?

DANIEL:     It's repulsive.

MARY:     It's full of case-histories, all of them authentic.

DANIEL:     How can they publish such things?

MARY:     How can they do such things?

DANIEL:     It's pure sensationalism! A pack of lies! (*He throws the book down on the table and moves away*)

MARY:     Daniel, you're the only one I've got. I want to believe you. There'll be no more lies between us. (*She gets up and goes to him*) I know you can't have done those things. You watch the others doing them and you have to keep your mouth shut. That's what happens, right? (*She puts her arms around him*) Look at me. (*He looks at her*) Your eyes are good and innocent. You aren't like them. I know you aren't. But . . . how could you go along with such animals? Couldn't you get out when you knew the truth? Poor Daniel, you must have suffered! I'll help you escape from this black pit. Now that there aren't any secrets between us, we'll be all right. (*She begins to weep in his arms*) We'll be all right, Daniel.

DANIEL:     (*weakly*) We live in terrible times, Mary. They only do their . . . job. If they are to blame, the whole of society's to blame. (*He pulls away, goes to the armchair*)

MARY:     (*taken aback*) Are you justifying them?

DANIEL:     They aren't deliberately cruel. The prisoners must confess.

*He sits and puts his head in his hands.*

MARY:     By whatever means?

DANIEL:     They must confess.

MARY:     What? Lies?

DANIEL:     (*looks at her*) What do you mean, lies?

MARY:     They force them to tell lies.

DANIEL:     Is that what the book says?

MARY:     Yes.

DANIEL:     (*after a moment's pause*) They regard them as enemies to whom no quarter can be given. The rest doesn't matter.

*Pause. Mary looks at him without blinking.*

MARY:     (*leaning against the back of the armchair*) Daniel, it's sheer cruelty. The book describes torture through the centuries, but not just to make people talk. It's appalling. Can you imagine? Millions and millions tortured: eyes gouged out, tongues torn out, people impaled, stoned, beaten to death, dismembered, crucified, buried alive . . . burnt alive. . . . And it wasn't to make them talk. It was to punish them, to sacrifice them to the gods! And now, this very minute . . . I'd rather not even think about it! What are they doing this very minute at your headquarters? (*Strongly*) To what terrible god are they making sacrifices?

DANIEL:     Mary, please. . . .

MARY:     (*excitedly, pointing to the book*) Do you know what the bronze bull was? They'd put a man inside and light a fire beneath it. The bull would snort. And the iron maiden? Outwardly, the image of a bride . . . the most monstrous of weddings. The bridegroom died slowly, pierced by spikes, in the darkness of that metal tomb. And the despicable, repugnant things they did to women . . . severed breasts, rapes. . . . (*Daniel gets up, tense*) Evil for the sake of it, a thirst for blood, a cowardly and filthy wish to torture defenceless people.

DANIEL: In those days too, the whole of society was involved. Everyone was to blame.

MARY: Not everyone. There were always those who condemned it. And many, a considerable number, who tried not to be involved. (*Softly*) Like you . . . an unwilling accomplice; like me, an ignorant accomplice. But all of this is going to stop, Daniel. You have to turn your back on them. Tomorrow you hand in your notice. I shall start teaching again. We'll find some other way to earn our livelihood. Don't you want to?

*Lights up stage-right. Dr Valmy is seated and is dictating to the Secretary who is sitting next to him. While he speaks, Mary and Daniel are absolutely still, their expression and movements frozen.*

DR VALMY: If time would only stand still. For long enough to let us think, not to regret a moment of sudden anger. In the heart of a man and woman a lie is a maggot that eats away at the bonds that hold them together. But when it has eaten too much, it is even worse to learn the truth. As a doctor, I would at that moment have told my patient: don't say a word! But the need to confess and drown himself in his wife's tenderness swept him along like a surging tide. For time is our impulses; time is ourselves and we cannot make it stand still.

SECRETARY: We cannot make it stand still.

*Lights down stage-right, leaving the Doctor and the Secretary in shadow.*

MARY: (*repeats*) Don't you want to?

DANIEL: (*after a pause, not looking at her and very nervously*) I saw Dr Valmy.

MARY: What?

DANIEL: The day before my leave. He found the cause of my problem.

MARY: (*trembling*) Go on.

DANIEL: It's a kind of self-inflicted punishment, do you understand?

MARY: What exactly?

DANIEL: I wish . . . you had guessed yourself.

MARY:      Tell me.

DANIEL:      I had to do . . . something terrible, Mary. Your friend's husband wouldn't talk. Paulus ordered me to torture him . . . in the most horrible way.

MARY:      (*horrified*) You?

DANIEL:      Yes.

MARY:      You as well?

DANIEL:      Yes. (*Mary supports herself on the arm of the chair, all strength drained out of her*)

MARY:      What did you do?

DANIEL:      The worst thing you can do to a man.

MARY:      I don't understand.

DANIEL:      Imagine the very worst thing. And, because I did it, something inside me has punished me and left me in the state that I left him. Or someone has. . . . Because there's another person inside us, to punish us. Another person. (*Mary's eyes are full of fear. She moans quietly. With difficulty she sits in the armchair and closes her eyes*) Mary, I'm worthless. For the last few days I've had time to think and it's useless trying to justfy what I've done. But I want you to know how sorry I am. You can't imagine my self-disgust. (*He moves towards her, supports himself against the armchair, pauses*) Help me become this other person inside me. I've no one else in the world but you. (*He picks up courage to take her hand. She begins to weep*)

MARY:      (*weakly, without looking at him*) Give up the job.

DANIEL:      I'll try, Mary. I'll do something . . . to escape from this black pit.

MARY:      Atonement won't be easy.

DANIEL:      (*full of fear*) Will you stay with me?

*Mary moans, places her hands to her face. We begin to hear the grand-mother singing. She enters singing the earlier jingle. Daniel gets up, concealing his distress. The grandmother looks at them and goes to the radiator.*

GRANDMOTHER:      Little Daniel's soaking. I'll change his nappy. (*She takes a nappy. Mary looks up slowly*) I had to clean him up and powder him. All that weeing makes him very sore.

*Suddenly Mary cries out, a prolonged cry which becomes a frightening shriek. Daniel rushes to her, The grandmother stops.*

DANIEL:    Mary!

MARY:    Children too, Daniel. Children!

DANIEL:    Mary, please!

GRANDMOTHER:    (*stepping forward*) What's wrong with her?

MARY:    (*convulsed*) They sacrificed children. They burned them alive.

DANIEL:    (*holding her*) Mary!

MARY:    They banged an enormous drum to drown their cries.

DANIEL:    Calm yourself.

MARY:    (*shouting*) Ah! To drown their cries. (*She cries out again, while Daniel struggles to make her sit up straight.*)

GRANDMOTHER:    (*holding her*) Mary!

MARY:    How they screamed! The child's terrible screams when they broke its legs, in the concentration camp!

DANIEL:    Mary, Mary! (*He tries in vain to control her*)

MARY:    In front of its mother!

*She goes on crying out. Suddenly, she collapses. Daniel lifts her in his arms and goes out stage-left. Far away the sound of Chopin's 'Nocturne'. The grandmother, concerned, watches them exit. She looks around the room and sees the book. She goes to the table while taking out her glasses. She picks up the book and looks at the cover. She opens it and looks at an illustration. She closes it and stares into space. The Secretary continues to write. Dr Valmy is still.*

## Part Two

*'The Twist' played loudly on the piano. The curtain rises on a stage in shadow.
The lights come up on the office. Daniel comes up the stairs stage-left. He sees
there is no one there, hesitates, goes to the door back-stage, listens. He almost
decides to open it but changes his mind. Finally he sits on the sofa and nervously lights a cigarette. Pause. The piano stops playing suddenly and the door
opens. Paulus enters and closes it. Daniel gets to his feet.*

PAULUS:     Ah, so you're back, then? (*Shakes hands*) How did the week go?

DANIEL:     (*smiling*) It was far too short.

PAULUS:     (*laughing and advancing to put some papers on the table*) But like
            a new penny, eh? I'm glad. (*He sits and looks at some papers*) Is your
            mother well? And your wife and child?

DANIEL:     Fine, thanks. All of them.

PAULUS:     You are just in time. Volski hasn't come back from the South, and
            we've made some new arrests. We received some information; we are
            getting close to their top man. (*Daniel approaches him and extinguishes
            his cigarette in the ashtray*) Sit down. (*Daniel sits*) We could do with a bit
            of success. That stupid business with Marty, they didn't like it upstairs,
            but. . . . (*He searches amongst the files and picks out one*) You'd better
            read it. (*Gives him the file*) Take a good look and come back tonight. (*He
            gets up, and Daniel does the same*) Pay close attention to the stuff on
            Gauss. He's your man.

DANIEL:     Has he been arrested?

PAULUS:     Of course. (*He takes Daniel by the arms, affectionately*) Good to
            have you back, son. Do you want to say hello to the others?

DANIEL:     I'll see them tonight.

PAULUS:     (*accompanies him to the door*) Fine. Eleven o'clock. And welcome
            back. (*He leaves Daniel and turns away*)

DANIEL:     (*with an effort*) Mr Paulus. (*Paulus turns at once and looks coldly
            at Daniel, as if expecting him to speak*)

PAULUS:      Yes?

DANIEL:      Mr Paulus. I'd like to ask a favour.

PAULUS:      What is it?

DANIEL:      (*approaching him*) The fact is, sir, I've hardly slept at all . . . and I'm still feeling pretty bad.

PAULUS:      You don't look too bad.

DANIEL:      I feel exhausted.

PAULUS:      Dr Clemens found nothing wrong. What is this favour?

DANIEL:      I'd like to have some leave.

PAULUS:      For how long?

DANIEL:      In theory . . . unconditional. Until I'm completely well.

*Pause. Paulus thinks it over, goes across to sit at the table. He comes back and looks at Daniel.*

PAULUS:      Sit down. (*Daniel sits down. Paulus looks at his watch and glances towards the door*) Six months ago Dalton was sick, remember? They had to inject him every four hours; he'd collapse on the sofa every so often; he couldn't cope with the fever. But he never wanted to stop work.

DANIEL:      I'd never compare myself with someone else.

PAULUS:      But I would. You are better than Dalton. What's wrong with you? (*Silence*) Daniel, you have an outstanding record, and soon a chance for promotion. You mustn't confirm what some are saying already.

DANIEL:      What's that?

PAULUS:      That this old man was wrong, that you were my favourite when you didn't deserve it. Don't let them take your patch. Show them who you are. I understand you, my boy. You are going through a moment of weakness. No one ever escapes it, but one goes on. Hold on to me and you'll find it's easier. (*He gets up*) Stop thinking about it. Study the file. I'll see you tonight.

DANIEL:      (*getting up as well*) You are very kind, Mr Paulus. Believe me, I'm very grateful.

PAULUS:      (*laughs*) I knew you wouldn't let me down.

DANIEL:      But the fact is. . . .

PAULUS:      Yes?

DANIEL:      If you'd only give me a few days more. Look at my hands. Look at them shaking. Maybe I'm not as strong as you think.

*Paulus sits down again slowly. Daniel remains standing.*

PAULUS: (*without looking at him*) If things were quieter, I might be able to give you leave. But now it's out of the question. They've even criticized me for giving you a week; a moment of weakness on my part. We are far too few for all the things we have to stamp on. I need you here. Do you still insist?

DANIEL: It's the only way, believe me!

PAULUS: (*looks at his watch, looks at Daniel*) All right. I've spoken as a friend, but now I speak as your superior. Request denied. You may go.

DANIEL: (*after a moment*) I don't know if I can cope.

PAULUS: (*annoyed*) Why are you so stubborn? (*He gets up*) I'm going to give you a good piece of advice. At times like these, failing to cope is the same as helping our enemies.

DANIEL: What?

PAULUS: Precisely that! (*He goes around the table to Daniel*) Do you think I don't know what's happening? You suddenly feel sorry for those fools. But if they were in our shoes, they'd be as hard on us. That means you sympathize with them.

DANIEL: You know very well I don't.

PAULUS: I know nothing anymore, son. Suddenly, you see them as human beings. It couldn't happen if you remembered the things they do, how dangerous they are for all of us. Just you take care. We can't protect those who are simply exhausted or those we suspect of wavering. Among such people, traitors are bred.

DANIEL: You can't accuse me of that. It's a different situation.

*He is interrupted by the opening of the door. Luigi and Marsan enter in shirt-sleeves.*

MARSAN: Excuse me, Boss. He's given us an address. We ought to go at once.

PAULUS: He could be lying again.

LUIGI: We've got to check it out.

PAULUS: Take Dalton with you. (*To Marsan*) Put more pressure on him. He's always lying.

MARSAN: Right, sir. Good to see you, Barnes.

*He leaves, closing the door. Luigi meanwhile picks up his jacket and puts it on.*

LUIGI:     I'm glad to see you, lad. (*He shakes Daniel's hand*) See you tonight, then.

*He slaps him on the shoulder and exits quickly by the stairs stage-left. Paulus thoughtfully rubs his eyes. He walks up-stage, stops and turns.*

PAULUS:    Why are you still here?

DANIEL:    I was trying to tell you, Mr Paulus, that you misjudge me.

PAULUS:    I understand you perfectly and I warn you to be careful. (*He approaches, lowering his voice*) And you know how we have to deal with detainees.

DANIEL:    (*taken aback*) Is that a threat?

PAULUS:    On the contrary: I'm doing my utmost to help. I wouldn't want to see you in their miserable shoes.

DANIEL:    There's not a single reason why I should be, unless you decide to invent one.

PAULUS:    Invent one?

DANIEL:    You know what I mean.

PAULUS:    Can't you see you are speaking just like one of them, when they protest their innocence? 'I don't feel well, you're inventing it all. . . .'

DANIEL:    But that's quite different.

PAULUS:    I'm not so sure. (*He sits down*) If that's the case, you won't mind telling me why Lucila Marty went to your house eight days ago.

*Daniel takes a backward step, stunned.*

DANIEL:    Are you mad? She . . . my wife used to teach her.

PAULUS:    I know.

DANIEL:    (*he goes to the table, puts down the file and leans towards Paulus*) So what are you talking about? She wanted to help her husband.

PAULUS:    You never told us.

DANIEL:    But it's absurd. If a policeman can't feel reasonably sure he is above suspicion, who will want to join?

PAULUS:    On the other hand, only when he knows he might be suspected, will he act as he really should. (*Gets up, goes across to Daniel*) Bear it in mind. (*He takes the file, gives it to him*) Take it. It's not that you've lost my confidence; it's just that we need to take great care. (*Daniel takes the file*) I'll see you tonight.

*Mr Paulus walks quickly upstage, opens the door and leaves, closing it behind him. Dr Valmy appears stage-right, illuminated by a spotlight. Daniel draws his hand across his face and leaves by the staircase, stage-left. The office light goes out.*

DR VALMY:     That's how the conversation must have gone. She didn't tell me that; like other bits of the story, I learned about it later on. She came a few days later to tell me other things. It happens far more often than the layman thinks; a patient confides in us, and, almost at once, the other player in the story enters the consulting room. It sometimes helps us find the cure. But on this occasion, what could I do?

*The light grows stronger in Dr Valmy's office. Mary is sitting on the sofa. Dr Valmy approaches.*

MARY:     I hope I'm not being a nuisance.

DR VALMY:     *(sitting on a chair)* I'm not in any hurry.

MARY:     But you won't tell my husband I came to see you.

DR VALMY:     Of course not. I promise.

MARY:     What am I to do, Doctor?

DR VALMY:     To a certain point, your problems can be overcome. But you are going through an extremely negative phase. When precisely was it that you felt this need to scream?

MARY:     When he confessed to me the things he'd done.

DR VALMY:     Was it you who persuaded him to ask for leave?

MARY:     I told him he should ask for extra leave.

DR VALMY:     And did you expect them to grant it?

MARY:     I wanted to believe that they would.

DR VALMY:     Was it after you learned the outcome that you started vomiting?

MARY:     No. The day before.

DR VALMY:     Do you think there was a specific cause?

MARY:     Yes.

DR VALMY:     Are you sure you aren't pregnant?

MARY:     I'm quite sure. You know the things he's done.

DR VALMY:     You relate it to all that?

MARY:     Am I wrong?

DR VALMY:     I don't think so. But why not tell me everything, Mrs Barnes?

MARY:     That evening, I waited for him anxiously. He arrived in time for dinner, but he didn't want to eat. (*She gets up*) I'd been speaking to his mother previously. (*Lights up on the Barnes' household. The vase on the table is empty. Mary moves stage-left. She turns*) If you can call that speaking.

*She steps from Dr Valmy's office into the sitting-room of the house, walk-ing impatiently back and forth. Dr Valmy is left in shadow. Mary looks at her watch. The grandmother enters stage-left with her knitting and two nappies. She puts them on the radiator to dry. Mary watches her.*

GRANDMOTHER:     If I hadn't washed these, we'd have no nappies at all.

MARY:     Why are you putting them there? What if someone calls?

GRANDMOTHER:     (*failing to hear*) The other day I dropped one from the balcony. On the way down it got caught on the first-floor window. I had to go and fetch it. (*She switches on the table lamp*) Their house is a palace. (*She sits down to work*) They didn't seem very pleased. They were prob-ably telling me to be more careful, but I couldn't understand. (*She looks at Mary*) You know I don't hear sometimes.

MARY:     Gran!

GRANDMOTHER:     What?

MARY:     (*pointing to the nappies, raising her voice*) Why don't you put them on another radiator?

GRANDMOTHER:     (*as deaf people do, she listens open-mouthed*) Another radiator?

MARY:     Yes.

GRANDMOTHER:     This is the hottest. It dries them quicker.

*She counts stitches in a whisper. Mary walks up and down.*

MARY:     Daniel's late. (*She looks at the grandmother, who goes on knitting.*)

GRANDMOTHER:     (*singing quietly*)

> 'If your nose is blocked, and you're feeling down,
>
> And your head is spinning round and round,
>
> Try "Clear Head", it stops the pain,
>
> You'll soon be feeling right as rain. . . .'

*Meanwhile, Mary goes to the nappies and feels them. Her face contorts.*

*She turns towards the audience, staring into space. When the grand-mother is about to end her song, Mary feels sick. The grandmother watches her. Mary turns towards the radiator and doubles up. The grandmother leaves her knitting and gets up.*

GRANDMOTHER:     Again? (*She goes to her*) I'll get you something.

MARY:     No. It's all right.

*She moves away, goes to the seat by the telephone and sits exhausted. The grandmother, intrigued, follows her slowly.*

GRANDMOTHER:     Are you pregnant again?

MARY:     (*looks at her in astonishment*) No!

GRANDMOTHER:     You . . . well, it would be nice . . . a pair of them . . . a little girl. (*Mary looks away, shaking her head*) Have you mentioned it to Daniel?

MARY:     What?

GRANDMOTHER:     You being sick.

MARY:     (*getting up quickly*) I'm not expecting a child. Never again!

*The grandmother gives a sigh, goes back to the sofa to resume her work. Mary paces nervously.*

GRANDMOTHER:     (*sits down*) No child. (*Mary looks at her, goes to sit by her. The grandmother counts the stitches in a whisper*)

MARY:     Gran, there may be changes.

GRANDMOTHER:     Changes?

MARY:     Not the kind of changes you expect. Daniel may be giving up his job.

GRANDMOTHER:     What did you say?

MARY:     Daniel wants to leave his job. (*Speaking very close to her ear*) He was going to ask them tonight. (*She puts her hand on her shoulder*) Would you like that? I'd go back to my school, and he would look for another job.

GRANDMOTHER:     Going to give his job up?

MARY:     (*strongly*) Yes!

*Pause.*

GRANDMOTHER:     You are putting ideas into his head.

MARY:     You have to understand. He's ill because he can't put up with it. (*The grandmother looks at her with an increasingly anguished expression)* We don't want it happening to the child.

GRANDMOTHER:      The child?

MARY:     He mustn't grow up like his father. The two of us have to save them. Daniel promised he'd give it up. I pray to God he'll keep his word.

GRANDMOTHER:      I can't hear you.

MARY:     The terrible things they do there! *(The grandmother averts her eyes but doesn't go back to her work)* I'm sorry, but I'm so alone. But you know. I know that you know. You've known Paulus since you were young. . . . *(Pause)* Or was it that you didn't know? Maybe you were just like me, not knowing. *(Pause)* Or maybe you didn't dare believe it. But you helped him fall into the trap and you have to help him escape. *(Grandmother's eyes are moist)* I know how sad it is, to see your son like this, at the end of your life. I love you so much. *(She embraces her)* We have to help him, both of us. At least, to save the child. Help me. Help us!

GRANDMOTHER:      *(without looking at her)* I can't hear you . . . not a single word.

MARY:     *(looking at her, without hope, thinking)* My God!

*She gets up, goes to the chair by the telephone, leans against it. She looks at the grandmother, who hasn't moved and who is beginning her knitting again with some difficulty. Mary has heard something and looks up.*

MARY:     He's here.

*Daniel enters, carrying the file.*

DANIEL:      *(crossing to and kissing his mother)* Mother.

GRANDMOTHER:      Hello, son. *(Continues working)*

DANIEL:      Mary.

*He goes towards the bookcase, avoiding her eyes, and places the file on it. He is about to take the pistol from his inside pocket when his eyes meet Mary's and, looking away from her, he turns from the bookcase without taking out the pistol. Mary watches him go to the chair, down-stage left, where he sits. She advances towards him. Seeing she wants to speak, he cuts her short.*

DANIEL:      Give me a drink.

MARY:     Aren't you drinking rather a lot?

*She goes towards the bookcase.*

DANIEL:     Don't worry. I know where to draw the line.

*Mary opens the drinks cupboard. While she is pouring she looks repeatedly at the file. He is aware of it.*

Won't you have one?

MARY:     (*in anticipation*) Is there something to celebrate?

*He smiles and grunts. She closes the cabinet and gives him the glass.*

DANIEL:     Thanks. (*He drinks*)

MARY:     What happened?

DANIEL:     It went quite well. Let's talk later.

MARY:     Shall we go inside?

DANIEL:     It's fine here.

MARY:     But your mother. . . .

DANIEL:     She isn't wearing her hearing-aid. She can't hear.

MARY:     She can still see us.

DANIEL:     (*gets up, takes a few steps*) Good stuff this. Are you sure you don't want some? (*He goes to the drinks cabinet and opens it*)

MARY:     (*raising her voice*) Daniel, what happened?

DANIEL:     I told you. (*He begins to pour himself a drink*)

MARY:     You've told me nothing. Did they give you leave?

DANIEL:     I think they will.

*He closes the cabinet and leans against the bookcase as he drinks.*

MARY:     (*going towards him*) You aren't telling me the truth.

DANIEL:     Mary, Rome wasn't built in a day.

MARY:     (*twisting her hands*) They've turned you down!

DANIEL:     It's a matter of a couple of days. (*He leaves his glass on the shelf*)

MARY:     (*desperate*) God help us! (*Turning to The grandmother*) Help me! (*The grandmother looks at them for a moment*)

DANIEL:     (*moving forward*) Don't bring her into it.

*Mary struggles to contain herself, turns and moves away.*

MARY:     Do you have to go back tonight?

DANIEL:     Yes.

*Mary sits sadly, on the chair beside the telephone. Daniel takes his glass and returns to the chair stage-left.*

MARY:     Are there new detainees? (*The grandmother looks at them*)

DANIEL:     No. (*Pause*)

MARY:     You are lying again. (*Pause*) We are lost.

DANIEL:     (*darkly and without looking at her, playing with his glass*) Mary, could you go on living with me like a sister?

MARY:     (*looking at him, fiercely*) Lost!

*Pause. Daniel sighs deeply. The grandmother, knitting once more, begins to speak.*

GRANDMOTHER:     Does Mr Paulus send me his regards?

DANIEL:     What? (*Daniel and Mary exchange glances*) Yes, he does.

GRANDMOTHER:     (*carrying on with her knitting*) It's strange that we've never seen each other since. He used to be so attentive. You must remember it.

DANIEL:     (*gets up*) Yes, Mother. (*He goes to sit by her, while she continues speaking*)

GRANDMOTHER:     When your father died, he behaved quite properly. The very least he could do. He hadn't behaved very well before.

DANIEL:     No?

GRANDMOTHER:     He never forgave us getting married. He was courting me himself, you see, and it came as a great shock. He even spoke of taking revenge. He was so aggressive and bitter. And then he joined the police-force and we didn't see him again for ages. But when your father died, he started to come to the house. He never spoke of marriage, even though I was still attractive. I was, you know. I was very attractive once. He got tired, of course, because he wasn't getting anywhere. But still he went on trying, until one day I had to send him packing. It was some years later when he came again and said he could help to get you into the Security Police. By then, of course, I'd lost my looks. It was obvious that I didn't matter anymore, and nothing was going right for us. That's why I let him do us a favour. (*Long pause. Mary hangs on her every word*) No doubt you wanted to be something else, but you were still young. Always do what you want to do. Happiness is the only thing that matters. (*Daniel squeezes her hand affectionately. She glances at her knitting and gets up*) I'm going to see the baby, make sure he's lying properly. (*She moves stage-*

*left, stops*) You haven't seen him today. Are you coming?

DANIEL:     (*gets up*) Yes, mother. (*He steals a glance at Mary, picks up the file and goes across to his mother. Mary gets up, looking at them*)

GRANDMOTHER:     It won't be long before he has a sister, eh? (*Mary and Daniel avoid each other's eyes, disturbed. Daniel empties his glass and puts his arm around his mother*) My son!

*They leave. Mary sinks into the armchair, deep in thought. A spotlight picks her out. The room returns to shadow as the light fades. Dr Valmy gets up and approaches.*

DR VALMY:     Would you like to have another child?

MARY:     No, no.

DR VALMY:     Are you sure?

MARY:     (*not really looking at him*) How can I have a child now?

DR VALMY:     Are you saying that because of your husband's condition?

MARY:     I wouldn't want to bring another child into the world. He'd never forgive me.

DR VALMY:     What feelings do you have towards your husband?

MARY:     I'm not sure. Sometimes he seems a stranger. At other times, he fills me with resentment. It's very strange, but sometimes I. . . . (*Hesitates*)

DR VALMY:     What?

MARY:     I feel I want to laugh at him.

DR VALMY:     Are you still fulfilling your marital obligations?

MARY:     No.

DR VALMY:     Would that be his or your fault?

MARY:     He never suggests it, and I prefer it like that.

DR VALMY:     You mean he fills you with disgust?

MARY:     (*impatiently*) It's difficult to say. I used to love him blindly. Now I hardly sleep, and he sleeps well because he drinks. There are nights when I look at him and I say to myself: 'nothing's happened. I adore him.' And I feel an enormous desire to wake him up and kiss him.

DR VALMY:     So do you do it?

MARY:     I woke him once. But I turned away and ran to see the child. I told him I thought I'd heard it crying.

DR VALMY:     (*pause*) Do you have many dreams at present?

MARY:     I'd call them nightmares.

DR VALMY:     Do you recall any?

MARY:     Yes.

DR VALMY:     Could you describe one?

MARY:     I'll do my best. I was at home. . . .

> *A mysterious light fills the room. Dr Valmy withdraws quietly to the shadowy area stage-right, where he sits.*

My mother-in-law came in with the baby, but it wasn't a boy.

> *The mother-in-law enters stage-left pushing the cradle and leaving it by the telephone. Mary speaks to her.*

It's cold in here.

GRANDMOTHER:     I want to watch the television and I didn't want to wake her.

MARY:     (*getting up*) She might catch cold.

GRANDMOTHER:     Give her a tablet. (*She goes out singing*)

> 'Try "Clear Head", it stops the pain,
>
> You'll soon be feeling right as rain. . . .'

MARY:     (*bending over the cradle*) My little Daniella! Aren't you my lovely little girl! (*She arranges the clothes*) Let's get you tucked in properly. Now go to sleep, my little one.

> *Daniel enters back-stage. He carries a book and doesn't seem to see Mary. She straightens up and says 'hello'. Without answering, he goes to the bookcase, places his hand inside his jacket where he keeps his revolver and takes out a large pair of scissors, which he puts down. He sits on the chair by the telephone and flicks through the book. Mary approaches him.*

MARY:     Daniella's getting cold. (*She goes to the bookcase and picks up the scissors*) What did you buy them for? (*She takes the scissors to him*)

DANIEL:     (*takes them from her*) To cut the pages. (*He pretends to do it*)

MARY:     But they aren't stuck.

DANIEL:     (*smiling*) I bought them to cut the baby's hair when she grows up.

MARY:     You can't see. I'll put the light on.

DANIEL:     Thank you. (*He reads.*)

*Mary goes to the lamp and pulls the cord. The light comes on. Paralyzed by the current of electricity, Mary twists and cries aloud but cannot release the cord.*

MARY:     Daniel, I'm burning up! For pity's sake! (*Daniel goes on reading*) Daniel! (*He turns to her*) Put the light out! Quickly! (*Daniel gets up, calmly, goes to her.*)

DANIEL:     I'll have to cut your fingers off.

MARY:     What are you doing?

DANIEL:     It's not going to hurt. (*He cuts, she screams. The light goes out*) Not a trace of blood.

MARY:     (*looking at her fingers*) No. (*Staring at him, moving away. He holds the scissors out to her*)

DANIEL:     Here. You ought to have them.

MARY:     No! (*Daniel advances. She moves away quickly*)

DANIEL:     If you move away, how can I give them to you?

*He strikes out at her but misses.*

MARY:     (*moaning, moving away*) Please!

DANIEL:     Come here.

MARY:     (*moving quickly towards him, arms held wide*) All right. Kill me if you want.

*Daniel smiles, goes to the radiator and picks up the nappies. Then he goes to the cradle.*

DANIEL:     He's going to need them. (*He pushes back the hood of the cradle and opens the scissors*)

MARY:     (*running to stop him*) No! Not him!

DANIEL:     But you really want a girl.

MARY:     (*running stage-left, calling out*) Gran!

*The grandmother enters at once.*

DANIEL:     Put the light on. I can't see.

GRANDMOTHER:     (*going to the lamp*) Whatever you want, son.

MARY:     Don't touch it!

*The grandmother switches on the lamp and turns away.*

GRANDMOTHER:    Is that better?

DANIEL:    That's much better. (*He rocks the cradle. The grandmother goes over to him.*) Go to sleep, little Daniel. Sleep peacefully.

GRANDMOTHER:    We'll give you a tablet. (*Sings quietly as they take the cradle out, stage-left*)

>   'If your nose is blocked and you're feeling down,
>
>   And your head is spinning round and round. . . .'

*The lights fade while the light comes up on Dr Valmy's office, stage-right. Mary goes to sit opposite him. Pause.*

DR VALMY:    Have you had any other dreams like that?

MARY:    Yes, I have.

DR VALMY:    Do you think about them often?

MARY:    I rarely think of anything else.

DR VALMY:    Was it the history of torture he was reading in the dream?

MARY:    No.

DR VALMY:    Have you been reading it recently?

MARY:    It seems to have disappeared.

DR VALMY:    How is that?

MARY:    My husband read it, trying to make sure I didn't know. I never saw it afterwards.

DR VALMY:    Do you think he disposed of it?

MARY:    (*disagreeing uncertainly*) I think he tried to find it once, without success. Neither of us spoke of it again.

DR VALMY:    So you don't know what your husband was reading in the dream?

MARY:    Oh, yes.

DR VALMY:    What was it?

MARY:    A book he bought very recently. On psychiatry.

PAULUS:    (*thoughtful*) Of course.

MARY:    What should I do, Doctor?

DR VALMY:    I'd like to know if you've thought of some solution?

MARY:    I've thought of many things. Separation for a while. Going back to school.

DR VALMY:     I'm glad you've thought of that. Being apart, contact with the children could be very beneficial. If you wish, I'll try to get your husband to agree to it.

MARY:     No. You don't understand. I've thought of all those things but none of them appeal to me. I can't be bothered. I feel a total lack of interest, a great indifference . . . for everything.

DR VALMY:     For your son as well?

MARY:     (*weeping*) Poor child! Will he forgive me for bringing him into this terrible world?

DR VALMY:     You see? You do still care about something. In that case, set aside your pain; fight for your son. Do that, Mrs Barnes, I guarantee, he'll help you to forget.

MARY:     I'm afraid not, Doctor.

DR VALMY:     What do you mean?

MARY:     It's a terrible thing to say. I feel at times that I no longer love my son.

DR VALMY:     What?

MARY:     No, because he's his. In his face I see his father's face. That of an executioner.

DR VALMY:     Get rid of such unhealthy thoughts. These things are not inherited.

MARY:     (*desperate*) I know they aren't. I know.

DR VALMY:     Your son is innocent and has a mother who can stop him becoming an executioner.

MARY:     In order to become a victim?

DR VALMY:     I beg you, try to help yourself. In this world of ours there are more than victims and executioners.

MARY:     My husband has a mother too, who should have stopped him. Why should I be any better than her? I always believed that life was so magnificent and all it is is a trap that always catches us. We should never hand it on.

DR VALMY:     Life can be splendid, believe me. Join up with those who try to make it so! There are more of them than you imagine. You've come here to see me. That means you still have faith and hope.

MARY:     No. I'm like the person who turns to a father, crying out because she's drowning. But the father calls to me from the shore and tells me I should swim, although I have no strength. (*She looks at him with the expression of a helpless animal. Dr Valmy sighs, takes out his pad and begins to write a prescription*)

DR VALMY:     You must be patient. Take this for the time being. You'll see for yourself, it's very effective. Come back next week. Or whenever you want to talk. (*He gives her the prescription*)

MARY:     (*taking it and getting up*) Thank you.

DR VALMY:     (*getting up, shaking hands*) Take courage, Mrs Barnes.

MARY:     (*moving stage-right, turning*) Goodbye.

DR VALMY:     Goodbye. (*Mary goes out. The Secretary reappears with notepad and pencil*) What could I do? When I gave her the wretched prescription — that as often as not conceals our embarrassment —, it occurred to me that the world was sick, and I couldn't cure the world. But she meanwhile was drowning in that sea of which she spoke, the victim of terrible dreams which dragged her down. I've been able to piece together what happened after her visit. It was her final one. She left and I never saw her again.

*Lights up down-stage. Dr Valmy and the Secretary exit stage-right. Pause. Mary, wearing a coat, enters stage-right and crosses the stage. Lucila Marty enters stage-left. She is dressed in black and walks past Mary without looking at her. Mary stops, turns and watches her as she walks past.*

MARY:     Lucila!

*Lucila stops without turning or showing surprise. Mary approaches her but doesn't dare speak.*

LUCILA:     (*half turning, without looking at her*) What do you want?

MARY:     You told me the truth, and I called you a liar. I'm sorry.

LUCILA:     Nothing's solved by saying sorry. He can't come back to life.

MARY:     (*taken aback*) He's . . . dead?

LUCILA:     (*looks at her with a mocking smile*) Didn't your husband tell you? It seems he had a heart attack . . . at the police station.

MARY:     I . . . didn't know. . . .

LUCILA:     I can't say I'm surprised. Goodbye. (*She is about to leave. Mary stops her*)

MARY:     Don't go like this. I know I can't do anything, but . . . I want you to forgive me, please . . . for what my husband did to yours.

LUCILA:     (*strongly*) Do you want me to forgive him?

MARY:     No. I can't forgive him either. In a way, I have no husband. We suffer together.

LUCILA:     Together? No! My suffering belongs to me, and you've no right to share it. You've never been held by the Secret Police and you never will. They haven't tortured your husband: he's the one who tortures. (*Pointing to her clothes*) You'll never know the meaning of this.

MARY:     Lucila, I'll try to understand. I promise. (*Lucila wants to leave*) For pity's sake! Let me be your friend. I'll learn to share your suffering. If we can, we'll comfort each other. Lucila! My child! (*She weeps*)

LUCILA:     Don't cry. I have no tears anymore and yours are going to make me laugh. There's no solution to this, Miss. Goodbye. (*She moves stage-right*)

MARY:     It was you who sent me the book, wasn't it? (*Lucila stops, doesn't answer*) It was you.

LUCILA:     I don't know what you are talking about.

MARY:     Thank you for sending it, Lucila.

> Lucila hears these words, half-turned away, and exits stage-right. Mary takes a few paces forward and watches her as she walks off. Daniel enters stage-left. He wears a raincoat and a hat. He stands behind the park-bench, watching Lucila. Mary turns to go on her way and stops, taken aback, when she sees Daniel. She walks slowly to the bench.

DANIEL:     What were you talking to her about?

MARY:     Can't you imagine?

DANIEL:     I told you, you mustn't see her ever again. It's dangerous.

MARY:     What does it matter! (*She sits on the bench and looks down*)

DANIEL:     Why have you been seeing Dr Valmy?

MARY:     Have you been following me?

DANIEL:     Yes.

MARY:     (*looking at him, understanding*) I can't believe it. (*Laughing*) You are jealous.

DANIEL:     (*he sits on the other end of the bench*) Try to understand.

MARY:     It's absurd. Why should it matter if you aren't a man?

DANIEL:     But I love you, Mary.

MARY:     Empty words!

DANIEL:     No, as long as we live! I'll find a way out of this mess, I promise. Listen: I know there are vacancies in the overseas branch. I'll apply for a posting. Paulus will agree, I'm sure. Once abroad, I can resign. They won't be able to stop me then. I swear to you, I'll do it. There must be forgiveness somewhere. I have to look for and deserve it. Give me yours, even though I don't deserve it yet.

MARY:       How can I? How can that poor young widow? And he can't do it, because you killed him!

DANIEL:     (*looking down*) I didn't tell you. I didn't want to make you suffer more.

MARY:       All that is just as empty.

DANIEL:     It isn't, Mary!

MARY:       And what about the poor flesh that's passed through your hands for years on end? You never mention it. You talk about me being made to suffer a little more or a little less. It's laughable. I feel the pain of all that flesh every second of the day and night. That's why I went to Dr Valmy. I can't think of anything else.

DANIEL:     Nor can I, Mary.

MARY:       Especially at night. (*Lights slowly up on the office*)

DANIEL:     At night?

MARY:       At night I try to imagine who at that very moment you've got in your clutches. And I imagine it's myself. But you imagine nothing. You do it. Every night you've had to go back to do your butcher's work. Tell me: what do you feel when you make them scream?

DANIEL:     I've got to go back in order to escape from it.

MARY:       Do you feel that it's your flesh that screams?

DANIEL:     (*looking around*) Lower your voice. There are people passing.

MARY:       Does it matter?

DANIEL:     (*looking towards the left of the stage*) Don't move. Do you see that man? Pretend you aren't looking.

MARY:       I don't see anyone.

DANIEL:     He's just turned off the path. I'm sure it was Marsan.

*She sighs disconsolately. Paulus enters the office by the door at the back and stands before the table, in full light, his arms crossed, his thoughts far away.*

We've got to leave the country.

MARY: Wherever we go, another Paulus will be waiting.

*Chopin's 'Nocturne' is heard in the distance. Mary's fingers caress the edge of the bench. Daniel is bold enough to place his hand on hers. She bursts into tears. Silence.*

DANIEL: Yes, Mary. It was here. You were crying then too. I've failed to dry those tears; it's all been an enormous lie. But that, at least, was true. . . . That was true.

MARY: (*gets up*) Let's go.

*She walks to the side of the stage. He follows her. She turns and looks at the bench. He glances at it too. Both go out. Paulus is still in the office, motionless, in full light. Stage-right lights up on Dr Valmy and the Secretary. The piano music continues.*

DR VALMY: (*dictating*) The reader will recall that the patients in my first case-history were neighbours of Mr and Mrs Barnes: people of good position, without children, who came to see me about the various symptoms which announced the boredom of their lives: insomnia, a lack of appetite, vague anxieties, a mutual weariness. They proposed for themselves a temporary stay in the sanatorium, and I agreed. I thought that a change might benefit their health. . . .

SECRETARY: Their health.

DR VALMY: But at this point in the story I wonder if someone reading it will not neglect this first case. The fact is, I often begin to read a book at a page which I find interesting, rather than at the beginning. That's why I ought to say that the present case does not in my opinion make complete sense without regard to the other one, and that, at bottom, they might be the same. So now, I can tell you the rest. My patient decided to speak to the Boss once more, and that was the beginning of the end.

*Down-stage in shadow, including the bench and the consulting-room. Dr Valmy and the Secretary leave. Paulus turns stage-left and waits. The piano music stops suddenly. Daniel climbs the stairs and takes his hat off.*

PAULUS: You want to see me?

DANIEL: I'd like to have a few minutes.

PAULUS: Sit down. (*Daniel puts his hat on the peg, crosses to the chair, waits*) Sit down. I'm tired of sitting. What's it about?

DANIEL: I want to ask a favour.

PAULUS:     You want to ask for leave.

DANIEL:     (*laughs*) No. That's all over. You saw it for what it was: one of those moments of weakness anyone can have. I'm fine now. (*Half-heartedly*) I doubt that you can complain about my behaviour nowadays.

PAULUS:     True enough. You've done good work. (*He walks back and forth*)

DANIEL:     (*smiling*) Do you trust me, then?

PAULUS:     I always have.

DANIEL:     If it weren't the case, I wouldn't dare to make my request.

PAULUS:     What is it?

DANIEL:     I'm bothered about my wife. She didn't know what was really going on, and now that she does she's edgy, nervous . . . sick. You can't expect her to understand at once, when what she needs is much more time.

PAULUS:     Of course.

DANIEL:     I see it as my job to put her mind at rest, and I think I can achieve it. But not here. It's best to take her somewhere else, to make her feel that both of us are far away from what upsets her. I thought I might be able to work in the foreign branch. I wouldn't ask if I were on my own, but I've got a family. Could you help me once again? The country doesn't matter. Wherever I can be most useful.

PAULUS:     (*watching him closely*) You can be most useful here.

DANIEL:     Perhaps I can't with a wife who's such a burden.

PAULUS:     You've done very well recently.

DANIEL:     (*nervously*) Even so. . . .

PAULUS:     I'll put it another way. A transfer would cause surprise and, maybe even suspicion. And it wouldn't do to cause suspicion now, by my making such an ill-timed suggestion.

DANIEL:     What if I made the request directly?

PAULUS:     I'd have to speak to it, and I very much doubt I could give it support.

DANIEL:     (*shaken*) But why?

PAULUS:     (*comes up behind him, places his hands on his shoulders*) It's not for your wife, is it?

DANIEL:     I've explained it already.

PAULUS:     Let's say it's for both of you. (*He straightens up and goes to the table*) Right. You had a nice little script prepared, but now you know my answer. I'll see you tonight.

*He sits and begins to look at some papers. A long silence. Suddenly, someone cries out from behind the door back-stage, a muffled and barely audible moan. Paulus is unmoved. Daniel trembles.*

DANIEL:     I shan't be back tonight.

PAULUS:     What do you mean?

DANIEL:     I'm not going to torture anyone again. (*Paulus drops the papers on the table*) You'll have to throw me out if you won't let me retire. If you'd rather think me a deserter, lock me up.

PAULUS:     So it's come to this?

DANIEL:     Yes.

PAULUS:     Because of your work?

DANIEL:     How can you call it work?

PAULUS:     What is it then?

DANIEL:     A crime.

PAULUS:     (*looking towards the door*) Lucky for you we're on our own. I'll do what I can to help, but listen to me, fool. I didn't invent torture. When you and I were born, it was there already. Like pain, like death. All right, it might be brutal, but we are in the jungle.

DANIEL:     Against human beings?

PAULUS:     Such concern for human beings? You've seen them here: most of them are worthless. In the whole of our history no progress has been made unless innumerable crimes have been involved.

*A cry off. Both look towards the door.*

DANIEL:     You mean innumerable martyrs.

PAULUS:      Don't be stupid. Every undertaking has its martyrs . . . and its torturers.

DANIEL:     It's the torturers who make it stink.

PAULUS:     (*shaking his head sadly*) You are like a child; you see the world as a story of goodies and baddies. But a torturer is often the martyr who survives; and a martyr the torturer who doesn't die in time. As any one of us could be tomorrow . . . martyrs, torturers. . . . Words they use for propaganda. But now we're alone, I'll tell you the truth. (*Another cry. Paulus looks towards the door*) The most important thing is to be right. When that happens, the methods don't matter.

DANIEL:    What if we aren't completely right?

PAULUS:    (*quietly*) You can never be completely right. Even so, we need to use what weapons we've got, as our enemies use theirs. Daniel, they are natural weapons. Some people die, mauled by a wild beast. A crane might crush some poor worker. (*Another cry. Paulus raises his voice*) Another person screams for months on end, eaten away by cancer. You won't get rid of pain in the world. So are you going to leave it all to chance? You have to take control of chance and use it.

DANIEL:    Then why don't we make it public? Why isn't torture part of our law?

PAULUS:    People are incredibly childish. They'd never understand.

DANIEL:    No. The truth is they begin to understand. People accepted it in ancient times when they were more naíve than now. But now we have to keep it out of sight, like some grotesque child. To protect it, you must lock the doors and speak in whispers. In public you are forced to look like some kind soul who loves his fellow men. What a fraud this is! You are an imposter. A lie that bears its burden on its back. (*Cries off*)

PAULUS:    (*annoyed*) What burden?

DANIEL:    The burden of keeping quiet. You are like a madman wanting to be rational, but not quite mad enough to shout it out. But never mind. Your victims will pay. Their cries will compensate for those you dare not make.

*Pause. They look towards the door.*

PAULUS:    You poor fool. It's not my portrait you are painting; it's your own. You think yourself so brave telling me this; but you know I have no wish to do you harm. (*He gets up angrily*) You are the one who doesn't dare to shout outside; you the one who will not say a word. (*He walks around the table. Another cry. He leans to whisper*) You are trapped. There's no escape. You're a member of the Secret Police until you die. (*He moves away*) You can thank me that I'm soft enough to want to help you still. I intend to save you in spite of yourself. Because I've chosen power, understand? To devour instead of being devoured. And I'm taking you with me. (*He approaches, puts a hand on Daniel's shoulder*) The crisis gets worse, my boy, but maybe you'll get through it. Don't come back tonight. Rest. By tomorrow you'll have worked things out.

DANIEL:    I shan't be here tomorrow.

PAULUS:    (*red with anger*) Give me your gun and your badge. At once!

*Daniel gets up, trembling. He puts them on the table.*

DANIEL:     There. All yours.

*Paulus goes to the phone and starts to dial.*

Am I the first, Mr Paulus?

PAULUS:     What do you mean?

DANIEL:     Am I the first to leave the service?

PAULUS:     (*suddenly putting down the phone*) You are getting on my nerves! But you won't succeed. (*Shouts*) You'd better think about it. If you think it through, you'll be back tomorrow. (*He paces up and down. Shouts*)

DANIEL:     Don't you see I can't? What's happening here doesn't just destroy the ones who suffer. It also destroys the ones who cause the suffering. (*Shouts*)

PAULUS:     Only someone as sick and feeble as yourself. (*Shouts*) The rest of us are fine. (*Shouts. Paulus goes quickly to the door and opens it*) Take him to another room. Of course I mean it!

*He slams the door shut, comes back. Daniel looks at him intently.*

DANIEL:     (*after a moment's pause*) Dalton's having trouble with his head. Do you know when it began?

PAULUS:     No.

DANIEL:     After what he did to the prisoner, Rugiero.

PAULUS:     So?

DANIEL:     Volski's having problems with his stomach and he's always in a bad mood. Marsan's a nasty piece of work; a real appetite for women scared to death. I prefer not to speak of Luigi. As for Pozner. So strong, so well-balanced, Pozner . . . the brute. Did you know he wakes up screaming in the night?

*As he speaks, Paulus sits on the sofa, his mood dark.*

PAULUS:     You are telling me nothing new.

DANIEL:     (*smiling triumphantly*) You said that they were fine.

PAULUS:     I told you a lie.

DANIEL:     (*thinking for a moment and taking a deep breath*) Send me to the foreign branch. I don't want to cause any trouble here, not if I can avoid it.

PAULUS:     You'll stay with us.

DANIEL:     (*taking a step towards him*) Do you want to destroy me? You are giving me sufficient cause!

PAULUS:     No. Your colleagues are sick, but so is the whole world. Somewhere out there the respected father of some family is also appalled by what he's done, a stomach-ulcer, perhaps, or shouting in the night. He'll know the reason why if he knows anything at all. Maybe he thinks he doesn't earn enough, or maybe he feels he's somehow responsible for everything we are doing here to protect him. The world is just the same, out there or here. That's why the man's a fool who thinks our work demands some special person or that we somehow make them here. Look at me: I've been that kind of fool. Each one of your companions has disappointed me, and you the most of all. I had such faith in you. You were different, like myself. You should have stayed sane! But now you have to act. You are sick, like them. It's many years since I learned to be alone.

DANIEL:     How many, Mr Paulus?

PAULUS:     Why do you want to know?

DANIEL:     Why did you choose this profession?

PAULUS:     Why did I choose. . . ? What are you talking about?

DANIEL:     There are those who get sick in here and those who are sick when they get here. You were sick when you came.

PAULUS:     Sick? What with?

DANIEL:     With spite. (*Pause*)

PAULUS:     (*not looking at him*) Son, you must be mad!

DANIEL:     (*after a moment*) My mother sends her regards.

*Paulus looks up, eyes fixed on Daniel.*

Do you want me to give her yours, like I always do?

PAULUS:     If you find that amusing.

DANIEL:     You never seem to forget. It's very strange. It would make more sense to forget it after all this time. Is it quite so hard to forget she turned you down?

PAULUS:     (*looking at him with surprise and getting up*) Shut up!

DANIEL:     I even thought at times that you were my real father. Just now you called me son. Don't call me it again! I see you clearly now. You've never stopped hating the man who was my father. (*He laughs nervously*) Doesn't it make you laugh? The strong man is really a rag doll. The faultless politician hides a grudge. Ever since then he simply wants revenge for all that hurt. Above all on his rival's son, who could have been his son but was someone else's.

*Paulus approaches, fists clenched.*

PAULUS:     (*close to him, shouting*) Shut up!

DANIEL:     (*excited, shouting*) You helped me join in order to destroy me! You got me into the Secret Police in order to destroy me! All right, so you've succeeded. The son pays on his parents' account. The highest price, which you would have made my father pay and I'm condemned to pay instead. It's what you wanted, isn't it? When you ordered me to torture poor Marty, that's what you really wanted.

PAULUS:     (*shaken*) What?

DANIEL:     You should be pleased. Now I'm just like him! I can never be for my wife more than just a brother. (*Strangely disturbed, Paulus closes his eyes*) But even so, I'm still a man.

*Paulus suddenly seizes Daniel by the lapels, shaking him roughly.*

PAULUS:     Will you shut up!

DANIEL:     A man's spirit can't be silent; a man's spirit throws caution to the winds. I can feel my strength coming back. This wretch of a human being informs you that you're a bastard.

*Paulus hurls him onto the sofa. They look at each other, breathing heavily. The telephone rings. Paulus goes to the table to pick up the phone.*

PAULUS:     Yes? (*His tone changes*) Whatever you say, sir. The thing is we are short-staffed. But we are working day and night. I promise you, sir, that. . . . Give me four more days. In four days I'll have the statement. I'll bear it in mind. As you say, sir.

*He puts the phone down, remains thoughtful. Daniel gets up.*

DANIEL:     It's not only spite. It's fear too. You are caught in the trap as well. Goodbye. (*He goes to take his hat*)

PAULUS:     Daniel. (*Daniel turns. Paulus steps towards him*) I shan't deny what's perfectly obvious and I shan't resort to lies. In spite of everything my motives are more honest than all that shit you'll find in there. That's my strength, and there's nothing else I need to know. You belong to the Secret Police and you always will. (*He takes the revolver and the badge. He puts the revolver inside Daniel's jacket*) Keep the gun. And the badge. (*He puts the badge in Daniel's raincoat pocket*) You may be right in one respect. It might be best to send you abroad. I am quite fond of you, despite what you believe. You might recover there. And after what you've said I must admit I'm not too keen on you being here. I'll reconsider the matter. We'll have to wait for the right moment. In the meantime you'll have to carry on. Until tomorrow night then. Now go home.

*Daniel has listened, smiling triumphantly. He goes to the peg and takes his hat.*

DANIEL:     I'll take you at your word, Mr Paulus.

*He puts his hat on and goes down the stairs, stage-left. Paulus watches him impassively and then goes out through the door back-stage, an erect and vigorous figure, as the lights fade on the office and come up on the Barnes household. Mary is sitting on the chair by the telephone, deep in thought. Pause. The grandmother enters stage-left pushing the cradle, which she leaves by the phone.*

MARY:     (*She gets up*) Won't he be cold in here?

GRANDMOTHER:     Eh? . . . I've wrapped him in his shawl. I didn't want the television to wake him up.

*The grandmother goes out as she came in, humming her customary tune. Mary, somewhat puzzled in a way she doesn't understand, watches her go out. She goes over to the cradle, bending over it.*

MARY:     You mustn't get cold, my precious. (*She arranges the shawl*) There. Nice and cosy. Go to sleep now. You aren't to blame for anything. You are mine. Mine and no one else's. Your mother loves you. Because you belong to her . . . just her.

*She straightens up, bothered again by a vague memory. She looks stage-left and looks at the cradle once more, uneasily. Suddenly she turns towards the door up-stage, expectant, waiting. Pause. Daniel enters and she breathes a sigh of surprise. Daniel looks at her from the doorway, his eyes bright with the spark of a possible release.*

DANIEL:     Hello.

MARY:     (*whispering*) Hello.

*Daniel goes to the bookcase and, without taking his eyes off her, places his revolver in its usual place. She takes a step back.*

DANIEL:     Is he asleep?

MARY:     Yes. (*He moves towards the cradle. Mary instinctively reaches out to stop him*) Don't disturb him.

DANIEL:     (*stopping, speaking quietly*) Mary, it seems impossible . . . but I'm going to manage it. We can still have a future.

MARY:     (*disturbed*) I don't understand.

DANIEL:     I've spoken to Paulus. (*He goes to the door stage-left and makes a gesture*) Is she watching television?

MARY:     Yes.

DANIEL:     You were right, Mary. I was such a coward I could never have broken free. But I felt so desperate today I summoned up my courage. That bastard had to listen. To everything. In the end he promised to let me go, to the foreign branch.

MARY:     (*looking straight at him*) Don't you have to go back?

DANIEL:     Not tonight. I refused point blank. Tomorrow, yes. (*Mary looks down. Daniel comes nearer*) I know, Mary, it's a hard price to pay. But until now I was paying for nothing, and finally he's had to compromise. It'll be for a couple of days . . . and he won't dare say anything. (*Close to her*) Mary, it's a wonderful release. To be a man again I had to shout the truth right in his face. And now I'm sure. I can tell. We'll both break free if you can help me. (*He puts his arm around her. She trembles. He whispers to her*) I can tell, Mary. I could tell when I was there, and now that you are here, I know that this is something extraordinary. (*He strokes her arms*) My patient, long-suffering wife. . . . (*He tries to kiss her. She turns her head away, her eyes staring*) Come. (*He tries to take her stage-left. She pulls away, breathing heavily*)

MARY:     What do you want?

DANIEL:     (*he approaches, smiling*) Mother's happy with the television. The baby's fast asleep. It's as if we were alone. (*He takes her hand*) If you want we can start all over again today. You've been so understanding, so good. Go on being the same. I need you now. I love you more than ever.

MARY:     (*pulls away, goes to the cradle*) No.

DANIEL:     Mary. We can start to be free. I'm your husband. Daniel.

MARY:     No, no. You are someone else. Another person.

DANIEL:     What?

MARY:     You are someone else.

DANIEL:     (*going towards her*) We need each other.

MARY:     Don't touch the baby.

DANIEL: (*close to her*) He's my child. (*He shakes her by the arms*) And you are my wife.

MARY: Let me go. Let me go. (*She cries out, frees herself*)

DANIEL: Mary! (*Beside herself, she takes the child from the cradle*) What are you doing? Leave him alone. (*Holding the baby tight, she moves back-stage*)

MARY: Stay away. He's mine, mine. You shan't touch him.

DANIEL: What's wrong with you?

*Close to the bookcase, she suddenly takes the revolver and, holding the child tight, releases the safety catch. She points the gun at him.*

MARY: Stay away from us.

DANIEL: What are you doing? Give me that!

*He steps forward. She points the gun and backs away quickly, passing between the sofa and the small table in order to circle the room and ends up down-stage left.*

MARY: If only we'd never met! Go to sleep, my baby. I'll protect you. If only you'd never been born! Forgive me, my precious. I'll protect you. He shan't do us any harm. You'll be able to play with all the children in the world.

DANIEL: Mary, control yourself! (*He steps forward*) Give me the gun.

MARY: (*she raises the gun, shouts*) Stay where you are.

*Daniel stops. The lights fade on the sitting-room and come up on the down-stage area. Dr Valmy and the Secretary enter stage-right. Mary and Daniel remain motionless, frozen in their gestures and attitudes. Dr Valmy dictates.*

DR VALMY: If only we could stop the march of time. If we could think before it proves too late. He might have thought, 'What's to become of my wife, my child?' And she, 'If I shoot, I'm completely lost.' But when poor human beings get to the end of their tether, they are swept along by a fierce tide and only wish to close their eyes, blind to what happens afterwards.

SECRETARY: What happens afterwards.

*As the last words are spoken, the man in the dinner-jacket and the woman in the evening gown enter stage-left. As they speak, Dr Valmy sadly watches them. Suddenly, lights up on the auditorium.*

MAN:      (*clicking his tongue and shaking his head disapprovingly*) You aren't playing fair, Doctor.

WOMAN:      (*her voice, like her companion's, betrays a certain unease*) Do you really want to shatter our nerves with these unlikely stories?

MAN:      You are forcing us to interrupt again.

WOMAN:      (*to the audience*) Pay no attention, my friends. We've already told you the story is a lie.

MAN:      And even if something like it occurred, it wasn't nearly as bad. We know that sometimes people go too far, maybe even come to blows.

*He smiles at his own joke. Dr Valmy makes a gesture. A Male Nurse enters stage-left and approaches the couple from behind.*

WOMAN:      But there's no point in making a fuss over something so unimportant.

MAN:      Stay calm. We assure you the doctor's fooling you.

WOMAN:      (*sadly*) You should never forget to smile.

*The Male Nurse takes them by the arm. They look at him, disconcerted. He moves them gently towards the wings.*

MAN:      (*resisting and turning to the audience, sadly*) Never forget to smile.

*Pulling him away, the Male Nurse takes them both out. Lights down on the auditorium.*

DR VALMY:      As the reader will recall, this was how my first case history ended. I had decided to recount the second to a group of patients at the sanatorium and, getting to the moment when the wife suddenly seized the revolver, the couple from the first case called me a liar. I reminded them in vain that they were the Barnes' neighbours; they attempted to use that fact to contradict my story. I discharged them the following day. It's true. How could I diagnose them as mentally unbalanced simply because they refused to accept as real the events I've just described? In this strange world of ours, such incredulity cannot be classified as madness. There are millions of others exactly like them. Millions who choose to ignore the world they live in. But no one calls them mad.

SECRETARY:      Mad.

DR VALMY:      The couple have returned to their comfortable way of life; and when they meet the Grandmother in the hallway, they laugh and gossip more excitedly. As for my present story, I managed to complete it, thanks to information from a former fellow student, a doctor with the Secret

Police. There, after all, under physical pressure, people speak the truth. So. To return to our story. The ending is near and has to be told. The events occurred when we were sending our space station into orbit.

*The Secretary and Dr Valmy exit stage-right. Lights fully up on the Barnes' household.*

MARY:     Stay where you are.

DANIEL:     (*in tears*) Mary!

MARY:     Go back to them. You'll always go back. Your boss knows it and you know it too. Because you want to, you want to.

DANIEL:     That's what the driver said. Paulus has deceived me. I'll never recover.

*He stares at Mary obsessively. His arms fall limply at his side. Tears run down his face.*

MARY:     You are just a monster.

*Daniel accepts the accusations: he closes his eyes and bows his head.*

DANIEL:     There's no escape.

*He opens his eyes and looks intensely at his wife, his son, the revolver.*

MARY:     (*crying out*) Don't move. (*Daniel moves forward slowly. Mary calls out again*) Don't come near me.

*He continues to advance, his eyes fixed on her. Overcome by irresistible fear, she cries out again as she simultaneously presses the trigger. Daniel falls, almost smiling. He succeeds in almost sitting up in order to look at her.*

DANIEL:     Thank you.

*Mary fires again. The child starts crying. Mary drops the gun and holds the baby close, looking in anguish at Daniel's body. With the second shot an unreal light begins to fill the office. Chopin's 'Nocturne' can be heard in the distance. The grandmother rushes in stage-left, looks at her daughter-in-law, at the revolver, and runs to her son's body, kneeling beside it.*

GRANDMOTHER:     Daniel! Daniel! My son! My son!

*She begins to weep. The office door opens and Paulus enters, going to the table where he stops. Marsan, Pozner and Luigi follow him in. All of them wait, motionless. The grandmother straightens and looks at Mary, her eyes full of hate.*

GRANDMOTHER:     Murderer!

*She gets up, never taking her eyes off Mary, hurries to the phone and nervously dials a number. The piano music is louder. There is no sound of the phone ringing in the office, but Paulus picks up the receiver and listens. The grandmother says something inaudible and hangs up. Paulus puts the phone down and gestures to Marsan and Pozner who nod and begin to go down the steps at the front. He gestures to Luigi, who nods and goes down the stairs stage-left, while Marsan and Pozner enter the Barnes' sitting-room to observe Daniel's body. Pozner bends to confirm that he is dead. Marsan approaches Mary, picks up the gun with a handkerchief and steps back, his eyes fixed on her, indicating that she should move. In the office Luigi reappears stage-left, leading Lucila. Mary moves slowly stage-right. She stops in front of the grandmother, kisses the child with great tenderness and hands him to her. Then she steps down from the stage and begins to climb the stairs, preceded by Pozner and followed by Marsan. The piano, without stopping, begins to play Brahm's 'Cradle Song'. The grandmother sits on the chair, weeping, rocking the child, glancing at her son's body.*

GRANDMOTHER:     (*almost inaudibly*) Once there was a little boy, prettier than the sun, whose name was little Daniel . . . and little Daniel was handsome and good, and he had a mother who loved him . . . and his mother used to say: 'my little Daniel will grow up strong and big as a captain.' And little Daniel would smile. . . . 'And because he's such a good boy, the whole world will love him and be his friend.' And little Daniel would smile. . . .

*Meanwhile, Mary arrives upstairs in the office. She and Lucila exchange meaningful glances. Both women, facing the audience, contemplate the emptiness of their future, surrounded by the impassive faces of the men. The stage begins to darken except for the light that illuminates Mary and the soft glow that falls on the empty bench. In the darkness, Grandmother's final words are heard. The piano continues playing.*

**ALMOST A GODDESS**

# Jaime Salóm

Born in Barcelona on Christmas Day, 1925, Jaime Salóm Vidal is probably Spain's most successful and productive dramatist writing today. Educated in the city of his birth, he completed his medical studies in the late 1940s, specializing in ophthalmology and, following in his father's footsteps, worked in Barcelona as a full-time ophthalmologist until the beginning of the 1990s.

Fourteen years old at the end of the Civil War, Salóm has been greatly affected by the values embodied in the Franco regime. As a student in Barcelona he was already trying his hand at writing plays, although his first professional production did not take place until 1955, when *The Message* was premièred at the Teatro Arriega in Bilbao. During the 1960s he wrote fourteen plays, eight of which were staged in Barcelona and four in Madrid, the latter establishing a connection with the capital city which would become more pronounced by the early 1970s. The early plays, in particular *Emerald Green* (1960) and *The Guilty* (1961), are really mystery-thrillers, reminiscent of the work of Agatha Christie, and give little indication, except perhaps in their intricate structure, of the level which Salóm's theatre would later achieve. His most outstanding plays were *The Trunk of Disguises* (1964), in which the three stages of a man's life are evoked, *The House of the 'Chivas'* (1968), which ran for more than 700 performances in Barcelona, and *The Heirs Apparent* (1969). All three plays point to a much greater seriousness and technical assurance in Salóm's theatre.

During the 1970s Salóm wrote seven plays, of which six were produced in Madrid and only one in Barcelona. The best-known of these is probably *Bitter Lemon*, premièred at the Teatro Marquina in Madrid in 1976. It concerns Juan's attempt to break out of an empty marriage, in which he feels trapped, in order to live with the woman he loves. In the end, however, he yields to the demands of conventional morality and social convention by returning to his wife. *Bitter Lemon* has often been seen, like *The Heirs Apparent* and *The House of the 'Chivas'*, as an attack on the Franco regime and its advocacy of so-called traditional values in any circumstances. Salóm would himself argue that his main interest lies less in the political implications of this and other plays than in the very human dilemmas in which the characters find themselves. *Bitter Lemon* also provides a very good example of the dramatist's developing stage technique. The action of the play moves constantly between the objective reality of Juan at home with his wife and daughter, and the inner reality of his thoughts in which episodes from his life with his lover, Barbara, are recalled. Its shifting, episodic structure therefore reflects the conflicting world of Juan's home and social life, distinguished by its cold formality, and the turbulent world of his passions. Since 1970 Salóm's style has been characterized as 'psychological expressionism' and has also been compared with that of Buero Vallejo.

In the course of the 1980s five plays appeared, of which the best-known is *The Cock's Short Flight*, a particularly interesting play, especially as its protagonist is Nicolás Franco, father of the dictator. In part Salóm's purpose was to draw a contrast between the repressive nature of the Franco regime and the liberal-minded, amorous father who left his wife, Pilar, in 1907, in order to live with another woman. On the other hand, Salóm's interest, as in *Bitter Lemon*, lies predominantly in the character of the robust and non-conformist Nicolás.

Salóm's retirement from his practice as an ophthalmologist in 1990, combined with his move to Madrid, where he lives with his actress wife, Montse, has led to a new burst of creativity. He regards *Almost a Goddess*, premièred in Madrid in 1993, as his best work for the theatre, and it is certainly a magical piece. Salóm's interest in his characters as human beings explains why, unlike dramatists whose work is rooted in the problems of the dictatorship, he has not 'dried up'. To meet him is to become aware of an enthusiasm for the theatre that is still essentially that of a young man. At an age when most dramatists have nothing more to say, he is still brim-full of ideas.

# ALMOST A GODDESS

A Play by

**Jaime Salóm**

## Characters

Elena

Salvador

Paul

An Actor

Other Man

# Dramatis Personae

ELENA:   A woman whose age is difficult to determine, approaching maturity, but whose body remains young, desirable and attractive. Her expression is piercing, her complexion like honey. She is intelligent and mischievous, extremely lively, dazzlingly ambitious and proud. There is about her a timeless feeling, verging on the immortal.

SALVADOR:   A young man of twenty-five, good-looking, with a small moustache and elegantly dressed. In spite of being Spanish, there is something South American about him. He is dark, impassioned, at times demented, transported to regions only he is allowed to occupy. There is nothing about him of the comic and ludicrous Dalí of later years. He has an extreme shyness which overwhelms him in certain situations, as well as stimulating him in others.

PAUL:   About twenty-two. Refined, a snob, elegant, somewhat decadent, a mixture of openness and perverseness, of angel and devil.

AN ACTOR:   In outward appearance he looks like Paul, but his long hair and beard give him the appearance of Christ as we see him represented in Christian tradition. At times he seems lit from within, outside the actual moment in which he is living, the effect perhaps of the drugs he has consumed over many years. At other times he seems innocent, even child-like.

OTHER MAN:   Somewhat older than the others, between thirty and fifty. He will play a number of different parts as indicated by the text.

NOTE:   The same actor will play the parts of AN ACTOR and OTHER MAN.

# The Setting

A very large room, like an enormous quadrangular store. The whole of the back wall is covered by an Impressionist painting which depicts a beach, the sea and the clear blue sky of a summer's day.

To the right of the audience a great window facing the bay (the window is real), through which we can hear the sound of the sea and the cries of the gulls at dawn and at nightfall, as well as smell the salt of the Mediterranean. In front of the window is a sofa on which Elena, facing the sea, will rest and sleep. To the left, painted on the wall, the whitewashed wall of a fisherman's hut with its door and window-frame painted marine blue. In front of it, as though sheltered from the sea breezes, are four or five wooden armchairs, the kind that are found in a garden, in which at given moments the characters will sit and take the sun.

# The Play in One Act

*Elena is asleep on the sofa. Salvador, Paul and Other Man are relaxing in the armchairs, taking the sun. The first is reading the paper, the second has his eyes closed, the third, who is wearing sunglasses, is smoking a cigarette. Elena opens her eyes, sits up and faces the first ray of sunlight that comes through the glass and lights up her face.*

ELENA:     I always sleep facing the dawn, with the window open. So the first ray of light can wake me up when it shines through the rocks on the headland at the furthest, eastern end of the bay. I'm sure that first ray of sunshine contains the secret of what will happen on that same day and so I observe it carefully, touch it with my fingers, caress it seeking to find the hidden meaning of its mysterious light.

*She gets up and goes to the window, bathed by the light of the sun.*

I am a first-class medium. People say it, and I believe them. In Paris they used to ask me to reveal the dark currents of the subconscious and forecast the future. But I still cannot tell what this first ray of sunlight wants to reveal, what it hides amongst its shining particles. Every morning I ask which day will be my last. It's not that I'm afraid of death, merely curious about the great experience that the end of the road will surely mean. Fortunately, the Tarot cards will take me a little closer.

*She lays out the cards on the sofa, using her right hand to arrange them in circles from right to left. Then she places them in one large circle, divided into twelve piles. Salvador gets up from the armchair, stands behind Elena and observes the cards as she deals them.*

ELENA:     (*without stopping and without looking at him*) What is it, my darling?

SALVADOR:     I'd like to know what today has in store. I have a great canvas prepared, on which I want to paint the dream that made me restless all night long. Watches, lots of watches, silent, soft, collapsing over a wall made from rhinoceros horns and sea urchins. Today could be for me a frenetic day of mystical, ammoniacal joy.

ELENA:     You'd best paint nothing. All you do is doomed to failure, you could become ill. No, wait . . . there's another card.

*She deals a card.*

The sun! It changes everything. Go to your studio, don't stop, not even to eat; don't sleep, don't pee. The sun is the strongest card of all; it has supreme power, is never influenced by any other card.

*She deals a card.*

And now the face of God. Kiss me.

*He kisses her.*

Hurry to your studio. I shall be with you, as always.

*Salvador turns away to face the armchair but remains standing.*

Every morning he asks me the same thing. He cannot make a single brush stroke unless the Tarot cards give him their permission. . . . Oh, I believe in them too, in the esoteric world that lies behind this false reality we touch with our fingertips. The only truly real things are money . . . and death.

*She returns to the cards.*

SALVADOR:     (*to Paul*) Paul Eluard?

PAUL:     (*getting up*) Yes?

SALVADOR:     I knew you as soon as I came in. You're a very famous man, an important poet amongst the surrealists, and an expert in buying paintings, especially new work. I am a painter and I'd like to show you my work. I'm sure it has an appeal for you.

PAUL:     To whom do I have the honour of speaking?

SALVADOR:     Dalí.

PAUL:     The name seems to ring a bell.

SALVADOR:     (*to Elena*) That's not what happened, Elena. One night a dealer took me to the ballet Tabarin. He pointed out a man accompanied by an extremely glamorous woman wearing a sequined dress. He told me who he was and insisted on introducing us.

PAUL:     (*to Salvador*) *Un chien andalou.* Of course! An interesting film you made with Buñuel. Placing a rotting donkey on top of a grand piano was a wonderful idea!

SALVADOR:     (*to Elena*) I should never have approached him, never have indulged in such exaggerated praise. How could I be an admirer? I'd never even read one of his poems.

ELENA:    You were later on! You used to claim he was the greatest living poet.

SALVADOR:    Except for myself! I can't think why I allowed him to buy my paintings.

PAUL:    You mean you are a painter too?

SALVADOR:    (*to Elena*) Inform him I'm the greatest genius ever!

PAUL:    If you wish, we could lunch together one of these days.

SALVADOR:    I leave Paris tomorrow. For a village on the coast in Catalonia. I have my studio there. If you'd like to come this summer, do. There you could see my work.

PAUL:    I'd be delighted. . . .

ELENA:    (*to Salvador*) You see? He was very nice to you.

PAUL:    We'll postpone until the summer, then, the pleasure of getting to know each other.

SALVADOR:    It was simply a polite invitation, a completely empty gesture. He took it at its face value.

ELENA:    You made a great impression. As soon as he came back from Switzerland, he spoke constantly of your elegance.

SALVADOR:    He came for a cheap holiday, nothing more.

ELENA:    How can you say that? You became great friends, you got to know him well. He was a kind and generous man.

SALVADOR:    At the time he hadn't a bean to his name.

ELENA:    Nor did you!

SALVADOR:    I admit he was an astonishing, legendary being. One only had to see the elegance with which he drank, the way he admired beautiful women.

ELENA:    He was always an admirer of beauty.

SALVADOR:    The most elegant women longed for him. . . .

ELENA:    What do *you* mean by an elegant woman?

SALVADOR:    A woman who shows contempt for one and shaves her armpits.

*Salvador sits in one of the armchairs.*

ELENA:    He was right. Paul was an astonishing, legendary being. . . . I met him in Clavadel, a Swiss sanatorium to which, on account of my con-

stantly poor health, my family had sent me. I was seventeen years old. . . .
My God, I can't believe I was once seventeen.

*She sits on the sofa and begins reading a book.*

PAUL:     (*To Other Man who is sitting next to him*) How long have you been a
patient here?

OTHER MAN:     More than two years.

PAUL:     And you aren't dead yet?

OTHER MAN:     (*nervously*) What sort of question's that? I've almost stopped
coughing and it's three and a half weeks since I spat up blood.

PAUL:     I'm sorry. I meant to say, aren't you bored to death? I've only been
here ten days and I can't stand any more.

OTHER MAN:     You'll get used to it. It's just like a fine hotel or a first-class
ocean liner. We dress for dinner, as you know already. . . .

PAUL:     I prefer to eat in my room.

OTHER MAN:     They often arrange quite interesting dances, and sometimes we
wear fancy-dress. Now and again a guest disappears, and his name is
never mentioned again. It's the only forbidden topic, death. Don't forget
it.

ELENA:     In this wretched place my only pleasure's reading. Dostoevsky.
Pushkin and Tolstoy too. My stepfather said he held me on his knee, when
we went to his house once. I was so young I can't recall it.

PAUL:     (*to the Other Man*) Who is that girl?

OTHER MAN:     Her name's Elena Diakonova. I saw it in the register. She's
Russian. Can't say I know her. She hasn't been here long. She doesn't
speak to anyone.

PAUL:     You mean she's shy?

OTHER MAN:     She probably despises us.

ELENA:     I also pray a lot. To the icons and the crucifixes I brought with me and
that cover the walls of my room. . . . Today I pray that they give me the
handsome young man I passed in the gallery the other day . . . I could
easily fall in love with him, be driven quite mad, if I haven't gone mad
already.

PAUL:     (*to the Other Man*) She has such great big eyes, like clear liquid,
capable of piercing walls . . . and such an exciting body, as if it were all a
continuation of her sex.

ELENA: The maid gave me the information I needed. His name is Paul, he's a poet, every week they send him books from Paris, he loves a good time, and he's very keen on casinos and women. In short, interesting.

*She gets up and sits in the empty chair next to Paul. She reads a book.*

PAUL: Would you care for a blanket to cover your legs?

ELENA: At last, the sun's come out after all these weeks of snow.

PAUL: I love the snow.

ELENA: I despise it. It snows in my city for months on end. The streets are filthy from people's feet and the wheels of carriages. Someday I'll live where I can lie in the sun and feel its warmth on my skin for twelve months of the year. What are you reading?

PAUL: The poems of Whitman. You?

ELENA: 'The Gambler'.

PAUL: You like playing cards?

ELENA: Tarot.

PAUL: I prefer baccarat. (*They laugh*) My father's a builder. He makes me work in the business, but I've got other plans. I don't really fancy spending my life on invoices and property.

ELENA: It must be very profitable.

PAUL: Of course. But money isn't important. Don't you agree?

ELENA: Up to a point. . . . My father went to Siberia, as many others did, in search of deposits of gold which no one ever found. It was one of the Tsar's tricks to populate the area. He died there without finding anything. On the other hand, my stepfather's very important. Thanks to his wealth I was able to meet in Moscow the greatest writers and poets. I wore expensive clothes, attended the balls at Court, and now I'm here till my lungs recover. Without such money I might have died . . . and then I wouldn't have met you.

SALVADOR: My father has greatly influenced my life. I've admired him, copied him and hated him. We've had many confrontations, the worst of all when he learned of my relationship with Elena. He even disowned me. He was an absolute atheist, shocked the entire city with his blasphemous opinions, and yet his moral values were stricter than those of any believer.

OTHER MAN: (*as Salvador's father*) Religion, my boy, is the province of women. In this family only the women go to mass. God doesn't exist. I have many books in my library which prove it with mathematical precision. Read Voltaire. He provides irrefutable arguments, and he is one of the greatest legal minds of modern times.

SALVADOR:    What about Nietzsche? He insists that God is dead. How can he speak of someone's death if he doesn't exist?

OTHER MAN:    Nietzsche was just a hot-head.

SALVADOR:    Father, you are a practical, rational man. Your feet are firmly on the ground. But I want to free myself from that, and conquer the irrational. . . . You can't understand it. That's because you're nothing more than a bloody bourgeois.

OTHER MAN:    (*sitting down*) Get out of my sight, you wretch!

*Salvador goes to one of the chairs. Elena is lying on the sofa. Paul is standing next to her.*

PAUL:    Am I being a nuisance?

ELENA:    I never sleep in the afternoon.

PAUL:    Nor I.

ELENA:    Why aren't you with the French girl? You spend hours talking and laughing with her. And she's pretty.

PAUL:    But not as pretty as you. (*Change of tone*) I'm afraid you won't be seeing her again.

ELENA:    When did it happen?

PAUL:    Last night. Everyone knew it was just a matter of time.

ELENA:    I'm sorry.

PAUL:    Do you mind if I sit here?

*He sits on the edge of the sofa.*

ELENA:    From then on Paul came to my room very often . . . after lunch, during the two-hour rest period the sanatorium insisted on. We would talk about books, painting, philosophy . . . or we'd make fun of the other guests. Sometimes we'd be silent for quite a long time.

PAUL:    Why so quiet? Tell me what you are thinking. I like to follow your train of thought.

ELENA:    My house in Russia is large. It has one blue drawing-room and another brown. My stepfather, Ivan, is a lawyer, a strong man with a grey beard and small round glasses in a gold frame. My brothers and sisters hate him for his overbearing manner and he often gets annoyed with them. I'm the only one he takes an interest in, he buys me clothes, brings me books, and sometimes even some jewellery. (*Short pause*) I was still just a child when he robbed me of my virginity. One evening, when only the servants were at home. My eldest brother came home first, and he knew as soon as he saw us. He hated my stepfather after that, because he'd wanted to be the first. He'd suggested it several times and he never forgave him for beating him to it.

PAUL:    (*incredulous*) What colour was the sofa?

ELENA:    Blue . . . or red. What does it matter?

PAUL:    (*smiling*) You'd remember the colour if what you've described had been the truth. (*He bends over her*) My little Elena. You still have the eyes of a young virgin . . . bright with perfect innocence . . . I know that no male hand has touched the silky warmth of your neck. . . . (*He strokes her neck*) . . . or ever caressed the sweet trembling of your breasts, or explored the delightful path that travels to your stomach, or trembled in the hair of your abdomen, or felt excitement in the warm folds between your legs. . . .

*As he speaks these words, Paul has been exploring Elena's body. She is as if electrified, feeling for the first time the enormous force of sexual arousal. For a moment they both share the same sensation. Then Paul draws back.*

It's the cruellest lie you've ever told me. If I thought it were true, I'd stop taking my medicine, so my illness could finish me off the sooner the better.

ELENA:    It was, I do admit, a lie. I'd told the story on several occasions, I suppose to create more interest because I felt so young and boring. At times my brother was the one who enjoyed me, my stepfather the one who found us. But to be quite honest, I knew nothing then about desire and even less with regard to sex. I discovered it that afternoon, like a burning and painful whiplash. I suddenly awoke to what it was to be a woman as Paul's fingers explored my flesh and opened deep inside me a great abyss that would never be filled.

PAUL:    What are you hiding?

ELENA:    Nothing.

PAUL:    (*taking the hand she is keeping closed*) Open it. I want to see what it is.

ELENA:    It's something private.

PAUL:    What's yours is mine.

*He makes her open her hand and sees a piece of crumpled paper.*

ELENA:     Brute!

PAUL:     The drawing of a man. Who is it?

ELENA:     It's written underneath. Portrait of a young poet, seventeen years old.

PAUL:     Who is he?

ELENA:     You'll have to guess.

PAUL:     I'll buy it. I intend to collect pictures. This will be my first.

ELENA:     It's not for sale.

PAUL:     I'll pay for it with a kiss.

*He kisses her.*

SALVADOR:     Last night I had a strange dream, which will be repeated through-out my life. Dreams are much more honest than all the things we experience when we're awake.

I was a king. I am a king and will always be so, with my crown of gold and precious stones, even when I choose not to wear it. I above, the rest below, a flock of sheep, their feet full of calluses, enjoying Christmas holidays, snots up their noses, their food re-heated, smelling of sweat like children in school where they learn such pointless absurdities. A king to whom each night they brought a beautiful maiden of his kingdom, arrayed in dazzling clothes and lovely pearls. The king didn't touch her, merely watched as she slept at his side. He didn't need a girl to satisfy his love. A king is a king, sufficient unto himself. And when the sun came up, he'd take his sword and with a single blow cut off the girl's head. But then, when a beautiful girl was brought whose intelligence even outshone her dazzling beauty, something very strange occurred. The girl made an image of wax on which she fixed a sugar nose, and she placed the image in the bed, dressed in splendid clothes and jewels. The king lay down beside the figure and, as was his wont, didn't touch it. In the morning he cut off the head, at a stroke, and the sugar nose fell off with the force of the blow. The king then ate it, was amazed by its sweetness, and said that if he'd known the girl was so sweet, he wouldn't have killed her. The girl herself, having hidden under the bed, appeared then, and so it was the king discovered he could love a woman, married her, and they lived happily ever after.

*Paul and Elena say goodbye.*

PAUL:     When does your train leave?

ELENA:     At twenty past eight. The car is waiting to take me to the station. When are you leaving?

PAUL:     Tomorrow. I'll be in Paris at midnight. My parents will meet me at the station.

ELENA:     What will they think of our engagement?

PAUL:     Mother will feel intensely jealous, especially when she reads your prologue to my book of poems. But when she knows you, she'll adore you as much as I do. The last two years in this sanatorium have been the happiest of my life.

ELENA:     Mine too.

PAUL:     If only I'd possessed you completely.

ELENA:     Your words and caresses have possessed me already. I've given myself to them completely. . . . But I also want to keep myself for you until we marry.

PAUL:     When might that be?

ELENA:     Oh, very soon.

PAUL:     Everyone says there's going to be a war. The situation in Russia isn't clear at all.

ELENA:     No one can keep us apart. (*She shows him a book*) This book you wrote when I was with you is our most passionate act of love. . . .

*They kiss passionately.*

SALVADOR:     (*to Other Man as Buñuel*) Of course, Buñuel! How many times do I have to say it? We'll make a much more daring film than *Un chien andalou*.

OTHER MAN:     So when the hell do we start?

*Paul sits on one of the chairs, Elena stretches out on the sofa.*

SALVADOR:     I'm painting endlessly. There isn't time for anything else. In a few days time my dealer is coming to Cadaqués, with Eluard and his wife. I have to have the paintings ready.

OTHER MAN:     Have you met Eluard's wife?

SALVADOR:     No.

OTHER MAN:     A proud and disagreeable creature. She struts around like a goddess, judging, condemning, forgiving as she fancies. She revises Paul's poems with a most annoying concern for detail. And the entire surrealist group asks her opinion about their work, as if she were infallible.

SALVADOR:     She must be very intelligent.

OTHER MAN:    Or they flatter her because they fancy her. They reckon she's attractive. I can't think why. She's a tiny, nervous thing. . . .

SALVADOR:    I'd say she doesn't appeal to you.

OTHER MAN:    I detest her.

SALVADOR:    The girl's beginning to interest me. I cannot stand ordinary people or simpering women who agree with everything one says.

OTHER MAN:    She's a puffed-up flea.

SALVADOR:    And you're a beast. You should take up boxing permanently.

OTHER MAN:    I can hit much harder on the screen than in the ring.

*He poses like a boxer in front of an impassive Dalí.*

ELENA:    (*sitting on the floor, with her back against the sofa, she is writing a letter*) My dearest Paul. I don't know when you'll receive my letters — Moscow is so far from France — but I'm writing three a day. I need to speak to you, as if you were still at my side in my room in the sanatorium. I was welcomed with all the joy you can imagine, although my stepfather, as practical as usual, felt he had to work out — I'm not sure if he was serious or not — how much each ounce I'd gained in the sanatorium had cost him. I told them all about you, I showed them your photograph and read them some of your poems, which they really liked. My stepfather expressed the opinion that poets, however good they are, are always starving to death, incapable of keeping a girl like myself in the style she's accustomed to. My brother for once agreed with him and couldn't for the life of him understand why I should prefer an unknown foreigner when there's such a choice of young men in Moscow. Although I tried to calm them down by explaining what you are like and insisting how much I love my little Paul, my brute of a brother flung the window open, pointed to a regiment of soldiers marching below, and told me that's where I should choose from.

PAUL:    (*sitting in an armchair in the sun, writing*) I have been called up. Because of my state of health, they've made me an auxiliary, which has left me feeling quite ashamed. The youth of France are fighting it out on the battlefield, and here am I doing an administrative job, almost a civilian. I've requested a more active post, which would make me feel more useful and more in touch with the horrors of war. . . .

ELENA:    (*writing*) Each day I'm feeling more alone. I cry, I hardly sleep, and my nerves are so on edge I could scream. I pray for you every day in the hope that this terrible war will not affect you too much.

PAUL:    At last they have sent me to a hospital a few kilometres from the front.

The wounded arrive in their thousands and although I try to help them as much as I can, I feel that my place is really in the trenches. My health isn't so bad that I can't hold a rifle like the rest of them.

ELENA:  Your letter has made me ill. Forget your pride and think of our love which matters more than anything. The only thing that matters is your life. Don't risk it. Your bravery consists of staying where you are, with the lower bourgeoisie. Don't get carried away by the foolish enthusiasms of the masses.

PAUL:  I'm going to ask them to move me to the front line.

ELENA:  If you do that, if you value my love so little, I shall be just as stupid and volunteer as a nurse. I wouldn't have the strength, of course. I would die, a slow suicide for which you alone would be responsible.

PAUL:  I've been assigned to the 95th infantry regiment.

ELENA:  No, no, no. I absolutely forbid it.

PAUL:  Will you marry me?

*Salvador, without moving from his seat, releases a loud guffaw.*

ELENA:  You were my husband before we met, have been since, and will always be as long as I live.

*Salvador laughs again.*

PAUL:  They'll give me four days leave to get married.

ELENA:  I've just had my twenty-first birthday. I don't need my family's permission to do what I want. I'll catch a train and cross half of Europe to lie in your arms, my little sweet boy, my darling husband.

OTHER MAN:  (*as Buñuel, to Salvador*) What are you laughing at?

SALVADOR:  If you only knew, you'd kill yourself laughing. (*He laughs again*)

OTHER MAN:  Stop laughing. It gets on my nerves.

SALVADOR:  Don't make such a silly face. (*He laughs*) It makes me laugh even more. (*He laughs*)

OTHER MAN:  (*shaking him by the shoulders*) Stop it!

*Salvador is frightened for a moment, then laughs again. Other Man angrily turns away from him. Meanwhile, Elena and Paul are centre-stage. They are getting married.*

ELENA:  I've become a Catholic. I've changed religion in order to marry Paul.

I suppose in the end one God is not much different from another. But I did want a church wedding, like my parents, like any believer.

PAUL:    I've never been a believer. To please her I took communion for the first time from the priest of the regiment.

ELENA:    I take Paul as my loving husband.

PAUL:    I take Elena Diakanova as my loving wife.

ELENA:    I do.

PAUL:    I do.

*They kiss, then lie on the sofa to make love.*

SALVADOR:    (*laughs for a moment, then to Other Man*) Imagine, as if it were one of your films, the most correct people you know ... my father, the president of the Republic ... with an owl on top of his head, as if it were a hat. (*He laughs*)

OTHER MAN:    I can't see the joke.

SALVADOR:    Wait a moment ... and on top of the owl, between its little ears ... (*He can't stop laughing*) sheep droppings (*He laughs*), one of my turds ... (*He laughs, then stops suddenly*) Don't you think it's funny?

OTHER MAN:    (*very serious*) No.

SALVADOR:    I can't understand it.

*He laughs again.*

OTHER MAN:    You are mad.

SALVADOR:    The only difference between a madman and me is that I'm not mad.

ELENA:    They were two days of pure joy. Paul was an insatiable lover. He made me discover a love I could never remove.

PAUL:    I simply loved you.

ELENA:    But when his leave was over, my worries about our separation were even greater.

*She embraces him to say goodbye. Gets up.*

He didn't want me with him at the station.

*Paul moves away from her.*

I stayed in our hotel room, watching him through the window as he walked through the rain and disappeared down one of the streets ... wondering if I'd ever see him again. . . .

*She anxiously consults the Tarot cards.*

The death card hasn't appeared. He's not going to die.

*She kneels against the sofa, weeping.*

Thank you, God. Thank you.

*Paul has sat down in one of the chairs.*

SALVADOR:     (*to Other Man as Buñuel*) It's their car. They've arrived.

OTHER MAN:     How do you know?

SALVADOR:     It's the taxi from town. 1929 model. It's the only one. They've stopped in front of the Hotel Miramar. We must get ready to receive them. They'll be here soon.

OTHER MAN:     I came to write a script and we haven't started. I don't care a damn about the Eluards.

SALVADOR:     I intend to make a great impression. I'll wear my best shirt, my white silk shirt.

*He removes his jacket to reveal a white silk shirt.*

Open at the neck so they can see the hair on my chest. And my sister's pearl necklace.

*He puts it on.*

And an ear-ring.

*He looks at himself in an imaginary mirror.*

How do I look?

OTHER MAN:     Go to hell!

*Other Man sits down angrily.*

SALVADOR:     I don't like it much either. I ought to shave my armpits, as elegant women do. And I need some good perfume . . . but I only have eau de cologne.

OTHER MAN:     (*cursing under his breath*) How stupid can you get!

SALVADOR:     The most expensive of perfumes contain the excrement of animals, to make them more erotic. I'll annoint myself with dung, with the scent of goat. . . .

OTHER MAN:     Ugh! Go away! You stink!

SALVADOR:    It does smell a little too much. And I've cut myself shaving under my arms! They are almost here. What can I do?

*He laughs loudly.*

I know. A geranium.

*He puts a geranium in his ear and bows ceremoniously to welcome Elena.*

Madame. . . .

ELENA:    (*to Paul*) Why insist on destroying our love?

PAUL:    Love has to be free to be fulfilled. It is not a chain, nor an exclusive agreement. Love is not a limitation, simply a starting point to broaden our experiences.

ELENA:    And for that you've brought me to the world's end.

PAUL:    We've come to see some paintings.

ELENA:    The paintings don't concern you. You fancy the painter.

PAUL:    You'll like him too. He's a good-looking fellow.

ELENA:    But why, Paul? Isn't my love enough?

PAUL:    I have never loved and cannot love anyone other than you, but it's exciting to share one's desire with other men.

ELENA:    And you aren't afraid it might be risky?

PAUL:    You falling for him? The very idea!

ELENA:    It wouldn't be the first time.

PAUL:    But you always come back to me. We should take advantage of our freedom, abuse it.

SALVADOR:    (*bowing ceremoniously, offering Elena the geranium*) Madame. . . .

PAUL:    My dear Salvador. . . . (*He embraces him*) This is my wife.

SALVADOR:    Welcome. (*He laughs absurdly*) A pleasure to meet you. (*He laughs. Elena looks at him severely*) A great pleasure. (*He cannot stop laughing*)

OTHER MAN:    He laughs whenever he's nervous. He can't stop.

ELENA:    Do I have to put up with it!

PAUL:    (*referring to Buñuel*) You already know the great film-maker.

PAUL:    (*half-turning, without acknowledging him*) What is that terrible smell?

SALVADOR:      A wonderful perfume I've recently invented.

ELENA:      It stinks. (*To Paul*) Let's go.

*She throws the geranium to the floor and prepares to leave.*

SALVADOR:      I'd like you to see the wonderful landscape. . . . (*He laughs*) It's the most beautiful place on earth.

PAUL:      Please excuse her, she's extremely tired after the journey.

SALVADOR:      I want to show you my pictures too.

PAUL:      In a little while. We'll all have a nice shower, with lots of soap, and a change of clothing . . . clean, of course . . . and we'll meet again this evening.

*Elena is already lying on the sofa. Paul goes across to her.*

SALVADOR:      She is wonderful, Buñuel. Wonderful.

OTHER MAN:      Don't come near. You stink of shit.

SALVADOR:      Did you see the perfect line of her neck and her back? And her legs? (*He laughs*) Did you notice her legs? (*He laughs*)

OTHER MAN:      She's nothing but a common, puffed-up bitch.

SALVADOR:      And you're an unfeeling brute.

OTHER MAN:      You've never understood women.

SALVADOR:      And what do you know! We'll see what you do when you don't have me to write your scripts. No one will ever remember you.

OTHER MAN:      Keep away, or I'll spew my breakfast up.

*Other Man goes to sit in the armchair furthest away.*

ELENA:      We'll leave for Paris this very minute. I cannot stand this clown a moment longer.

PAUL:      Elena, please. . . .

ELENA:      He smells disgusting, he laughs like a moron. I've never met such a disagreeable person.

PAUL:      I expect he wanted to create an impression. His silliness was part of the effect.

ELENA:      You can say that again.

PAUL:      You must see he's not an ordinary person.

ELENA:      For God's sake, he seems more like an expert in the tango.

PAUL:    Maybe he's a good painter. He's preparing an exhibition for a Paris gallery.

ELENA:    You know perfectly well that I know talent when I see it. I guarantee he's nothing more than a talentless dauber.

PAUL:    You shouldn't prejudge him. When we go to see him this evening. . . .

ELENA:    I'm not going.

PAUL:    Of course you are, my little one. You are far too intelligent to let yourself be carried away by an impulse. You'll be nice to him, engage him in a long conversation so he can overcome his shyness. I assure you, you'll find him very attractive.

*He embraces her. She looks directly at him.*

ELENA:    You want him so much?

PAUL:    Let's just say that your pleasure is also mine.

ELENA:    My dear Paul . . . I sometimes wonder how, being so dissolute, you manage to remain so pure.

*Elena goes to lie on the sofa. Paul follows her and sits close to her.*

I could see it written in his bright eyes, like a child about to do something naughty. A capricious child who wanted to repeat with Salvador what had happened with Max . . . whom he'd brought home from Germany just after the war, and who shared our bed for quite some time. . . .

*Elena gets up.*

It was an exciting time. Max's excitement infected me, and Paul was happy to enjoy the passion we offered him every night, and without for a moment becoming jealous. Until it was Max who began to be jealous. And what was Paul's reaction to it? That of a bad-tempered child. He got some money from his father and went off on a long trip, leaving us to-gether.

PAUL:    And the two of you came looking for me.

ELENA:    Because your father asked us to. He paid all our expenses.

PAUL:    You abandoned Max to come to me.

ELENA:    Don't kid yourself. He got tired of it all and so he left.

PAUL:    Admit it. Neither Max nor any of the other men you had satisfied you as much as I do.

ELENA:    Don't be so conceited.

PAUL:     Our love will always dominate any other act of love, whoever performs it with you or me. Your climaxes are and will always be mine, whoever inspires them.

ELENA:     There are times when I can't decide if you are so weak that you need all this to give you pleasure . . . or so strong that you don't give a damn. . . .

*Salvador laughs noisily.*

SALVADOR:     Sit here.

*He puts a cushion on the ground and immediately moves it.*

Or better here. You'll have a better view of the bay.

*He laughs.*

It's hot. Are you thirsty? Would you like some water?

*He laughs.*

ELENA:     I'd like this silly laughing to stop.

SALVADOR:     But I can't control it. (*He laughs*) I can't . . . I can't.

*He laughs and then begins to cry and puts his head in her lap.*

ELENA:     Don't worry, I'll help you.

*She caresses his hair as if he were a child.*

PAUL:     Why bother, Elena? We made a mistake. The fellow's completely useless . . . for making love like any normal man, or completing the pictures for an exhibition he'd agreed to. . . .

ELENA:     But his paintings are fantastic, Paul . . . I could make him the greatest figure in surrealism.

PAUL:     I'm not even sure he is a surrealist. I rather think he paints outrageous things simply to shock the bourgeoisie. Let's go to Paris.

ELENA:     I'm staying.

PAUL:     You mean you actually like this fool?

ELENA:     I like the way he paints.

PAUL:     It wouldn't be revenge on me for making you come here in the first place?

ELENA:     Perhaps.

PAUL:     All right, if that's what you want. . . . Goodbye.

*He smiles.*

When you've had enough of masturbating him, you'll be back. . . .

ELENA:     They all left. Only I stayed behind in Cadaqués that September, having assured them that everything would be ready for the Paris exhibition.

SALVADOR:     (*to Elena, offering her grapes*) Do you like grapes? The vineyards are in season now. These are the sweetest grapes on earth. Shall we walk over the rocks?

ELENA:     (*eating the grapes*) Provided you are serious, and we can talk like friends. Give me your hand. The path is rather steep. I might fall.

*He takes her hand.*

SALVADOR:     There. The touch of your skin has cured my laughing at last. You are a goddess.

*He kneels at her feet and kisses her shoes.*

ELENA:     (*ironically*) Shall I take my shoes off?

SALVADOR:     I love your shoes. I passionately long for the leather of your tiny shoes. I want to kiss them until my lips ache.

*He kisses them frenziedly.*

ELENA:     Now I'm the one who can't stop laughing. (*She laughs*) Can I be as mad as you? Give me your hand, so the touch of your skin makes me better.

*They sit facing the sea.*

Give me some more grapes. I love their colour and the smell of your sea.

*Pause. The sound of distant shots.*

What's that?

SALVADOR:     Hunters. The season has begun. Each shot is a wounded bird, breaking its flight to become immortal.

ELENA:     I hate blood.

SALVADOR:     It fascinates me. Only through death is eternal love achieved.

*Pause. Distant and repeated gunshots. Sound of the sea. Cries of gulls. Elena eats more grapes.*

ELENA:     What are you thinking about?

SALVADOR:     About killing you. A tiny push would be enough for you to lose your balance, the sharp rocks would pierce your flesh, and your blood would turn red the deep blue of the Mediterranean . . . which would possess you in the most perfect act of love in the world. The particles of grape clinging to your lips would give eroticism a philosophical, transcendent dimension.

ELENA:     Would such a vision give you pleasure?

SALVADOR:     The greatest of my life. I have always dreamed of cutting off the head of the beautiful woman who lay at my side.

ELENA:     Then kill me. No one will blame you. It will simply be an accident.

*She gets up as if expecting him to push her over the cliff.*

SALVADOR:     Let me first taste the flavour of your nose.

*He kisses her nose.*

A true wonder of Nature! So sweet! It's made of sugar!

*Momentously, though always with a touch of ridicule.*

You and I shall be together for eternity. I shall be the sea, accepting you in an act of perfect anthropophagy. . . . I have just taken Holy Communion, and you have become the flesh of my flesh, of the greatest painter of all time. . . . Our great act of love has been consummated thus.

ELENA:     Is it true what Paul says . . . that you've never possessed a woman?

SALVADOR:     Much better to say I have been a hermaphrodite Narcissus, sufficient unto myself to fulfil my most exaggerated fantasies.

ELENA:     But now you and I are a single flesh. Possess me, destroy me, tear me in pieces. . . .

*Her words make him feel a certain preoccupation. She understands.*

SALVADOR:     But if I can't, promise me you'll never tell a soul.

ELENA:     I promise.

SALVADOR:     Undoubtedly, you still love Paul.

ELENA:     I shall always love him. Both of us shall love him. It shall be the ideal that gives our union meaning.

*They kiss passionately.*

PAUL:     (*writing*) My lovely little Russian doll. I have purchased a beautiful flat, at enormous cost, for when you return from Cadaqués. Yesterday, I met a young woman in the street who possessed the healthy look of an apple and the kind of simplicity in life and in love that was deeply moving. I thought of you the whole night long, and I wanted her body to be yours because it was you and only to you that I was making love. I love you and will always love you. Paul.

ELENA:      (*furiously throwing Tarot cards on the sofa*) A long life, gold, happiness, fame, success, more gold. (*To Salvador, who is seated, curled up at the other end of the sofa*) Do you hear, Salvador? The cards predict the most amazing future. Look: gold, gold, money, fortune, money!

SALVADOR:      And you?

ELENA:      Oh, yes, for me too. Your Paris exhibition will be a huge success, and then there will be many more. Europe, America, the entire world will be at our feet. They will cover us with honours and cheques worth millions. Museums will fight for our paintings. Books will be written about your genius . . . we are going to become a myth.

SALVADOR:      The exhibition is in March.

ELENA:      Paint day and night. You must dazzle them to have them at your feet.

SALVADOR:      I am the king. I've known since my childhood that I am the king.

ELENA:      (*linking her arm with his*) And these two hands together, our sceptre.

*They both begin to laugh hysterically.*

ELENA:      Tomorrow I leave for Paris.

SALVADOR:      You are going back to Paul.

ELENA:      To prepare for your exhibition. You shall join me as soon as you've finished your work.

SALVADOR:      Oh, please don't leave me! I shan't know how to buy my train ticket, or telephone, or pack the pictures, or fill in the forms at the border.

*Elena lies down on the sofa.*

OTHER MAN:      (*as Salvador's father*) Salvador!

SALVADOR:      My father wants to see me. For days he's been sending messages.

OTHER MAN:      Salvador!

SALVADOR:      I'm tired of him and of all the family.

ELENA:      Don't go.

SALVADOR:      That would be useless. He's extremely stubborn. He'd persist until he'd spoken to me. Though I know very well what he's going to say: that he's a notary.

OTHER MAN:      I am a notary.

SALVADOR:      It's the first thing he always says. As if I gave a damn.

OTHER MAN:    I am a notary.

SALVADOR:    And one cannot upset the people we know.

OTHER MAN:    Your reputation is ours too, and the things you do reflect on both your sister and myself.

SALVADOR:    It is my life.

OTHER MAN:    To a certain extent. You know I've been patient with your antics, the extravagance of your paintings, the fantastic dreams that will put you in the madhouse. But now we are dealing with something else: your scandalous relationship with that woman and her husband. You have to end it immediately. What have you got to say?

SALVADOR:    I'd kill myself laughing if she hadn't cured my laughing.

OTHER MAN:    A Russian! Everyone knows that Russian women are free and easy, and lack the slightest notion of fidelity. Besides, she hasn't a penny to her name, nor a roof over her wretched head. And what success have you achieved with your painting?

SALVADOR:    I've a contract with a Paris gallery.

OTHER MAN:    Let me see it.

SALVADOR:    I can't think where I've put it.

OTHER MAN:    When you get there, you'll end up in the street with nothing. Your little dove will go back to her husband, and you, you idiot, will have to come home with your stupid pictures on your back.

SALVADOR:    Have you finished, father?

OTHER MAN:    I have not. This time you've gone too far. Forget you have a family. You'll not get a peseta more. Let's see if your silly, shameless ways allow you to survive.

SALVADOR:    (*producing some money from his pocket*) I don't need your rotten money. You see, you see? The advance from my exhibition.

OTHER MAN:    And what afterwards?

SALVADOR:    Afterwards, whether you like it or not, I'm going to marry the Russian.

*He leaves his father open-mouthed.*

ELENA:    Why would I marry a man like that, so complex and arrogant, and the worst lover I've ever known?

PAUL:    (*approaching the sofa*) For money, my little girl.

ELENA:     How so if he only has debts?

PAUL:     You shall become the most money-minded woman of all time. You shall also succeed in loving him.

ELENA:     I shall?

PAUL:     There are many forms of love, my little one. Exclusive possession of a totally helpless genius who owes you everything is one of the most attractive.

ELENA:     I only want to go back to the sanatorium and be like I was when I was young, you coming to my room after lunch. . . . (*Reliving an earlier scene*)

PAUL:     Why so quiet? Tell me what you are thinking.

ELENA:     Portrait of a young poet, seventeen years old.

PAUL:     I'll buy it.

ELENA:     It's not for sale.

PAUL:     I'll pay for it with a kiss.

*He kisses her.*

SALVADOR:     (*sitting at the foot of Elena's sofa*) Thank you, God, for making her so beautiful. No one, not even the great Raphael, could capture her beauty. . . . Only I shall do so, because I shall always stand before you in ecstacy.

PAUL:     (*to Elena, both of them standing*) Do you like it? The windows provide the best view of Paris.

ELENA:     It's wonderful.

PAUL:     Buñuel lives nearby. I've bought a revolver, with a handle of mother-of-pearl, to defend you against him.

ELENA:     I doubt he'd dare attack me again.

PAUL:     But have you forgotten Cadaqués? He's a most disagreeable, violent person.

*The Other Man and Salvador both join them and the scene in Cadaqués is re-enacted.*

ELENA:     I'm tired of your coarseness.

SALVADOR:     Apologise to the lady.

OTHER MAN:     (*as Buñuel*) I've always found it rather coarse that a woman's thighs should form a gap beneath her crotch.

ELENA:    Get out at once, you oaf.

OTHER MAN:     No cheap slut throws me out.

SALVADOR:    Buñuel!

PAUL:    I won't allow you to insult her.

*Elena attacks Other Man. He reacts by grabbing her throat with the apparent intention of strangling her.*

ELENA:    Scoundrel!

OTHER MAN:    Bitch!

*The others pull him away.*

OTHER MAN:    I didn't want to kill her. Only to see the pink tip of her tongue. . . .

*He laughs.*

ELENA:    (*to Salvador*) Get this creature out of my sight.

PAUL:    Pig! Wretch!

OTHER MAN:    Don't make me regret not having squeezed a little bit more. Bastards!

SALVADOR:    Get out!

*Other Man and Salvador sit down.*

ELENA:    I adore the bedroom.

PAUL:    I chose the furniture, piece by piece, from all the antique shops in Paris.

ELENA:    The bed is huge.

PAUL:    I had it built to specifications . . . I suppose, as a lover, Salvador is as much a disaster as ever.

ELENA:    Let's not discuss it. What about your adventures?

PAUL:    As always, a great disappointment.

*Short pause. They look at each other.*

I've longed so much for your body.

ELENA:    And I for yours, Paul.

*They embrace.*

SALVADOR:    (*carrying a great bunch of roses*) Elena, Elena!

PAUL:     (*going to meet him. Elena goes to the sofa, recalling memories*) Elena isn't here, Salvador.

SALVADOR:     I've just arrived in Paris. The journey was quite impossible. I had to change trains at the frontier. I lost my ticket, ripped my suitcase, and encountered a completely stupid taxi-driver who couldn't understand a word.

PAUL:     I've seen your paintings.

SALVADOR:     They arrived safely then?

PAUL:     They are truly magnificent. The dealer believes he can sell them all.

SALVADOR:     So much the better. These roses have cost me my last franc.

PAUL:     Elena is at the new house in Montmartre. I'll give you the address.

SALVADOR:     I'll go tomorrow, or the day after. The anguish of waiting is more delicious than meeting again.

PAUL:     The flowers will die.

SALVADOR:     You give them to her. I haven't the courage to see her yet.

*He gives the flowers to Paul and beats a hasty retreat.*

ELENA:     Salvador's arrival astonished the surrealist group, in which Paul was one of the most active members. They worshipped his work, asked him for articles and drawings for their journal. . . . They met periodically at the café Cyrano de la Place Blanche, under the chairmanship of André Breton, their high priest.

OTHER MAN:     (*as André Breton*) More Pernod! It's the only drink the bourgeoisie will never touch.

SALVADOR:     I prefer vermouth with lots of olives.

PAUL:     And I a Curaçao.

OTHER MAN:     I insist. We shall all drink Pernod!

*Elena serves them. They take their glasses and add water.*

The wretched yellow lemon is transformed by water into milky white. It gives it a surrealist dimension which is quite unique. . . . To our health!

*They drink.*

ELENA:     They were there for hours, making a racket, swearing their movement would destroy everything else.

*The sound of the men's voices, almost in unison, shouting as if they were in a tavern. When Elena speaks they are silent.*

OTHER MAN:     Complete spiritual freedom! Banish the writer, banish the poet, banish man himself!

SALVADOR:     Only the marvellous is beautiful. Long live the imagination.

PAUL:     Down with talent. We have no talent. Talent does not exist.

ELENA:     A complete lie! Never did so much talent exist as in those men crowded against the café counter.

OTHER MAN:     My friends, we are faced with a great dilemma: we either persist with our anarchist stance, or we join the only truly revolutionary movement: Marxism.

ELENA:     I, who had visited my family after the Revolution, had my own ideas about the Marxist system of my country, although I must admit I always hated politics.

PAUL:     If we do not join the revolutionary movement, all our efforts will go up in smoke.

ELENA:     Paul joined the Communists, as did many of his friends. He was always an idealist, the only one who put his principles into practice. . . .

SALVADOR:     I only believe in the individual, and in Art. I am and have always been a king.

*He drinks.*

ELENA:     There was a long silence in the café Cyrano.

SALVADOR:     Our ideal is confusion and the critical-paranoia of man, not putting ourselves at the service of the art of propaganda. . . . Our whole revolution is above theirs, which is limited precisely because it belongs to the proletariat. Revolution yes, but our, total revolution.

*Applause.*

ELENA:     It suddenly dawned on me that he was truly a king.

SALVADOR:     You fools, every alliance depersonalises. To join with others is to die.

ELENA:     Despite his apparent madness, he knew precisely what he wanted and was going to achieve it.

SALVADOR:     There is only one thing in Art and in life, of which there is never enough: exaggeration!

*Renewed applause.*

ELENA:     In contrast, Paul was quiet, naïve. Perhaps my family was right when it came to poets.

*The group in the café has dispersed.*

SALVADOR:    (*to Elena*) We are leaving.

ELENA:    But your exhibition opens tomorrow.

SALVADOR:    To a small hotel in the south. We shall lock ourselves in our room until the advance runs out.

ELENA:    And do what?

SALVADOR:    Make uninterrupted love. I shall stroke your nipples, count your freckles one by one, smell your pubic hair. . . .

ELENA:    And paint.

SALVADOR:    I shall paint hundreds, thousands of portraits of you. . . . We shall both paint.

ELENA:    But I don't know how.

SALVADOR:    You shall paint through me, as I shall make love through you. . . . We shall be as one, even if, to be so, we must consume each other.

PAUL:    (*writing*) Thank you for writing, my dear little Elena. I am glad you are free and happy. I cannot nor do I wish to hold on to you. But do not forget I've loved you since we were both seventeen and that now, as then, I am still seventeen. Give my regards to Salvador.

*Elena is lying on the sofa. Salvador has his back to her, facing the audience, as if he is painting.*

SALVADOR:    Is it day or night?

ELENA:    What does it matter?

SALVADOR:    Can I open the window?

ELENA:    Of course not. Keep on working.

SALVADOR:    I've been locked up here for days, painting endlessly. And I'm cold. Put more wood on the fire.

ELENA:    You need to work on the left arm. It's out of proportion.

SALVADOR:    The arm is sublime. A landmark in the history of Art.

ELENA:    Here. I melted some amber yesterday, to add to your colours.

SALVADOR:    What will they bring us to eat today? The usual pig swill?

ELENA:    I'm afraid so.

SALVADOR:    I am sick of the hideous meals in this hotel — of melting butter, mustard and parsley. I want muscatel, sardines. I want to wash in the water of the Mediterranean, have the sun lick me dry. I want to swallow sea-urchins by the dozen. I shall place one on top of my head and become the new William Tell. . . .

*He throws away his bruch.*

Ki-ki-ri-ki. . . .

ELENA:     (*looking at the painting*) It's perfect.

SALVADOR:     Perfection cannot be achieved . . . but, thanks to you, I almost grasp it. Has Paul sent you some money?

ELENA:     A half of what he got from selling some African carvings. In dollars.

SALVADOR:     I love dollars almost as much as you. Dollars, dollars. I am avid for dollars. One has to despise money, but the only way to despise it is to have it first. Where are you going?

ELENA:     To get some air.

SALVADOR:     I'm coming with you.

ELENA:     No, my little one. You have to finish the painting.

SALVADOR:     Ki-ki-ri-ki.

*Elena goes over to Paul. Salvador continues painting. Paul and Elena embrace.*

ELENA:     I am yours, completely yours.

PAUL:     I've dreamt of you every night, naked in my arms. Other women cannot diminish our love.

ELENA:     Nor any man ever make me forget you.

PAUL:     Does Salvador know you are here?

ELENA:     He never leaves the hotel. I made up a story to get away.

PAUL:     Have you helped him improve as a lover?

ELENA:     Do you still pursue your one-night stands, your orgies?

PAUL:     Only in order to find you.

ELENA:     You say it with such honest eyes, as if it were true. Your eyes are what fascinate most . . . well, your eyes and your poems. . . . Please, don't look at me like that, or I'll end up believing you. . . .

*Pause.*

Paul, we have to get a divorce.

PAUL:      But why?

ELENA:    Salvador needs me.

PAUL:      So do I.

ELENA:    But you can continue writing and loving and become the greatest French poet of the twentieth century. But if I leave him alone, he'll be destroyed by his own eccentricities. I am the umbilical cord, joining him to the real world. Without me he cannot breathe.

PAUL:      So?

ELENA:    I love him.

PAUL:    You think you love any good-looking man who comes anywhere near you.

ELENA:    Don't forget that he has genius.

PAUL:      What else does he have?

ELENA:    Besides all that, he's a king.

*Short pause.*

PAUL:      I've brought a cheque. It's all I can afford.

ELENA:    It will be enough.

PAUL:      Where will you live when you come back to Paris?

ELENA:    I don't know.

PAUL:      You can have the flat I rented for us. I couldn't live there without you. . . . Will we see each other again?

ELENA:    Why not?

PAUL:      You still believe in our love?

ELENA:    It's one of the lost things I long for most. You awakened me to love and desire, though you were the one who also soiled those feelings. . . .

PAUL:      But do you love him?

ELENA:    Salvador? I suppose I do . . . I'm not sure. Perhaps more than I think.

PAUL:      The man is quite absurd!

ELENA:    I admire him deeply.

PAUL:      But that isn't enough. Tell me, be honest. What do you want from him? The money he can offer you?

ELENA:    I shall make him the greatest genius of the century. . . . He is my challenge, the masterpiece for which I shall be remembered. And of course there is the money. One day I shall go to Siberia and cover my father's grave with banknotes, so he can rest in peace, his dream accomplished. Every day I ask God to grant me this and He guarantees it will come true.

PAUL:      You still pray to those icons you brought from Russia?

ELENA:      More than ever.

PAUL:      (*smiling*) You are still a child, keeping your treasures safe in a cardboard box.

ELENA:      Don't you believe it. More than anyone, you've made me what I am, a woman who only looks ahead, without roots or any kind of weakness.

PAUL:      That's what people will say who don't know you well. I know what you really are: sensitive, tender, sentimental . . . however much you try to hide it, pretending to despise everyone so as not to offer the love that oozes from every pore. . . .

ELENA:      No one thinks that. Not even me.

PAUL:      You are an adorable, detestable creature. You amuse yourself by fooling everyone, including yourself.

*They move away from each other. Elena speaks to Salvador.*

ELENA:      As soon as I turn my back, you stop painting.

SALVADOR:      I was simply starving. I couldn't go on.

ELENA:      No food until you've finished the painting.

SALVADOR:      It might take hours, or days.

ELENA:      It's for your own good.

SALVADOR:      (*like a child*) Please! Please! (*suddenly*) Then take your clothes off. If I can't see you naked, I can't paint.

ELENA:      As soon as you've finished, you can see all you want. Now paint!

SALVADOR:      Why are you so cruel to me?

ELENA:      Because I love you.

*Elena kisses him and lies on the sofa.*

PAUL:      I joined the army for the second time. I who have always been a pacifist have become the oldest lieutenant in the French army. But soon I shall be demobilised, go back to Paris and join the Resistance.

ELENA:      War, war, always some damned war. First in Spain when Salvador and I escaped by the skin of our teeth from the Anarchist patrols. Then the German invasion, our flight to the south, followed by our voyage to America.

SALVADOR:     I cannot go by sea. I am terrified of shipwrecks.

ELENA:     You'll do as I say, my precious.

SALVADOR:     Don't force me. I'm far too young to drown. I have still to paint my greatest works for posterity.

ELENA:     America is a wonderful country. Those fools will trumpet your appearances, buy your paintings and spread your fame throughout the world. Isn't your motto 'Avid for dollars'? Well there they are, in the banks, the strong-rooms, the salesrooms, the dealers' wallets . . . waiting for you to hold out your hands and receive them. Where are you going?

SALVADOR:     I need a life-jacket. I shall wear it throughout the crossing, even to sleep. The Atlantic shall not swallow me. It has so much water, it is so vast.

ELENA:     But not as vast as your talent.

SALVADOR:     That is true.

ELENA:     In that case, how can it swallow you?

SALVADOR:     You and I know it cannot, but does the Atlantic know? Bring me the bread.

ELENA:     Which bread?

SALVADOR:     I have asked the chef to make me a roll six feet long. The journalists can then report the arrival of an extraordinary man.

*Elena gives him the bread roll, six feet long. He takes it and places it under his arm.*

Ki-ki-ri-ki. . . .

OTHER MAN:     (*as a journalist*) Hold it there!

*Flash of a camera.*

SALVADOR:     Another one please, with the bread on my head, another William Tell.

OTHER MAN:     Why bread?

SALVADOR:     Because I don't have a sea-urchin. (*To Elena, almost in tears*) They'll ignore me. . . . The news of my arrival will appear hidden somewhere in the inside pages.

ELENA:     You have to paint. Just leave the rest to me.

*Salvador sits down, using the bread as a kind of support.*

PAUL:    My dear Elena: I am most upset by what happened to Salvador. The papers say he's been put in jail for what he did in one of the stores on Fifth Avenue.

ELENA:    Love of my life, there's no need to worry. On the contrary. It has been the beginning of a fame which will prove unstoppable. I had arranged that one of the large stores should offer him its window display, containing the latest fashion in bathrooms. He spent the entire night transforming it into a brilliant example of surrealism, but the following morning the cretins who ran the store thought that because they had paid him their filthy money they had the right to do anything. They dared to alter the great work of an artist with the addition of vulgar, bourgeois elements.

SALVADOR:    (*excitably waving the bread*) It is my work! No American dwarf, no matter how large his bank account, can alter in any way the work of a giant. How dare they dress my mannequins in such absurd clothes!

ELENA:    Of course, you are right. You are always right.

SALVADOR:    I shall empty the water from the bath, decapitate the grotesque dummies, flush the toilets.

ELENA:    Be careful, you'll smash the window.

SALVADOR:    I don't give a damn!

*Sound of breaking glass followed by the sound of a police siren.*

SALVADOR:    They've tricked me, abused my talent, attempted to strangle my genius. Call the police! Help! Police!

ELENA:    (*writing*) They released him almost at once. It was front-page news in all the papers.

PAUL:    (*writing*) I love you, I desire you, you are the only love of my life. Your adoring Paul.

ELENA:    None of the young American sportsmen compare with you in making love.

PAUL:    P.S. Last Tuesday Nusch and I got married. I think I've mentioned her to you . . . the insignificant, submissive girl who's lived with me for several years. . . .

*Elena, lying on the sofa, receives her secretary.*

OTHER MAN:    (*as the Secretary. He carries a briefcase*) I'm sorry. As you know, I was late getting to sleep.

ELENA:     The nights are for amusement, the mornings for work.

OTHER MAN:     Of course.

*He produces some papers from the briefcase.*

May I say it was just wonderful.

ELENA:     With me it is always wonderful. (*Changing tack*) To business.

OTHER MAN:     Mr MacMillan would like a portrait of his wife.

ELENA:     Who is he?

OTHER MAN:     He owns a chain of butchers shops. He's offering fifty thousand.

ELENA:     Make it the advance.

OTHER MAN:     Blady City wishes to buy a painting for its museum.

ELENA:     Where is this place?

OTHER MAN:     In Oklahoma. They're offering thirty thousand.

ELENA:     Far too little.

OTHER MAN:     Remember it is a 'cultural' transaction.

ELENA:     Who wants to go to Oklahoma to see it? Forty thousand.

OTHER MAN:     I can probably arrange it. A chocolate factory wants a poster design.

ELENA:     Fifty thousand and a percentage of all the extra chocolates sold.

OTHER MAN:     I've brought the money owing. In cash.

*He gives her an envelope. She puts it in her handbag at once, as if she fears someone will steal it.*

OTHER MAN:     Take care. Some of the notes are for large amounts. Here are some signed cheques. Shall I put them in your account?

ELENA:     I'll look after them. I don't trust banks, not even American banks.

*She places the cheques in her already bulging handbag.*

OTHER MAN:     As to the other matter. . . .

ELENA:     Let me see the photographs.

OTHER MAN:     (*giving them to her*) These are of two young men, these of a man and a girl. I've picked out the most attractive ones. This is what they charge.

ELENA:     Who do these people think they are? Can't they see what an honour it is? To take part in an erotic mass, conducted by the master; to be sodomised in the presence of a genius is a glorious experience. Most of our friends would be willing to pay a fortune. We'll pay their travel and hotel expenses.

*She returns the photographs.*

OTHER MAN:    (*giving her some different photographs*) These are for you.

ELENA:    (*studying them*) Not bad. I hope their performance matches their looks.

OTHER MAN:    They are young, strong and healthy. From the Yacht Club, various gymnasia and the Athletic Country Club.

ELENA:    I'd like this one, this one and this one. Not this one. He's good-looking but too skinny.

OTHER MAN:    (*putting the photos in his briefcase*) May I . . . come to your room tonight?

ELENA:    I'll call you if I'm in the mood. (*She kisses him on the lips*) Goodbye.

OTHER MAN:    As you wish.

ELENA:    Men, men, men . . . I am tired of men. How boring and monotonous they are! Provide me with a god!

OTHER MAN:    What?

ELENA:    You atheist, materialist unbeliever. The people in this country have no sensibility . . . only money. I knew a god. He was seventeen years old, had a lung complaint and was called Paul. What are you writing?

OTHER MAN:    Just to remind me. A god for a goddess.

*Other Man goes to his chair. Paul stands up.*

PAUL:    Paul died in Paris, in 1952. Thirty years after our divorce. Great personalities attended the funeral, like Cocteau, Picasso and Aragon. Messages of sympathy came from Neruda and Bertolt Brecht. There was a great display of grief and hundreds of admirers. . . . But you weren't there, Elena.

ELENA:    Paul, Paul. . . .

PAUL:    As you know, I was always against cheap patriotism, but was buried, paradoxically, as a national hero. School children were obliged to learn by heart my poem 'Liberty' which had been produced in pamphlet form by British pilots during the German occupation.

ELENA:    (*to Paul*) I can't believe I have to live without you. You were far away. We had little contact and many years had passed since we last made love. But I know that you were somewhere . . . that your love was there too.

PAUL:       I loved you till the final moment.

ELENA:       Why, if you were purity itself, did you teach me to deceive and lie so much?

PAUL:       My sweet child, whatever form love takes, it is always unique. Whatever we do, it is always alive and true.

ELENA:       Oh, Paul. What would I give to be able to weep!

*Thinking back.*

PAUL:       When does your train leave?

ELENA:       At twenty past eight. The car is waiting to take me to the station. When are you leaving?

PAUL:       Tomorrow. These last two years in the sanatorium have been the happiest of my life.

ELENA:       I take Paul to be my husband, marvellous, beloved Paul. . . . I do.

PAUL:       I take Elena Diakanova to be my wife. I do.

*They embrace.*

PAUL:       Now you must care for our daughter.

ELENA:       She can manage on her own.

PAUL:       You haven't spoken to her for ages.

ELENA:       She married a good-for-nothing. I gave them our Paris apartment so they wouldn't be out in the street. And what did she do? She secretly sold my pictures for any old price. I shall never forgive her.

PAUL:       And then there's your grand-daughter.

ELENA:       I have no grand-daughter. This tribe of mediocrities and petit bourgeois has nothing to do with me.

PAUL:       Promise me you'll visit her.

ELENA:       All right. But only to tell her what I think of her and to let her know she can forget her mother forever. Now you go too. Go!

*Paul leaves by the door and Elena kneels.*

ELENA:       God, you have extinguished the light of true love and left me only easy and empty affairs. And the cold brightness of money. My love for

Salvador has grown cold little by little until it has become as hard as metal. Only you, God, can give my life some final meaning, the meaning it had when I was a child, when my mother made me kneel at the side of the bed and pray for my father in Siberia. Do not fail me again now.

*She rises quickly, takes the pack of cards and deals them in order to see her destiny revealed.*

Gold, gold, success, fame. . . . Is that all there is? More fame, trivial love-affairs. . . . Where is Paul? And Salvador?

*She deals more cards.*

God, at last you appear to me, God!

OTHER MAN:     (*entering as the Secretary*) Madam.

ELENA:     What is it? I didn't call. Go away.

OTHER MAN:     The bills. . . .

ELENA:     Some other time.

OTHER MAN:     (*giving her some sheets of paper*) The sheets of paper you asked for.

ELENA:     What, only these? We need much more. Hundreds, millions.

OTHER MAN:     Will the master agree?

ELENA:     I'll make sure he does. Goodbye.

OTHER MAN:     I've brought you one last thing. The request you made some time ago. I've been successful.

ELENA:     Be more precise.

OTHER MAN:     Listen.

*The music from 'Jesus Christ Superstar'.*

ELENA:     The music is hideous.

OTHER MAN:     I'm sure you'll like it. It's just opened on Broadway. It's based on the New Testament. The theatre is sold out every night.

*He hands her a photograph.*

This is the leading man.

ELENA:     Jesus Christ!

OTHER MAN:     He has identified so much with the part, he seems an authentic reincarnation. When I managed to speak to him, he claimed he was the source of God.

ELENA:     I want to see him, I want to wash his feet and dry them with my hair, I want to put my arms around his waist, kiss his divine lips, I want him to possess me and whisper at the same time those words I needed to hear and no one has ever spoken. . . .

OTHER MAN:     We are talking about an actor. His name is. . . .

ELENA:     I don't want to know his name. I know who he is and that's enough.

OTHER MAN:     He is only twenty-four.

ELENA:     What does his age matter? Do we speak of the age of the sun, or the sea, or the gods? Go and find him. I want him now.

OTHER MAN:     I'm afraid that's quite impossible. The performance has just begun.

ELENA:     Then stop it, give the people their money back, compensate the theatre.

*She gives him her handbag.*

Take it. If it's not enough, give them one of Salvador's paintings. One of the small ones, of course.

*The music has stopped. Other Man sits. Salvador gets up and approaches Elena. He is carrying a sheaf of papers.*

SALVADOR:     Did you call me?

ELENA:     No. Leave me.

SALVADOR:     I'm doing what you asked me to. But I dislike signing sheets of paper before doing the drawing. How do you know that I'll ever want to do so many drawings?

ELENA:     If you don't do them, someone else will.

SALVADOR:     With my signature?

ELENA:     But don't you see? It's precisely the signature of a genius that really matters. What do provincial dealers and the petit bourgeoisie know about your art? They pay for your name and that's exactly what we are going to sell them. So they can hang the pictures over the fireplace in their apartments and arouse the envy of all their suburban neighbours.

SALVADOR:     I refuse to have my work displayed in the suburbs.

ELENA:     Are you going to defy me?

SALVADOR:     I am, I am. Of course I am!

*He throws the papers in the air.*

ELENA:     (*scolding him like a child*) Salvador! Come here at once! Pick those papers up!

SALVADOR:     (*reluctantly*) Whatever you say. I'll put my signature wherever you say and as many times as you want. The people who say I am mad might be right. For the first time ever I have acted like a madman by disobeying you.

*He hands her the papers.*

OTHER MAN:     (*entering as the Secretary*) Madam.

ELENA:     (*handing him the papers*) Put them with the rest in the chest in my bedroom.

OTHER MAN:     (*he takes the papers but doesn't leave*) Of course.

ELENA:     What now?

OTHER MAN:     He's arrived.

ELENA:     Who?

OTHER MAN:     The person that madam was expecting.

ELENA:     You mean. . . ?

OTHER MAN:     Indeed.

*Pause.*

ELENA:     Show him in.

*To Salvador.*

Kneel beside me. We shall thank God for honouring our household.

SALVADOR:     I have no wish to pray.

ELENA:     It is not to the icons in my room, nor to the image of our Lord in the chapel of San Patricio, but before Him, in person.

*Other Man enters again, accompanied by Paul dressed in stage costume as Jesus Christ.*

SALVADOR:     Where on earth did you find this nincompoop?

ELENA:     Do not blaspheme.

SALVADOR:     Does he really believe he is Jesus Christ?

PAUL:     (*as Jesus Christ*) You said it, man.

OTHER MAN:     Jesus Christ Superstar.

SALVADOR:     Get him to take the costume off. Let's see him naked. If I like what I see, I might even honour him and use him as a model for a new masterpiece.

PAUL:     Forgive him, Father. He knows not what he says.

SALVADOR:     It's you who don't know that, you cretin. You do not interest me. Go.

ELENA:     He's a guest of mine.

SALVADOR:     In my house. Out of my sight! Peasant!

PAUL:     No one's throwing me out, least of all a silly old fool like this.

SALVADOR:     Get him out of here!

ELENA:     *(to Paul)* Don't go, I beg you.

*(To Other Man, with reference to Salvador)*

Get him out!

*(To Salvador)*

I'll never forgive you for this.

*Other Man and Salvador leave.*

*(To Paul)*

Allow me to kiss your hand with all my heart.

*She kisses his hand and, without releasing it, leads him to the sofa. The music of 'Jesus Christ Superstar' is heard again. She helps him slowly remove his tunic. He is left wearing only trousers, his torso bare.*

ELENA:     How handsome you are, such warm skin, such tender eyes, such white teeth!. . . Are you really Jesus Christ?

PAUL:     I am just a singer who sings the same songs night after night. Though I'm not so sure that I'm not more than that. Sometimes I kneel in front of a mirror and pray to myself.

ELENA:     You're as handsome and as lovely as a god.

*She kisses him.*

PAUL:     I drink alcohol, I take drugs. Anything to escape the constant presence of Christ possessing me. I've even prayed to the Devil for help. The people worship me, applaud me, touch my clothes and request miracles. And do you know what bothers me most? I feel I can perform them.

ELENA:     Tonight you have performed one for me. The miracle of taking me back to when I was seventeen. When I wasn't the monster all of them have made me. You are just like Paul.

PAUL: Who is Paul?

ELENA: Someone who died some time ago . . . someone who lives inside me . . . and tonight you've brought him to life again, like Lazarus.

*They kiss and embrace on the sofa.*

OTHER MAN: Madam?

ELENA: Drive him to the theatre. As soon as the performance ends, bring him back.

PAUL: I'm afraid I can't. A prior engagement.

ELENA: Then break it. I'm not accustomed to taking no for an answer.

PAUL: Whatever you say.

*He kisses her hand and leaves with Other Man.*

ELENA: So began one of the most exciting periods of my life. My contact with him made me young again, my religious faith grew stronger than ever. . . . He was man and God, body and spirit, heaven and hell. Flesh divine. In his arms, as in Paul's, there was love and depravity, virtue and degradation. A perfect mix of sex and saintliness, mysticism and lust.

*She plays with the Tarot cards.*

OTHER MAN: He wasn't at the theatre.

ELENA: It's not possible.

OTHER MAN: I waited for him at the end of the performance. He'd slipped away.

ELENA: But why?

OTHER MAN: It seems his child was ill.

ELENA: Child?

OTHER MAN: Madam knows that he's married, that he has a wife and a child who's just gone into hospital.

ELENA: I don't know, nor do I wish to know. It doesn't matter what he does outside these walls.

*Suddenly.*

You can spend tonight with me. I'll expect you at eleven.

OTHER MAN: Thank you, Madam.

*Other Man withdraws.*

ELENA:     A few weeks later we returned to Spain. I did what I could to prevent it but Salvador was adamant. I had to agree.

SALVADOR:     I cannot go on painting in New York. There is too much noise, too many journalists, it is all too vulgar.

ELENA:     We could stay in the hotel bedroom, as we did before.

SALVADOR:     I need the light of the Mediterranean. These vampires suck my dreams, my colours, my secretions. They are going to suck me dry.

ELENA:     Don't lie. What you really want is to keep him away from me. But you shan't succeed. I'll love him until I die.

SALVADOR:     You and I will never die. Do you hear me, father? I am a king. I am still King of the Universe and so immortal. . . .

*He walks like a true king.*

Ki-ki-ri-ki!

ELENA:     I couldn't stand any more. My love for him was dead. Salvador was an old man. He was sick and always repeating himself. And so we bought the castle.

SALVADOR:     I cannot paint in a castle.

ELENA:     I want it for myself, to be far away from you and your constant shouting.

SALVADOR:     I shan't let you. You shall stay with me, even if I have to chain you down.

ELENA:     I want to spend my remaining years in peace and quiet.

SALVADOR:     You mean with your lovers!

ELENA:     Let me enjoy the pleasure of love. You never gave me any.

SALVADOR:     (*seizing her violently*) Ungrateful creature!

ELENA:     Do you want to hit me? Go ahead if that will calm you down!

SALVADOR:     (*releasing her*) You're a witch!

*He sits, weeping.*

OTHER MAN:     (*as Buñuel*) I didn't want to kill her. Only to see the pink tip of her tongue.

ELENA:     You pig, you wretch!

OTHER MAN:     Don't make me regret not having squeezed a little harder.

*Other Man sits down.*

ELENA:    (*to Paul in the part of Jesus Christ*) The castle stands high on a hill, like a small fortress no one can enter without my permission. But for you it will be open day and night.

PAUL:    You can't see the sea from here.

ELENA:    (*she takes him by the waist and leads him to the window*) Close your eyes. You'll smell the salty air, hear the cry of the gulls and the sound of the waves against the rocks.

PAUL:    I feel so tired. The flight from New York has exhausted me. I hate planes.

ELENA:    I had to see you.

PAUL:    The show will be closing soon. I can't live without the part. It's as if I'll be emptied from inside, as if my soul will be torn out. I'm Him, and without Him I'm nothing. A poor, out-of-work actor, kicking his heels in agents' offices.

ELENA:    I have made many men famous. With your talent, I shall make you the most wanted singer in the world. Love me and I'll give you everything. I know how to make money, lots of it. . . . And all of it for you.

*They embrace.*

Did John give you the cheque. Have you paid off your debts?

PAUL:    For the moment, yes.

ELENA:    Did you lose again?

PAUL:    I promise you I'll stop playing.

ELENA:    I'll sort it out. Don't worry. I have a reputation for being mean with money, but for you I shall be the most generous person you've ever known.

PAUL:    Come with me to America. We'll start a new life together.

ELENA:    If only I could!

PAUL:    You can do anything.

ELENA:    The castle is here.

PAUL:    It's just a pile of stones.

ELENA:    Salvador is here.

PAUL:    You hate him. He beats you, tortures you.

ELENA:     Above all, my life is here.

PAUL:     But it's something you can take with you, because it's yours. You carry it inside you.

ELENA:     You understand nothing. What I carry inside me, as you put it, is that man's painting. His work is my triumph. To renounce it as I harvest the fruit of so many years would be to destroy myself.

PAUL:     You sacrifice me to your own ambition.

ELENA:     More to the money we need to promote your career.

PAUL:     I shall earn it.

ELENA:     Someday, yes. I'll make you rich. But not straight away.

PAUL:     You have no faith in me. You don't love me.

ELENA:     And you? Do you have faith in me? Do you love me?

PAUL:     Yes.

ELENA:     Enough to divorce your wife and marry an old woman who will undoubtedly deceive you with any silly young man she fancies?

PAUL:     (*after a moment's hesitation*) Yes.

ELENA:     You see? You would also be sacrificing everything to your own ambition.

*Salvador gets up. He is very angry.*

SALVADOR:     She has no right to forbid me entrance.

OTHER MAN:     (*as the Secretary, cutting him short*) I'm sorry. Those are her orders.

SALVADOR:     (*yelling*) Elena. This idiot won't let me in. Me! Do you hear?

ELENA:     (*shouting back at him*) You know I want to be on my own. I don't wany anyone here.

SALVADOR:     I have to speak to you.

ELENA:     Very well. Arrange an appointment.

SALVADOR:     May I have an appointment?

ELENA:     In writing. I shall let you know which day is convenient.

SALVADOR:     Who's there with you?

ELENA:     What does it matter? Do I ever ask you who the young men are, the wretched queers you take home to liven up your orgies?

SALVADOR: (*handing to Other Man a piece of paper on which he has scribbled*) My request in writing.

OTHER MAN: (*to Salvador*) I shall give it to Madam and bring you her reply.

SALVADOR: I haven't signed it. My signature is worth a fortune. You shan't get rich at my expense.

*Salvador is annoyed. Other Man hands his request to Elena.*

ELENA: (*to Paul*) Excuse me, darling. The thought of receiving my oafish husband upsets me.

PAUL: I'll see you soon, my love.

ELENA: John will take you to the airport. You'll be in New York in plenty of time for tomorrow's performance. You'll find a surprise in the car. One of the master's wonderful paintings, the most valuable I have given you.

PAUL: You are too, too generous.

ELENA: Nothing is too good for you. We shall pray together.

PAUL: Like hell we shall! I'm not Jesus Christ. In a couple of weeks I shan't be Superstar. Don't torment me with these things.

*He goes out quickly. She kneels by the sofa and prays.*

ELENA: Please God make him come back soon, so that we may travel to the South of France, the Alps, the sanatorium where Paul and I first met. Oh, Paul, Paul. . . .

SALVADOR: At last you condescend to see me.

ELENA: What is it you want?

SALVADOR: To see you.

ELENA: You've seen me. Anything else?

SALVADOR: To tell you I can't live without you.

ELENA: Just as I cannot live with you. End of discussion. Was there something else?

SALVADOR: The blank sheets of paper you made me sign. Several dealers have received fake paintings signed by me. They have written to ask me to put an end to the whole scandalous business. If not, they refuse to sell my work.

ELENA: Don't worry. We shall find other dealers.

SALVADOR: You should recover the fakes and burn them.

ELENA:     It isn't possible.

SALVADOR:     They carry my signature. It's a question of my reputation.

ELENA:     You are nothing more than what I have wanted you to be.

SALVADOR:     I am the finest exponent of surrealism, the great genius of the century.

ELENA:     You are finished. You don't know what you are painting. It's nothing more than decadent and constipated pop art. It turns my stomach.

SALVADOR:     I saw you as my madonna. I placed you on the altar of my art, so everyone could worship you.

ELENA:     I only wanted to be a woman. The interview is over. Goodbye.

SALVADOR:     You are wrong. It's only just begun. I want to see the paintings.

ELENA:     Which ones?

SALVADOR:     The ones I gave you. The ones you hung on the castle walls. They aren't there now.

ELENA:     They are my pictures.

SALVADOR:     You've given them to Superstar. You thought he'd be the last great love of your life . . . and the boy's made a fool of you. Do you know where the paintings have ended up? In Christie's in New York. They were auctioned a week ago. He decided to take you for a ride as soon as he saw he couldn't get much more from you. You'll never set eyes on him again.

ELENA:     I don't believe you. . . .

SALVADOR:     (laughing) His wife is pregnant again. How they must have laughed at you while they were fucking in their bed!

ELENA:     (hysterically) It isn't true! It isn't true!

SALVADOR:     You are nothing but a ridiculous old woman, full of uterine frenzy.

ELENA:     And you an absurd old man, fit only to gaze on the arses of dwarfs and your circle of transvestites.

SALVADOR:     You dare lecture me in your bourgeois morality, you hysterical creature, you total grotesque?

ELENA:     It's your fault. For fifty years I've shared my bed with a man who's completely impotent.

SALVADOR:     You were a whore when I knew you first. Buñuel was right when he tried to strangle you. If only I'd done the same.

ELENA:    If it weren't for me they'd have put you in the madhouse.

SALVADOR:    You have fucked up my entire life. You only wanted my dollars. I hate you.

ELENA:    You pig! You pig!

SALVADOR:    You witch! You witch!

*They begin to struggle. On hearing their shouting, Other Man enters.*

OTHER MAN:    Have you gone mad?

*They have stopped struggling. They are on the floor.*

ELENA:    Since when do you enter without being summoned?

OTHER MAN:    I heard shouting.

ELENA:    I fell. The master was trying to assist me.

SALVADOR:    (*on his feet*) Help her up. And all of you go to hell! (*He goes towards the chairs*)

OTHER MAN:    (*helping Elena to lie on the sofa*) She's badly hurt. I'll call the doctor.

SALVADOR:    I forbid it. . . .

OTHER MAN:    Allow me to say that Madam is still as lovely as a madonna.

*He kisses her on the lips.*

ELENA:    Don't kiss me. I don't want you to kiss me anymore. You are dismissed! Get out!

*She lies motionless on the sofa.*

OTHER MAN:    They took her to the hospital, where a broken femur was diagnosed. She stayed there for a while and then they brought her home to the master's house to die.

*He goes out. Paul enters and stands next to Salvador.*

SALVADOR:    When I was a child I was in the fields one night and found a fallen star. I took it home and placed it in an old biscuit box. The next morning I opened the box to see my newfound treasure, and the only thing there was a worm. That's what you are, Elena . . . a shining star transformed in the end to a worm.

PAUL:    My angel, everything about you is lovely. Your eyes, your mouth, your breasts, your hair, your shoulders. Whatever you do fills me with love, whatever you do is perfect.

SALVADOR:    They claim what I am is due to you. It isn't true! It's the opposite. You are what you are on account of my genius. Only poets and painters can create angels or goddesses.

PAUL:    You are the soil to which I belong. Without you I lived in exile.

SALVADOR:    You promised that you'd never leave me, that you would die after me . . . I shall never forgive you for that.

PAUL:    She died on the twelfth of June. At dawn.

ELENA:    I always sleep with the window open. So the first ray of light can wake me up when it shines through the rocks on the headland at the furthest, eastern end of the bay. That first ray of light contains the events of the day, and so each morning I observe it carefully to learn its secrets, to discover the meaning hidden in that blinding light. Is this to be my last day of life? I ask the question every morning . . . but never before have I longed so much that this day should be the last. . . .

*Jesus Christ enters (this time played by Other Man), accompanied by Paul and Salvador. They remain standing alongside their chairs with the kind of respect people display at a funeral. Elena's eyes are closed. Long silence. Blackout.*